Contemporary Israeli Literature

ספרות ישראלית בת זמננו

Contemporary Israeli Literature
an anthology
edited by Elliott Anderson

poetry edited by Robert Friend
introduction by Shimon Sandbank
afterword by Robert Alter

The Jewish Publication Society of America
Philadelphia 5737 / 1977

555
A546

Contents

Grateful acknowledgment is made to the following: The Institute for the Translation of Hebrew Literature (Tel Aviv) for assistance with translations and for permission to reprint A. C. Jacobs's translation of "Distant Land," by Dahlia Ravikovitch; Bat-Sheva Sheriff's and Jon Silkin's translation of Anadad Eldan's "When You Gave Light"; Edna G. Sharoni's translation of Zelda's "Be Not Far," first published in the Hebrew Book Review *(Spring 1972); and Robert Friend's translations of Uri Zvi Greenberg's "Song of the Great Mind" and "No Other Instances" (from* To God in Europe*), which were first published in the* Anthology of Modern Hebrew Poetry, *ed. S. Y. Penueli and A. Ukhmani (Israel Universities Press). To* Ariel *(Jerusalem) for permission to reprint Aharon Appelfeld's "Badenheim 1939," translated by Betsy Rosenberg; Marcia Falk's translation of Dahlia Ravikovitch's "Pride"; Robert Friend's translation of Dan Pagis' "The Portrait"; Stephen Mitchell's translation of Amir Gilboa's "Samson"; and Betsy Rosenberg's translation of Tuvia Ruebner's "I Left." To the Israel P.E.N. Centre (Tel Aviv) for permission to reprint S. F. Chyet's translation of Haim Gouri's "Holiday's End," first published in* P.E.N. Israel 74, *ed. Richard Flantz. To the Carcanet Press (Manchester) and Dan Pagis for permission to reprint from* Selected Poems *(1972), by Dan Pagis: "A Lesson in Observation," "Twelve Faces of the Emerald," and "Fragments of an Elegy," in the translations of Stephen Mitchell. To Jon Silkin and Northern House Pamphlets (Newcastle-on-Tyne) for permission to reprint from* Against Parting *(1967), by Natan Zach: "He Apologizes," "King Solomon's Camel," "Sergeant Weiss," "A Song for the Wise Lovers," and "As Sand," in the translations of Jon Silkin. To Robert Friend and Daniel Weisbort for permission to reprint from* Modern Poetry in Translation, 22 *(Autumn 1974): Dan Pagis' "The Last" and "In the Laboratory," translated by Robert Friend, and Dahlia Ravikovitch's "How Hong Kong Was Destroyed," translated by Chana Bloch. Robert Friend also thanks Shlomit Rimmon, special assistant for the poetry anthology, who checked each translation against the Hebrew original; Shirley Kaufman and Ruth Nevo for their advice in connection with editorial choices; and he thanks Shlomit Rimmon, Shirley Kaufman, Ruth Nevo, Dan Pagis, and especially Shimon Sandbank, for their help with his own translations. The editor thanks Hillel Halkin for his cooperation in the preparation of this collection.*

Special thanks are due Irwin T. Holtzman, without whose generous support this anthology of Israeli literature would not have been possible.

Contemporary Israeli Literature

Contemporary Israeli literature: the withdrawal from certainty
Shimon Sandbank

1

In the midst of an elegant dinner party—uneasy, as were many Israeli social occasions immediately after the 1973 war—something unpleasant happens to Izy Ornan.

. . . almost irrelevantly, perhaps because of the embarrassment, the expectation, the startled faces, the lobster left untouched on the bulky, altar-like table—a sound escaped his mouth, perhaps a tremor, a supplication, an undefined something which burst out from within.

A strange silence fell. Heads turned, searching. Then a sudden tenderness made them look away.

And then, still trembling, astonished at the meaningless sound that had escaped from him, locked up perhaps for a long time, he recognized it as the moment a person knows himself. He was talking in a whisper, as if in self-defence:

"I don't know. I don't. I have been thinking, maybe. I have been afraid, yes. I had an uncle who used to tell a story about a certain Avreml. It doesn't matter. What he meant to say was that a man can wear himself out trying to decide whether he should get married or not. Doesn't matter. We've got something we carry with us wherever we go, and there's no escape, no escape. Sorry. I hope I'm wrong. I wish I were wrong. Only a question of time. Not even hope. For what, for nothing. No hope whatever. And whoever wants to can run away. If he can. Run away from himself. From ourselves. We can't even do that. And there's no hope. No. So, that's it? So there's no life? All's over? And were it not for wars, there would be no death . . . sorry. It doesn't matter. O.K., so there isn't much, but

3

surely there must be something. There's a bit of life. Who has the right to give it up? Even the tiniest bit. To say: I don't want children—that's easy. But to be a coward, yes. I claim my right to be a coward. And to have a home. And to love. And help each other. For what. Death eats us up every couple of years, but meanwhile . . . Perhaps there's greatness under the volcano. Perhaps."

Izy Ornan is the poet-protagonist of *A House for One* (1975), the latest novel by the Israeli author Yitzhak Orpaz. His bachelorhood, his impassioned inarticulateness, his basic nausea with the world and himself—partly overcome in this epiphanic episode—are all reminiscent of J. H. Brenner, the grim chronicler of early-century Jewish life in Palestine.[1] But though somewhat derivative, the sensibility and the style of the Orpaz novel are perfectly contemporary. A return to Brenner's soul-searching, his renunciation of easy truths, and his withdrawal from the pretense that one can understand and articulate one's experience, would have been unlikely twenty years ago. Only recently have literary attitudes in Israel begun to make such a frame of mind possible. In the pathetic, meaningless sound which Orpaz's protagonist emits, there is an admission that not only ideologies, but words themselves, have become inadequate.

2

It is perhaps late in the day for a modern literature to recognize the inadequacy of words. Didn't the literatures of Europe do so at the very beginning of a century now in its eighth decade? But the Hebrew language is a special case, because, rather than to slough off all meaning, its real problem has been to slough off its inbuilt sacred meanings. For thousands of years Hebrew existed only as a written language, steeped in religious tradition and permeated with biblical and talmudic associations. Its revival as a spoken language, with the rise of Zionism, required an adaptation to secular needs—a rejuvenated or newly created vocabulary for modern everyday life and a syntax to match the carelessness and fluidity of living speech. This has been a painful process, perhaps not yet completed to this very day. The creative energy that has gone into the process has left little initiative for a "modernistic" questioning of communication itself. To opt for silence, one must despair of language; to despair of language, perhaps one must first exhaust its possibilities. Hebrew literature, it seems, has not yet exhausted the possibilities of the Hebrew language.

4

1. His *Breakdown and Bereavement*, translated by Hillel Halkin, was published by the Jewish Publication Society in 1971.

A group of respectable Israeli literary critics—notably the late Baruch Kurtzweil—believe that the paradoxical use of a language of religious tradition to serve secular goals has been the bane of modern Hebrew literature. Kurtzweil thinks that ever since the Haskalah, the Jewish Enlightenment movement, Hebrew literature has been forced to use the language of the absolute religious imperative, only to contradict that imperative. To Kurtzweil, who was an orthodox Jew, this complex situation offered no advantage. What could be regarded as a splendid opportunity for a richly ironic exploitation of the gap between sacred etymology and profane usage was to him mere caricature and fakery—the use of the sublime to extol nihilism.

Others have stressed the "new virginity," in Gershom Scholem's phrase,[2] which Hebrew has acquired as a result of its development as a natural language. Modern Hebrew writers, says Scholem, "are free to wrestle with the words in a completely new emotional setting and on a level of freedom previously unattainable."

But this freedom, he notes, also involves a loss of form. "When language," he says, "is no longer forged, first and foremost, by the study of texts and through conscious reflection, but rather by unconscious processes in which the power of tradition is a minor factor at best, that language becomes by nature chaotic."[3] The "unconscious processes" to which Scholem refers are natural and involuntary. They depend on the changing needs of human communication. But language can also become chaotic through the *conscious* endeavor of writers determined to liberate it from tradition. Hence the apparent uneasiness with which Hebrew writers—even the most unorthodox—have been carrying out this "liberation" of the language, constantly oscillating between the poles of ancient text and modern colloquialism, rejecting the smooth familiarity of old, comfortable collocations for the immediate, rough impact of modern speech, but yearning for the splendor gone. Dame Hebrew, as the novelist Aharon Megged once said, has been a spoken language for a long time now, but she is still an aristocrat, still a lady. She has learned to perform all household jobs, but unlike that modest housewife, Yiddish, Dame Hebrew does them in her Sunday best. The same ambivalent feeling about the nature of Hebrew shows in a recent interview given by the novelist A. B. Yehoshua, in which he appears determined to drop his attempts to

5

2. "Reflections on S. Y. Agnon," *Commentary,* 44 (December 1967), 60.
3. *Ibid.,* p. 59.

imitate colloquial speech. "I think the answer—not just in my case—should be to return to a style as rich as possible. I've become allergic to lean Hebrew." The same allergy to lean Hebrew was already there in an interview Yehoshua gave ten years ago. But at that time he thought rich language was beyond his reach: "I'm incapable of experiencing the entire associative burden of the language, the way Agnon can, for instance." This new inclination to do what he thought he couldn't do ten years ago is, I think, highly significant.

3

The struggle to mold an idiom free from a tradition which has become irrelevant, and yet an idiom as regular and elegant as the language of tradition, has left little room for the more radical experiments undertaken in literatures that have been spared this dilemma. This may partly account for the nonmodernist character of much Hebrew literature, and particularly of much Hebrew fiction. But language is not the whole story.

Beyond and above it, the entire mental climate connected with the state of Israel, with its foundation, its wars, and other struggles, has made modernism a problem. For one central element in modernism is incompatible with this mentality—the element of doubt and irony, which conflicts with the passion and conviction of national movements. Nor does "dehumanization," in Ortega y Gasset's sense, go together with them. There has been little room, in the Israeli climate of opinion, for a "dehumanized" literature of pure aesthetic value.

It was only with the weakening of conviction that Hebrew literature could come closer to the mainstream of twentieth-century literature. In the following sections, I shall outline three important phases in the development of Israeli literature: the 1948 war generation, the "New Wave" of the 1950s and 1960s, and the literature of the present. These are by no means the only divisions possible, but they serve to set off the process of maturation, which is my main thesis. Both prose and poetry are included, but are dealt with separately.

4

"It goes without saying," said the late novelist Haim Hazaz at the

Hebrew Writers' Association conference celebrating Israel's twentieth anniversary, "that Israeli literature [should] be a responsible literature . . . a literature concerned above all with the individual and the community, with the people and the country, the people and their neighbors, the people and the diaspora, and similar subjects requiring seriousness, courage, and honesty. . . . Above all: books shouldn't be mere books, writers shouldn't be anonymous, shouldn't be lukewarm, comfortable people . . . they should be heroes of a national struggle, of a class-war, of culture; people of conviction and responsibility."

This came as recently as 1968, and was definitely anachronistic. Falling back on attitudes no longer in fashion, Hazaz voiced his discontent with fashion. The commitment to national and social causes which he advocated, the backbone of Israeli literature about the time of the foundation of the state, had long been questioned. Interestingly, however, this commitment had not really been done away with. It is a measure of the singular nature of literary life in Israel that Hazaz's words, incredible as they would seem in any other part of the Western world, could pass without much notice at an Israeli writers' conference in 1968.

Twenty years earlier, such ideas had been the norm. Any one of the many editorials and manifestos published in literary supplements or journals at the time of the 1948 war can serve to illustrate the socialist-realist approach of the period. That approach was perhaps stricter than the literary practice itself, which often digressed, as a free literature must, from ideology. "Our generation," wrote the novelist Moshe Shamir in an editorial for *Yalkut Ha-re'im* (*The Friends' Knapsack*), a short-lived magazine published on the eve of the war, "will be a generation writing realistic literature, searching and revealing. It will not necessarily be revolutionary in literary terms, but it shall, it must, follow the revolution of life." Earnest symposia, published by the literary weekly *Massa,* were devoted to the idea of "progressive art," and to the question of whether art was supposed to serve society and ideology or to be progressive through its very greatness as art. To forestall the attacks of traditionalists like Kurtzweil, who condemned the discontinuity between those "progressive" youngsters and the Jewish tradition, moderate leftists such as Aharon Megged declared they loved "not only what is faraway, the fighting Koreans, the liberated Chinese,

7

the oppressed blacks," but also new immigrants from the Jewish diaspora. Yigal Allon, now foreign minister, at a convention of Palmach (pre-State fighting units) veterans in 1953, praised the literature that "came out of the Palmach and served it." The Palmach, said Allon, "would have been unthinkable without our young writers and poets." Its writing, he said, was a test of the level of a Palmach unit no less than its training, weapons, or ammunition.

This confusion of art and life ("Our youth was not a mere 'phase'; it was culture, it was spiritual life"—Aharon Megged) did not necessarily result in real observation of life. This, perhaps, is a paradox inherent in all socialist realism; too preoccupied with revolutionizing life, it seldom looks at life itself.

Those writers seldom looked, for instance, at the living individual. Indeed one way of distinguishing them from later Israeli writers is to contrast (as many writers on the subject have done) their "collective" themes with their successors' concern for the individual. They defined themselves, says Robert Alter, "through a repeated sifting of the various social, political, and ideological materials that were the particular circumstances of the Israeli self at a fixed point in time."[4] Moshe Shamir's popular wartime heroes, Uri of *He Walked in the Fields* (1947) or Elik of *With His Own Hands* (1951), are more or less typical products of the youth movement and kibbutz, of the "religion of labor" and collectivist ideology.

At the same time, I am not entirely convinced that concern for the broad issues of society and the nation is peculiar to these writers. It is no less central, I suspect, to the literature of the fifties and sixties.[5] One could argue that even Amos Oz's latest collection of stories, *The Hill of Evil Counsel* (1976), has the birth of Israel, rather than any particular Israeli, for its real subject.

What *is* peculiar to the writers of the 1948 generation is their relative certainty about the values of their society. Although S. Yizhar, the most admired member of that group, had his misgivings about the treatment of Arabs, he did not question the very raison d'être of Zionism and Israel until *The Days of Ziklag,* his most ambitious (and, for the time being, last) novel, which came out in 1958.

Self-satisfaction is hardly a writer's best friend, and it certainly

8

4. "New Israeli Fiction," *Commentary,* 47 (June 1969).
5. This is Harold Fisch's thesis in his review "Unique and Universal," *Commentary* 54 (August 1972).

does not sharpen his perception. Lack of nuance, abundant rhetoric, and pomposity are some of the flaws which must be weighed against the attractive side of a literature passionately dedicated to a great vision. And, while "following the revolution of life," it was not, to use Shamir's above-quoted understatement, "revolutionary in literary terms." Quite the contrary.

5

The literature of the late 1950s and the 1960s reacted against such confidence. This second phase of Israeli fiction has been labeled the "New Wave" (the title of a study by the Israeli critic Gershon Shaked). In terms of our threefold division, it must be distinguished from a still newer wave of the 1970s. To be precise, some of its members are "new" and others are "newer."

A. B. Yehoshua, perhaps the best writer of the first New Wave, has repeatedly said that his group's major concern was to get away from all identifiable Israeli reality. "We were determined to leave out what was local, which had so overtaxed the literature before us." The result, in his case, was *The Death of the Old Man* (1962), a collection of allegorical fables, free of local flavor and diametrically opposed to the parochial naturalism of his elders. Though a wholesome corrective, this proved to be a dead end, because its Kafkaism was external gesture rather than inner necessity. It was later repudiated by the author himself and followed by another collection of stories, *Opposite the Forests* (1968),[6] more rounded and local in subject and color.

The original impulse to blot out all Israeli color and belong nowhere is most revealing. It is related to the kind of embarrassment one feels on meeting a typical fellow countryman abroad—the embarrassment of seeing oneself in a mirror. It is the very opposite of the 1948 generation's firm identification with their own values, and shows a weariness with those values.

Surely significant, however, is that this walkout, the withdrawal to a no-man's-land of existential angst, was so short-lived. In returning to the Israeli fold, Yehoshua opted to confront, not waive, the old values. In "Opposite the Forests," the title story of the second collection, the Israeli student who becomes the tacit accomplice of an Arab in burning down the Jewish National Fund forest (that is, the forest planted by his parents' generation) is no

9

6. The English version is titled *Three Days and a Child,* translated by Miriam Arad (Doubleday, 1970).

longer a destructive Everyman. He is, rather, the destructive *Israeli,* questioning his parents' lifework to the point of gloating over its ruin. Significantly, the destruction of the parents' dream is here related to guilt feelings toward the Arabs: a long-destroyed Arab village emerges out of the ashes of the burned forest.

Thus the younger generation's refusal to carry on the Great Work was not exactly the *Lo-ikhpatiyut* (devil-may-care attitude) for which their elders blamed them. Aharon Megged, whose many editorials in *Massa* serve as a fascinating chronicle of Israeli literature in the fifties, angrily quotes a manifesto by the then new *Akhshav (Now)* magazine: "Liberate Hebrew literature from its dependence on 'Jewish Life,' on the 'Great Work'! Let the writer be moved by the dictates of contemporary life. . . ." This double repudiation, of Jewishness and of socialism, shows, says Megged, a return to the notorious Jewish habit of self-denigration. It is, he says elsewhere, "an evasion of the need to face the problem of the day; a flight to the individual, to meaninglessness."

But it was not, of course. I cannot think, in fact, of a less "meaningless," less nihilistic body of mid-twentieth-century literature. And I cannot think of a more hilarious piece of criticism than Kurtzweil's attack on the "nihilistic" Oz: "If Satan had literary gifts, he would write like Amos Oz"(!). Even avant-garde magazines like *Akhshav* (founded 1957) and *Yokhani* (1961–1967), or their precursor *Likrat (Towards)* (1953–1954), with all their tirades against the literary establishment, gave "one's human duties" their full due. The critics in these journals, notably the highly influential poet Natan Zach, advocated fidelity to one's own inner life, a deliberate avoidance of what is public, a return to those neglected writers of the past who, unlike the popular names, had been "unable to quench their generation's thirst for grand certainties." Surely this had nothing to do with "nihilism."

It was, rather, the confrontation of one set of values by another. The "grand certainties" of the past were being questioned. At the same time, they were still strongly felt to be imperative, a necessary moral justification for unending political, military, and economic strife. Thus, there was plenty of occasion for pitting the disillusioned individual against them. Yehoshua's student, gloating over the ashes of the Jewish National Fund forest, is only a particularly

10

radical specimen in a long gallery of rebels who populate the novels of Megged, Yizhar, Hanoch Bartov, David Shahar, Binyamin Tammuz, and others in the 1950s and 1960s. But rebellion needs an object against which to pit itself, and the object was still very much there in those novels.

However, the object of rebellion now took on a more evasive form. Society and state became less explicit, more of a metaphor. Yehoshua's early allegorical Kafkaism, though later mellowed down, points to a change of style which was taking place. The grand certainties, though still very much there as objects of doubt, were now grappled with symbolically rather than directly. Guilt feelings about the Arabs, for instance, were no longer discussed as a moral problem (as in Yizhar's wartime novellas), but implied in a symbolic plot, as in the story "Opposite the Forests." The same holds for the Holocaust: first it was a direct, literal experience, as in Uri Orlev's *Soldiers of Lead* (1956); later it was treated more metaphorically in two novels by poets: Haim Gouri's *The Chocolate Deal* and Yehuda Amichai's *Not of This Time, Not of This Place* (both 1964).[7]

The dominant mode of the New Wave is thus symbolic. Outwardly this mode is a reaction against the explicitness of earlier Israeli prose. More intrinsically, it is a result, I think, of a split in sensibility between preoccupation with the individual self and inability to dissolve the commitment to supra-individual issues. As a result, it uses individual life to suggest broader social and national issues or, alternatively, makes "personal neurosis wear the guise of, fix on, national conflict" (Yehoshua). In either case, the result is symbolic.

The most obvious case in point is that of the novelist Amos Oz. The demonic power that permeates his stories is inner violence, which women possess, men suffer, and animals symbolize. But this private violence, as often noted, is closely interwoven with Israel's threatened military position. In his recent novella "The Hill of Evil Counsel," the same drives impel Ruth Kipnis, a respectable housewife, to elope with a British admiral and the Russian ladies from next door to rape her child. These drives are closely related to the totalitarian-messianic politics of the Kipnises' subtenant, a member of a dissenting terrorist organization on the eve of the 1948 war. And

11

7. Gouri's novel, translated by Seymour Simckes, was published by Holt, Rinehart & Winston, 1968; Amichai's novel, translated by Shlomo Katz, was published by Harper & Row, 1968.

it is on both planes—of sex and of politics—that Dr. Hans Kipnis's enlightened vision of nice family life and a nice state, with Martin Buber for president, is then shattered.

6

The first appearance of "The Hill of Evil Counsel" in the magazine *Keshet* in 1975 was followed by a highly perceptive, though perhaps excessively vehement, review by the novelist Amalia Kahana-Karmon. Her observations show some of the tendencies of what I earlier referred to as the "newer" wave, or the third phase in my scheme. The fact that she is older than Yehoshua or Oz shows that writers who represent one phase cannot always be classified by age. Nor are members of the "new" wave excluded from this "newer" style.

All things in Oz's world, Kahana-Karmon says, "are found and proved to be insubstantial, for a simple reason: they are of no interest in themselves. There is neither concern, nor love, nor tenderness, nor respect for them in themselves. Even all association with them, their use as mere props, is cautious, timid, reticent. Sooner or later they are bound to be sacrificed, deliberately, like pawns on a chess-board. Oz's eye is always on guard, always in search of something which exists beyond things, which alone is in focus. Something hostile, lurking, evil." The same holds for Oz's characters, she says. They are set in a time and a place, but they don't belong there. They don't exist for their own sake, but only to be threatened by a murderous transcendent being, absolutely determined to wipe them off the face of the earth.

The reviewer's subsequent psychological speculations (Oz, she says, painfully discovers himself in that murderous being) are less illuminating than the literary desideratum implied in what she says. Kahana-Karmon desires a return to a "concern for things," to the sights and sounds of the world, which Oz misses because of an obsession with what is beyond them, or because of a constantly inward-turned eye, which is the same thing.

This is not to be understood as a call to return to the realism of the 1948 generation. The respect for things in themselves, which the reviewer cannot find in Oz, is equally absent there. Yizhar, it is true, can beautifully convey the sheer physical magnificence of a horse on the run, or the sound of a well on a quiet night. In the last analysis, however, the writers of the 1940s, the 1950s, and the 1960s, both "realists" and "symbolists," both the old and the new waves, read their own vision, or myth—or antivision, or antimyth—into reality. They impose a scheme on it, be it a highly virtuous scheme not unlike socialist realism, or a less virtuous one, skeptical of the accepted norms.

Only recently has reality itself begun to come into its own in Israeli fiction. Kahana-Karmon's own collection of stories, *Under One Roof* (1971), and her one novel, *And Moon in the Valley of Ajalon* (1971), are subtle, nervous accounts of the strange shapes and colors of a vibrating world, ever reflecting the changing moods of her adolescent and middle-aged women in love. Her marvelously flexible syntax and her peculiar blend of ancient diction and up-to-date inflections of tone, hardly retainable in translation, serve to underline her very personal sensibility. Yitzhak Orpaz, in *A House for One,* has outgrown the excessive symbolism of his earlier novels, although his deliberate renunciation of an overall thematic pattern at times results in amorphousness. Yehoshua, too, has recently written one or two stories that are free not only from his early Kafkaism, but also from the later combination of local flavor and symbolic meaning. These stories, though involving army life and other collective experiences which tend to drag both writer and reader in the direction of ideology, are down-to-earth accounts of psychological states—not at all meant to be sacrificed, "like pawns on a chess-board," to any "transcendent being," murderous or otherwise. One could further mention, as examples of prose free from myth and symbol, some less recent phenomena in Israeli prose: Y. Knaz's gripping tales of Gothic pathology in rural life; Aharon Appelfeld's quiet, resigned account of lives truncated by the psychological aftereffects of the Holocaust; or the playwright Hanoch Levin's shabby men and women, ever engaged in a pathetic sadomasochistic battle of the sexes.

In an interview not long ago, Yehoshua connects the recent change in his own writing with a general change in Israeli mentality since the 1973 war. The Israelis, he says, have lost much of their self-confidence. There is therefore no point in repeating what he did in "Opposite the Forests"—pitting an alienated protagonist against a self-confident environment. Instead, his alienated protagonist can now return to the fold, which has itself become alienated from its former certainties. His characters, in other words, can now move to the center of Israeli life.

Like all generalizations, this one is only partly true. There is certainly much opportunity left for individual alienation in a country constantly thrown into conflict with itself by the force of circumstances. What is clear, in any case, is that the last war has put in question not only the original moral certainties but also the subsequent anticertainties, and has paved the way for a more receptive, more open frame of mind. All certainties gone, Israeli literature must do without the comfortable content and forms which those certainties made safe.

7

Hebrew poetry has lately suffered three major losses. The poets Avraham Shlonsky, Nathan Alterman, and Lea Goldberg have all died within the last seven years, leaving behind, as the only great survivor, Uri Zvi Greenberg, a highly individualistic expressionist who is also one of our most militant nationalists. Hebrew prose, too, has recently lost two of its great names: Nobel prizewinner S. Y. Agnon and Haim Hazaz. But while Agnon, with his unique blend of charming sageness and modern consciousness of crisis, still acts as a central influence on Hebrew prose, the three late poets have long served as targets for rejection. And the stronger their spell on young Israeli poets, the more violent has their rejection been. One could claim, indeed, that this rejection has made contemporary Hebrew poetry possible.

The most articulate and insistent spokesman of the rejection was the poet Natan Zach. In a series of essays in the fifties and sixties, Zach did for Hebrew poetry what T. S. Eliot did thirty or forty years earlier for English poetry. He blamed Alterman for the same mellifluous, mechanically regularized, inauthentic, generalized "poetic" verbosity that Eliot found in Tennyson and the Georgians. Like the New Critics, he advocated concreteness and adherence to time, place, and experience. Like F. R. Leavis, he spoke in the name of moral seriousness, commitment to feeling, empathy with others. "Alterman versifies," he said, "as a substitute for what he should feel."

Again like Eliot, Zach revised, along with the critic Shlomo Grodzensky, the canon of Hebrew poetry. As in Donne or Marvell,

14

the virtues now admired were those of ironic distance, lack of pompousness, colloquialism. These qualities proved to belong, not to the famous poets like Bialik (the pre-State "poet laureate") or Shlonsky, who rebelled against Bialik's authority and introduced a new, nonbiblical style, but to lesser poets: Ya'akov Steinberg, David Vogel, and Yehuda Karni.

The poets now in favor, unlike Alterman or Bialik before him, shied away from what was public, unable (to repeat Zach's words) "to quench their generation's thirst for grand certainties." This fact shows that the development of Israeli poetry ran parallel to the above-outlined development of Israeli prose. In terms of sheer output, poetry has been much richer than prose, perhaps because it does not require the leisure and perspective which prose requires. And its sheer volume explains, in part, the greater number of individual achievements. As in prose, modernism in poetry has been made possible by the withdrawal from ideological certainties. Shlonsky and Alterman[8] were as deeply steeped in socialist Zionism as were the prose writers of the 1948 generation (who were often their great admirers), and the reaction against their style, like the reaction against those prose writers, was inseparable from a decline in ideology.

Shlonsky and Alterman, however, were brilliant craftsmen. Alterman, in addition, was a much more complex poet than what I said may imply. Not unlike Brecht, but with greater integrity, he was torn between a highly refined private sensibility and a deep commitment to public ideas. Zach's dismissal of Alterman's work, like Eliot's one-time dismissal of Milton, is subjective historiography and cannot possibly detract from his importance.

The fact remains, however, that in the mid-fifties a group of poets headed by Zach, Yehuda Amichai, and David Avidan introduced a new style of poetry, marked by much that was antithetic to Alterman and his followers. Haim Gouri, the representative poet of the 1948 war and a disciple of Alterman, regretted, in an oft-quoted poem, that his generation "had no time." Zach and his friends now insisted on having time for themselves, on being less (and more) than mouthpieces for an era. This reductive tendency also involved a reduction in tone, which became understated, studiedly inelegant, ironicized through obvious rhyme or parodied liturgical allusion. English and American poetry, which had become the only body of

15

---

8. Lea Goldberg had been a nonideological poet all along.

foreign poetry accessible to many young poets and replaced their elders' favorites, Pushkin and Schiller, also influenced this new style.

This generalized account of the change, however, calls for at least two qualifications. First, the switch from overstatement to understatement was central, but not universal. Yehuda Amichai's natural gift for profuse imagery is often closer—in color, not in irregular syntax—to Dylan Thomas than, say, to Auden. And Dahlia Ravikovitch's exotic geography of the unconscious shows little ironic restraint. They do, however, participate in the general retreat from great issues, and in Ravikovitch there is hardly a reference to collective experiences. Second, the change described is not meant to draw an absolute line between the young and the old, for the simple reason that the old have often proved to be more capable of renewal than the young. Amir Gilboa, Abba Kovner, Anadad Eldan, T. Carmi, and Ozer Rabin, all 1948 poets in terms of their age—let alone Avot Yeshurun, who is now in his seventies—have turned out to be more susceptible to change than some younger people I have mentioned, who have either been chewing their cuds or stopped writing altogether.

8

In a sense, Israeli poetry, like Israeli prose, now shows signs of entering a third and "newer" phase. I don't think one could simply apply to it what we have said about prose—that it switched from a thought-scheme imposed on reality to a free observation of reality. But recent changes in poetry seem related to those in prose in a more oblique sense.

In a recent interview, Meir Wieseltier, a much-discussed younger poet and a central figure in the influential quarterly *Siman-Kri'a*, distinguishes his own poetry from that of his predecessors, who were "uncommitted" and "romantic" and took the self to be an "autonomous being." His own self, on the other hand, is "open, exposed in all directions, susceptible to constant influences and influxes."

One uncommitted romantic is, I suppose, Natan Zach. His dismissal—which began ten years ago in the very same *Akhshav* magazine that had published and celebrated him—is the sort of poetic justice no influential poet can escape. It is his turn now to be accused of being divorced from reality. Interestingly, however, fidelity to self is Zach's reality, which he finds lacking in Alterman; openness to the world is Wieseltier's reality, which he seems to find lacking in Zach. In this, Wieseltier's objection to Zach is surprisingly close to Amalia Kahana-Karmon's objection to Oz. Both the poet and the novelist want literature to expose itself—in very different ways, of course—to the direct impact of "things."

To Zach and his followers, authenticity meant a colloquial, "nonpoetic" style. This is still often accepted, either by Zach's many imitators or by independent talents such as Dan Pagis, who has moved away from a Rilkean romanticism to a dry, highly personal idiom. At the same time, a breakthrough is felt—in the poets Ya'ir Hurvitz, Mordechai Geldman, or Yona Wallach—to a more luxuriant language. I doubt if one can relate this point to the previous one and say that the new openness to a many-colored world calls for a more colorful language. This would be neat but inaccurate, particularly since the poets just mentioned happen to be perfect introverts, steeped in their utterly private worlds. But it is, I think, no accident that this change in style coincides with Yehoshua's earlier quoted words about the need to return to a style "as rich as possible." Both the poet and the novelist seem to feel that the limitation on expression owing to an overuse of colloquial layers of Hebrew, and an avoidance of its "higher" literary layers, is too heavy a price to pay for the direct impact gained.

We have come full circle and are back at what literature is really made of—words. The brief outline I have drawn now seems to confirm that contemporary Israeli literature is marked not by a distrust of words, but, on the contrary, by an ongoing discovery of the potentialities of language. Its paradoxical advantage, when compared with the literatures of Europe, lies in the many things it has not yet done with language. It has had neither a Joyce nor a Rilke, and it can look forward to many adventurous explorations of the undiscovered terrains of language. In the meantime, the achievement of Israeli literature appears in its present unembarrassed return to the treasures it had to relinquish in order to define itself as a contemporary, secular literature. Having reached relative freedom by denying its heritage, it can now come back to traditional forms and give them a pulse of life independent of tradition. The result should be extremely interesting.

FICTION

Badenheim 1939

Aharon Appelfeld

Spring returned to Badenheim. Bells rang in the nearby country church. The shadows of the forest drew back into the forest. The sun scattered the remaining darkness, and its light spilled out along the main street, from square to square. It was a moment of transition. Soon the holiday-makers would invade the town. Two inspectors passed from street to street, checking the flow of sewage in the drains. Over the years, the town had seen many tenants come and go, but its modest beauty was still intact.

Trudy, the pharmacist's ailing wife, stood at the window. She looked about her with the feeble gaze of a chronic invalid. The beneficent sunlight touched her pallid face and she smiled. A difficult winter, a strange winter, had ended. Storms played havoc with the housetops. Rumors spread. Trudy's sleep was disturbed by hallucinations. She spoke incessantly of her married daughter, while Martin assured her that everything was all right. That was how the winter passed. Now she stood at the window, resurrected.

The low, well-kept houses looked tranquil once again. Islands of white in a green sea. This is the season when you hear nothing but the rustle of things growing and then, by chance, you catch sight of

19

an old man holding a pair of pruning shears, with the look of a hungry raven.

"Has the post come?" asked Trudy.

"It's Monday today. The post won't arrive until afternoon."

The carriage of Dr. Pappenheim the impresario charged out of the forest and came to a halt on the main street. Dr. Pappenheim alighted and waved in greeting. No one responded. The street was steeped in silence.

"Who's here?" asked Trudy.

"Dr. Pappenheim has just arrived."

Dr. Pappenheim brings with him the moist breath of the big city, an air of celebration and anxiety. He'll be spending his time at the post office—sending off cables and express letters.

Apart from Dr. Pappenheim's appearance in town, nothing has happened. The mild spring sun shines as it does every year. People meet at the café in the afternoon, and devour pink ice cream.

"Has the post come yet?" she asked again.

"Yes. There's nothing for us."

"Nothing." Her voice sounded ill.

Trudy got back into bed, feverish. Martin removed his jacket and sat down next to her: "Don't worry. We had a letter just last week. Everything is all right." Her hallucinations persisted: "Why does he beat her?"

"No one beats her. Leopold is a very nice man, and he loves her. Why do you think such things?"

Trudy shut up as though she had been scolded. Martin was tired. He put his head on the pillow and fell asleep.

The first of the vacationers arrived on the following day. The pastry shop window was decorated with flowers. In the hotel garden Professor Fusshalt and his young wife were to be seen, also Dr. Schutz and Frau Zauberblit—but to Trudy they looked more like convalescents in a sanatorium than people on vacation.

"Don't you know Professor Fusshalt?" asked Martin.

"They look very pale to me."

"They're from the city," said Martin, trying to mollify her.

Now, Martin knew that his wife was very ill. Medicines would be of no use. In her eyes the world was transparent, diseased, and poisoned, her married daughter held captive and beaten. Martin tried in vain to convince her. She stopped listening. That night, Martin sat down to write a letter to Helena, his daughter. Spring in Badenheim is delightful, beautiful. The first vacationers are already here. But your mother misses you so.

Trudy's disease was gradually seeping into him. He, too, began to distinguish signs of pallor on people's faces. Everything at home had changed since Helena's marriage. For a year they had tried to dissuade her, but it was no use. She was in love, head over heels as they say. A hasty marriage took place.

Dark green spring was now ascending from the gardens. Sally and Gerti, the local tarts, strolled along the boulevard dressed for the season. The townspeople had tried at one time to throw them out—a prolonged struggle that came to naught. The place had got used to them, as it had grown used to the eccentricities of Dr. Pappenheim, and to the alien summer people who transplanted themselves here like an unhealthy root. The owner of the pastry shop would not let the "ladies" set foot on his premises, thus depriving them of the most delicious cream cakes in the entire world. Boyish Dr. Schutz, who liked Sally, once took some cakes out to the street. When the owner of the shop found out about it later, he made a scandal, but that led nowhere either.

"And how are the young ladies?" asked Dr. Pappenheim merrily.

Over the years they had lost their big-city haughtiness—they had bought themselves a modest house and dressed like the local women. There had been a period of riotous parties, but the years and the courtesans of the town had pushed them aside. But for their savings, theirs would have been a sad predicament. They had nothing left but memories, which they mulled over like widows on long winter nights.

"How was it this year?"

"Everything is fine," said Pappenheim cheerfully.

"Wasn't it a strange winter, though?"

They were fond of Pappenheim, and over the years they had become interested in his strange *artistes*. Here, on alien terrain, they grasped eagerly at anything.

"Oh don't worry, don't worry—the festival is packed this year—lots of surprises."

21

"Who will it be this time?"

"A child prodigy, a *yanuka*. I discovered him this winter in Vienna."

"*Yanuka*," said Sally maternally.

Next day, the vacationers were all over Badenheim. The hotel bustled. Spring sunlight and excited people filled the town, and in the hotel garden porters hauled brightly colored luggage. But Dr. Pappenheim seemed to shrink in size. The festival schedule was ruined again. He ran through the streets. For years these artistes had been driving him mad, and now they wanted to wreck him altogether.

After leaving their luggage at the hotel, the people moved on toward the forest. Professor Fusshalt and his young wife were there. A tall man escorted Frau Zauberblit ceremoniously. "Why don't we turn left?" said Frau Zauberblit, and the company did indeed turn to the left. Dr. Schutz lagged behind as though enchanted.

"Why do they walk so slowly?" asked Trudy.

"They're on vacation, after all," said Martin, patiently.

"Who is that man walking with Frau Zauberblit? Isn't that her brother?"

"No, my dear. Her brother is dead. He has been dead for years."

That night the band arrived. Dr. Pappenheim rejoiced as if a miracle had happened. The porters unloaded horns and drums. The musicians stood at the gate like trained birds on a stick. Dr. Pappenheim offered sweets and chocolates. The driver hurried the porters on, and the musicians ate in silence. "Why were you late?" asked Pappenheim, not without relief. "The car was late," they answered.

Dressed in a frock coat, the conductor stood aside, as if all this were no concern of his. He'd had a struggle with Pappenheim the year before. Pappenheim was on the verge of dismissing him, but the senior musicians sided with their conductor, and nothing came of it. The conductor had demanded a contract for the usual three-year period. The quarrel ended in a compromise.

In the past, Pappenheim had lodged them on the ground floor of the hotel, in dark, narrow rooms. There was an emphatic clause in the new contract providing for proper lodging. Now they were all

23

anxious to see the rooms. Pappenheim walked over to the conductor and whispered in his ear, "The rooms are ready—top floor—large well-ventilated rooms." "Sheets?" asked the conductor. "Sheets as well." Pappenheim kept his promise. They were lovely rooms. Seeing them, the musicians were inspired to change into their blue uniforms. Pappenheim stood quietly by and did not interfere. In one of the rooms a quarrel broke out—over a bed. The conductor chided them: "Rooms like these deserve quiet. Now get everything together before you go down."

At ten o'clock, all was ready. The musicians stood in groups of three, instruments in hand. Pappenheim was furious. He would gladly have paid them compensation and sent them packing, but he could not afford to. More than anything else, they reminded him of his failures. Thirty years gone by. Always late and unrehearsed. Their instruments produced nothing but noise. And every year, new demands.

The evening began. People swarmed over the band like hornets. The musicians blew and hammered as though trying to drive them away. Dr. Pappenheim sat in the back, drinking steadily.

Next day, the place was calm and quiet. Martin got up early, swept the entrance, wiped the dust off the shelves, and made out a detailed purchase order. It had been a hard night. Trudy had not stopped raving. She refused to take medicine, and finally Martin had tricked her into swallowing a sleeping mixture.

At approximately ten o'clock, an inspector from the Sanitation Department entered the pharmacy, and said that he wanted to look the place over. He asked strange questions. Ownership title. Had it come through inheritance? When and from whom was it purchased? Property value. Surprised, Martin explained that the place had been whitewashed and thoroughly disinfected. The inspector took out a folding yardstick and measured. Then, neither thanking him nor apologizing, he went directly out into the street.

The visit made Martin angry. He believed in the authorities, and therefore he blamed himself. The back entrance was probably not in good repair. This short visit spoiled his morning. There was something in the wind. He went outside and stood on the lawn. A morning like any other. The milkman made his rounds bucolically, the musicians sprawled in the hotel garden sunning themselves, and Pappenheim left them alone. The conductor sat by himself shuffling a deck of cards. In the afternoon, Frau Zauberblit entered the pharmacy and announced that there was no place like Badenheim for a vacation. She was wearing a dotted poplin frock, but to Martin it seemed that her late brother was about to walk through the door.

"Isn't that strange?" he asked, not knowing what he was asking.

"Anything can happen," she said as though she had understood the question.

Martin was angry. It was all because of Trudy.

The musicians stayed in the garden all afternoon. They looked pathetic out of uniform. For years they had been used to fighting with Pappenheim; now they fought among themselves. The conductor did not interfere. He put down his deck, and watched them. A gaunt musician took a pay receipt out of his vest pocket, and waved it at his colleagues. They showed him his mistake. From Martin's garden this looked like a shadow play, perhaps because the light was fading. One by one, long shadows unrolled across the green lawn.

At twilight, the conductor hinted that it might be advisable to go up and change into uniform. They took their time, like old soldiers worn out by long service. The conductor chatted with Pappenheim. For some reason, Pappenheim found it necessary to give a long-winded explanation of the festival program. "I hear Mandelbaum is on the program too. Why, that's a spectacular achievement—how did you manage it?" "Hard work," said Pappenheim, and turned to go into the dining room. The guests were already eating hungrily. The waitress watched the kitchen door sharply. Her orders were late. But the cynical old waiters praised the food with an air of self-importance. Trudy's condition was no better. Martin's endless talk was futile. Everything seemed transparent and diseased to her. Helena was a prisoner on Leopold's estate, and when he came home from the barracks at night, he beat her.

"But don't you see?" she asked.

"No, I don't see."

"It's only my hallucinations."

Martin was angry. Trudy frequently mentioned her parents and the little house on the banks of the Vistula. Her parents died, and all contact with her brothers was lost. Martin said that she was still immersed in that world, in the mountains, with the Jews. And this was, to a certain extent, the truth. She was tortured by a hidden fear not her own, and Martin felt that her delusions were gradually penetrating into him, and that everything was on the verge of collapse.

Next day it was made known that the jurisdiction of the Department of Sanitation had been extended, and henceforth the department would be entitled to carry out independent investigations. The modest announcement was posted on the town bulletin board. Without further ado, the clerks of the department set about investigating all places designated on their map. The detailed investigations were carried out by means of questionnaires sent in from the district head office. One of the musicians, who bore his Polish name with a strange pride, remarked that the clerks reminded him of marionettes. His name was Leon Semitzki. Fifty years ago he had emigrated from Poland with his parents. He had a fondness for his Polish memories, and when in good spirits he would talk about his country. Dr. Pappenheim liked his stories, and would sit with the musicians and listen.

The clouds vanished, and the spring sun shone warmly. A vague anxiety spread over the faces of the old musicians. They sat together and said nothing. Semitzki broke the silence all of a sudden: "I'm homesick for Poland." "Why?" Pappenheim wanted to know. "I don't know," said Semitzki. "I was seven years old when I left, but it seems like only a year ago."

"They're very poor there," someone whispered.

"Poor, but not afraid of death."

That night nothing happened in Badenheim. Dr. Pappenheim was melancholic. He could not get Semitzki off his mind. He too recalled those rare visits to Vienna of his grandmother from the Carpathians. She was a big woman, and brought with her the odor of millet, the smell of the forest. Pappenheim's father hated his mother-in-law. Rumors flourished. Some said that the department was on the track of a sanitary hazard, others thought that this time it might be the Tax Department masquerading as the Sanitation Department. The musicians exchanged views. The town itself was calm, cooperative, complying with all the department's requests. Even the proud owner of the pastry shop agreed to give information. There was nothing noticeably different, but the old musicians surveyed the town, imparting a strange unease.

At the end of April, the two reciters showed up. Dr. Pappenheim wore his blue suit in their honor. They were tall and gaunt, with an intensely spiritual look. Their passion was Rilke. Dr. Pappenheim, who had discovered them in Vienna seven years before, at once discerned a morbid melody in their voices which enchanted him. Thereafter he simply could not do without them. At first their recitals drew no response, but in recent years people had discovered their elusive melody—and found it intoxicating. Frau Zauberblit sighed with relief: They're here.

The reciters were twin brothers who, over the years, had become indistinguishable. But their manner of reading was not the same—as if sickness spoke with two voices: one tender and appeasing, the remains of a voice; the other clear and sharp. Frau Zauberblit declared that without the double voice, life would be meaningless. Their recitals were balm to her, and she would murmur Rilke to herself in the empty nights of spring, as though sipping pure nectar.

The musicians, who worked at dance halls in the winter and resorts in the summer, could not understand what people found in those morbid voices. In vain did Pappenheim try to explain the magic. Only Semitzki said that their voices excited his diseased cells. The conductor hated them—he called them the clowns of the modern age.

And meanwhile spring is at work. Dr. Schutz pines after the schoolgirl like an adolescent. Frau Zauberblit is engrossed in conversation with Semitzki, and Professor Fusshalt's young wife changes into her bathing costume and goes out to sunbathe on the lawn.

The twins are forever rehearsing. They can't do without the practice. "And I was naive enough to think that it was all spontaneous," said Frau Zauberblit.

"Practicing, practicing," said Semitzki. "If I had practiced when I was young, I never would have ended up in this second-rate outfit. I wasn't born here. I was born in Poland. And my parents didn't give me a musical education." After midnight, Dr. Pappenheim received a cable, worded as follows: *Mandelbaum taken ill. Will not arrive on time.* Dr. Pappenheim got up shaking and said, "This is a

27

catastrophe." "Mandelbaum," said Frau Zauberblit. "The entire arts festival is at stake," said Pappenheim. Semitzki tried to soothe them, but Pappenheim said, "This is the last straw." He sank into his grief like a stone. Frau Zauberblit brought out a bottle of Pappenheim's favorite French wine, but he wouldn't touch it, and all night long he moaned: "Mandelbaum, Mandelbaum."

And the investigations showed reality for what it was. From this point on, no one could say that the Department of Sanitation was ineffective. A feeling of strangeness, suspicion, and mistrust was in the air; still, the residents went about their usual business. The vacationers had their pastimes, and the local residents had their worries. Dr. Pappenheim was inconsolable over his great loss—Mandelbaum. Life was worthless since that cable had arrived. Professor Fusshalt's young wife declared that something had changed in Badenheim. The professor did not leave the room—his definitive book was about to go to the publisher, and he was busy with the proofs. His young wife, whom he spoiled like a kitten, understood nothing about his books. Her interests were confined to cosmetics and dresses. At the hotel they called her Mitzi.

In the middle of May, a modest announcement appeared on the bulletin board, stating that all Jewish citizens must register with the Sanitation Department before the month was out.

"That's me," said Semitzki. He seemed to be delighted.

"And me," said Pappenheim. "You wouldn't want to deprive me of my Jewishness, would you?"

"I would," said Semitzki, "but your nose is proof enough that you are no Austrian."

The conductor, who had learned over the years to blame everything on Pappenheim, said: "I have to get caught up in this bureaucratic mess all because of him. The clerks have gone mad, and I'm the one who suffers."

People started avoiding Pappenheim like the plague. He seemed not to notice, and rushed back and forth between the post office and the hotel.

Trudy's condition worsened the last two weeks. She talked on and on about death. No longer out of fear, but rather as if she were coming to know it, preparing to inhabit it. The strong medications that she swallowed drew her from one sleep to the next, and Martin saw her wandering off into the other regions of her life.

28

People confessed to each other, as if they were talking about a chronic disease which there was no longer any reason to hide. And their reactions varied from pride to shame. Frau Zauberblit avoided talking and asking questions. She pointedly ignored them. Finally she asked Semitzki, "Have you registered?"

"Not yet," said Semitzki. "I'll do it on a more festive occasion. You don't mean to say that I have the honor of addressing an Austrian citizen of Jewish origin?"

"You have indeed, sir."

"In that case, we'll be having a family party in the near future."

"Could you have thought otherwise?"

The sun stopped shining. The headwaiter himself served the white cherries for the cake. The lilac bushes climbed the veranda railing, and bees sucked greedily at the light blue flowers. Frau Zauberblit tied a silk scarf around her straw bonnet. "Brought in from Waldenheim this morning—they ripened early." "That's simply marvelous," said Frau Zauberblit. She adored these local voices.

"What are you thinking about?" asked Semitzki.

"I was remembering my grandfather's house—the rabbi from Kirchenhaus. He was a man of God. I spent my term vacations there. He used to walk along the river in the evenings. He liked growing things." Semitzki did not stop drinking: "Don't worry, children. Soon we'll be on our way. Just think—back to Poland."

Dr. Schutz ran about in a stupor. The schoolgirl was driving him mad. "Dr. Schutz, why not join intelligent company for an intelligent conversation?" said Frau Zauberblit. In academic circles, he was considered quite the prodigy—if a bit naughty.

"Have you registered?" said Semitzki.

"What?" he asked in surprise.

"Oh, you have to register, haven't you heard? According to the regulations of the Sanitation Department—which is, of course, a government department, a fine department, a department whose jurisdiction has been extended these last two months. And this most worthy department earnestly desires that you, Dr. Schutz, should register."

"This is no laughing matter, my dear," said Frau Zauberblit.

"In that case," he said, confused. He was the pampered darling of Badenheim. Everyone loved him. Dr. Pappenheim lamented his wasted musical talent. The prodigal son of his rich old mother, who never failed to bail him out at the end of the season.

A vague terror lurked in the eyes of the musicians. "Don't worry," said Dr. Pappenheim, rallying his courage, though he was feeling melancholy.

"But aren't we guests? Must we sign as well?" asked one of the musicians.

"It is my opinion," said Pappenheim dramatically, "that the Sanitation Department wishes to boast of its distinguished guests, and will, therefore, enter them in the Golden Book. Now that is nice of them—don't you think?"

"Maybe it's because of the *Ostjuden,*" said one of the musicians.

Semitzki rose to his feet: "What's the matter? You don't like me? I'm an Eastern Jew through and through—so you don't like me, eh?"

Badenheim's intoxicating spring is causing havoc again. Dr. Schutz is penniless, and has posted two express letters to his mother. The schoolgirl, it seems, is costing him a fortune. Frau Zauberblit and Semitzki sit together all day long. He might have been the only man left in the world. Dr. Pappenheim is depressed— the intoxicating spring never fails to make him sad. Frau Zauberblit has already rebuked him: "I'll defray the losses. Hand me the bill. If Mandelbaum continues to give you the runaround, I'll get the Krauss chamber ensemble." The twins wander through town looking cryptic. People at the hotel talk about them in whispers, as if they were sick. They eat nothing, and drink only coffee. The headwaiter says: "If only I could serve Rilke's death sonnets, maybe they would eat. That's probably all the food they can digest."

After breakfast, Frau Zauberblit, Semitzki, and Pappenheim decided unanimously to register at the Sanitation Department. The clerk did not so much as raise an eyebrow at Frau Zauberblit's declarations. Frau Zauberblit praised the department for its order and beauty. No wonder it had been promoted. Semitzki announced that his parents had come from Poland fifty years ago, and that he was still homesick. The clerk wrote all this down without a trace of expression.

That night Semitzki did not wear his blue uniform. The band played. Everyone saw at a glance that Frau Zauberblit had a sweetheart—she glowed like someone in love. The young wife of Professor Fusshalt was going mad. Professor Fusshalt was preoccupied with the book, and didn't leave his desk. She was fed up with the people in Badenheim. What was there to do here? Those readings again. They depressed her. One of the musicians, a cynic, tried to console her: "Don't be angry. In Poland, everything is beautiful, everything is interesting."

On the following day, Trudy's screams were heard in the street. From the hotel veranda, people watched the terrible struggle in progress. No one went down to help. Poor Martin fell on his knees in desperation, and begged: "Trudy, Trudy, be calm. There is no forest here—there are no wolves."

An alien night descended on Badenheim. The cafés were empty; people walked the streets in silence, as though being led along. The town seemed in the grip of some other vacation, from another place. Dr. Schutz led the tall schoolgirl about as though he were going to tie her up. Sally and Gerti strolled arm in arm like schoolgirls. The moist light of spring nights slithered on the pavement. The musicians sat on the veranda, observing the passing flow with sharp looks.

Dr. Pappenheim sat in the corner alone, reckoning sadly: The trio has deserted me again. Nobody will forgive me. And rightly so. Had I known, I would have planned it differently.

The deadline for registration was approaching. Three investigators from the district office arrived at the Sanitation Department. The conductor carried an interesting document in his vest pocket—his parents' baptismal certificates. Dr. Pappenheim was taken aback, and he said, "I would not have believed it." Strange, the conductor wasn't pleased.

"You're welcome to join the Jewish order, if you like. It's a fine old order," said Pappenheim.

"I don't believe in religion."

"You can be a Jew without religion, if you like."

"Who said so—the Sanitation Department?"

It poured that afternoon. They gathered in the lobby, and were served hot wine as on autumn days. Dr. Pappenheim was deep in a chess game with Semitzki. Toward evening, Frau Zauberblit's daughter arrived. From her father, General von Schmidt, she had inherited an erect carriage, blonde hair, pink cheeks, and a deep voice. She was a student at a lyceum for girls, far away from her mother.

General von Schmidt was still remembered there. He and his wife came to Badenheim the first year of their marriage, but von Schmidt had hated it, and called it Pappenheim, after the impresario. As far as he was concerned, it was no fit place for healthy people—no horses, no tennis, no hunting—no beer! They stopped coming after that and were gradually forgotten. They had a daughter. Years went by, and von Schmidt, who had started his career as a lieutenant, rose through the ranks. Soon afterward they were divorced. After the divorce, Frau Zauberblit, tall, slender, and suffering, appeared in Badenheim. That was the end of the matter.

The daughter stated at once that she had brought a document, a statement surrendering the so-called "rights of the mother." Frau Zauberblit studied the document and asked, "Is this what *you* wish?" "What my father wishes, and what I wish," she said, like someone who had learned a part. Frau Zauberblit signed. It was a hard and abrupt farewell. "Excuse me, I'm in a hurry," the daughter said on her way out. Her appearance shook the hotel. Frau Zauberblit sat mutely in the corner. A strange new pride seemed to show on her face.

Throughout the hotel, a secret was uniting the people. The conductor felt ill at ease for some reason, and sat down with the musicians. The twins were to perform that night. The proprietor of the hotel was arranging the small auditorium. They hadn't been seen on the veranda for two days now. Cloistered. "What do they do up there?" someone asked, and the headwaiter confirmed the fact that they had eaten nothing for two days. The people were standing by the windows, with the fading light on their faces. Pappenheim whispered, "They're rehearsing, aren't they wonderful?"

The silence of a house of prayer filled the small auditorium that evening. The audience was early, and Pappenheim darted back and forth between the doors as if that would make the twins come down before it was time. They came down precisely at eight o'clock, and took their place by the table. Pappenheim retreated toward the door, like a guard.

For two hours, they talked about death. They spoke in a calm, modulated voice, as if they had returned from hell and were no longer afraid. At the end of the recital, they stood up. The people bowed their heads and did not applaud. Pappenheim moved forward and took off his hat. He seemed about to fall on his knees.

Apple strudel was served in the afternoon. Frau Zauberblit had on her straw bonnet. Semitzki wore short trousers, and Pappenheim stood at the door like an unemployed actor. It seemed as if the old days were back.

At midnight, the *yanuka* arrived. The watchman refused to let him pass because he was not on the lists. And Dr. Pappenheim, who was amused, said, "But can't you see that he's Jewish?" When she heard, Frau Zauberblit said, "Everything is going according to plan. Isn't that wonderful?"

"You'll love him too," Pappenheim whispered.

"The impresario is a man of his word. By the way—in what language will the young artiste sing?"

"Why—Yiddish of course—he'll sing in Yiddish."

When Pappenheim presented him, they saw before them neither a child nor a man. He blushed; his suit was too long. "What's your name?" asked Frau Zauberblit, drawing near. "His name is Nahum Slotzker—and speak slowly," Pappenheim interrupted, "he doesn't understand German." Now they saw wrinkles around his eyes, but his face was the face of a child. The adults confused him.

"Where are you from—Lodz?" asked Semitzki in Polish.

The boy smiled and said, "From Kalashin."

It was a strange evening. Frau Zauberblit was like an amorous young girl. Semitzki paced the corridor like a retired gym instructor. The conductor shuffled cards and joked with the cook. The cook gave him freshly baked poppyseed cakes. She was of mixed parentage. Orphaned at an early age, she had been for several years the mistress of Graf Schutzheim, until his death.

"Do you think they'll let me come too?" she asked slyly.

"There's no question about it. Who will cook for us in the land of cold?"

"But I'm not wholly Jewish."

"Well, I'm not wholly anything."

"But your parents were both Jews, weren't they?"

"Yes, my dear, Jews by birth, but they converted to Christianity."

Next day, the patroness of the twins arrived in town. Frau Milbaum was tall and elegant, and she had an aura of majesty. Dr. Pappenheim was extremely glad to see her. He was always glad to see people returning to Badenheim.

The secret surrounds them little by little, a dread born of other intimations. They tread lightly, and speak in whispers. The waiters serve strawberries and cream. The frenzied shadow of summer is spread out on the broad veranda. The twins sit beside Frau Milbaum, flushed and silent. They look like children in a roomful of adults. Pappenheim has planned a full program, and there is a strange sense of anticipation in the air. The old people die between one interrogation and the next. The town swims in alcoholic fumes. Last night at the café, Herr Furst fell down and died. For years he had passed through the streets in his magnificent clothes. Next door, at the lottery house, another man died by the roulette table.

And the interrogations proceed quietly at the Sanitation Department. This is the center, and all the strands radiate from it. The department is now omniscient. They have maps, periodicals, a library—a person can sit and browse if he wishes.

The conductor registered at the department and came back smiling. They showed him a closetful of contracts, licenses, and credentials. Strange—his father was the author of an arithmetic book in Hebrew. "They know everything, and they're happy to show a man his past," said the conductor.

A barrier was erected at the town gate. No entrance, no exit. But it was not a total blockade. The milkmen delivered milk in the morning and the fruit truck unloaded its crates at the hotel. Both cafés were open, and the band played every evening. Yet it seemed that another time, from another place, had broken through and was quietly entrenching itself.

The banquet given for the *yanuka,* the child prodigy, began late. The guests filed through the corridor, lamplight on their faces. There were soft, woolly shadows on the carpet. The waiters served ice cream in coffee. The tables were laid in the hall. A few musicians

34

played to themselves in the corner. Tongues of darkness climbed the long, narrow windows.

Frau Milbaum sat on her throne, and green lights flashed from her green eyes. People avoided her look. "Where are my twins?" she asked in an undertone. No one answered. They seemed caught in a net. The twins were talking to Sally. Sally, in a long, flowered dress, was making faces like a concert singer. The twins, who seldom conversed with women, were embarrassed, and started to laugh.

Sally told them about the first festivals. Gerti appeared and said, "You're here." "Please meet two real gentlemen," said Sally. The twins offered their long, white hands. The *yanuka* sat mutely in the corner. Dr. Pappenheim explained in broken Yiddish that the banquet was about to begin. Everyone was anxious to hear him sing.

The guests drank heavily. Frau Milbaum sat enthroned, and now there was venom in her green eyes. So here, too, her life was becoming involved. She thought that there was a plot against her. That morning she had registered at the Sanitation Department. The clerk did not take her titles into account, the ones bequeathed her by her first husband; and he did not so much as mention her second husband, a nobleman of the royal family. There was nothing on the form but her father's name.

Semitzki was chattering away gaily in faulty Polish. He turned good-naturedly to Frau Milbaum and said: "Come and join our jolly circle. You'll find it amusing, I believe." Her look was metallic. "I am obliged," she said.

"A fine society—Jewish nobility." Semitzki was relentless.

"I understand," she said without looking.

"We would be delighted to have the lady's company," Semitzki continued to pique her.

"Don't worry, the duchess will get used to us," whispered Zimbelmann the musician.

"She registered, didn't she? What's all this distance about?" added someone from the corner.

Frau Milbaum scanned them with her green eyes. "Riffraff." She finally spat out the word.

"She calls us riffraff," said Zimbelmann. "Riffraff she calls us."

The waiters served cheese wedges and Bordeaux wine. Dr.

Pappenheim sat with the *yanuka*. "There's nothing to fear. These are all very nice people. You'll stand on the stage and sing," he said, trying to encourage the boy.

"I'm afraid."

"Don't be afraid. They're very nice people."

The conductor emptied one glass after another. His face was turning red. "We're going to your native land, Semitzki. We must learn to drink."

"They drink real alcohol there—not beer soup."

"What will they do with a goy like me?"

"Don't worry, they'll only circumcise you," said Zimbelmann, but felt he had gone too far. "Don't worry. The Jews aren't barbarians for all that."

Dr. Langmann approached the duchess and said, "I'm getting out of here tomorrow."

"But aren't you registered at the Sanitation Department?"

"I still consider myself a free citizen of Austria. They have to send the Polish Jews to Poland. That's the country for them. I'm here by mistake. One is entitled to a mistake now and then, isn't one? You're also here by mistake. Are we to forfeit our freedom on account of a mistake?"

Now she scrutinized Sally and Gerti as they led the twins into a corner. "Whores," she glowered at them. The twins were greatly amused and as gay as two boys stumbling upon a wild party.

After midnight, they set the boy on the stage. He trembled. Dr. Pappenheim stood over him like a father. The boy sang about the dark forest, the haunt of the wolf. It was a kind of lullaby. Seated around the stage, the musicians stared dumbly. The world was collapsing before their very eyes. Someone said, "How wonderful!" Semitzki sobbed drunkenly. Frau Zauberblit approached him and asked, "What happened?"

At that moment, Sally felt an oppressive fear. "Dr. Pappenheim, may we go as well? Is there room for us?"

"What a question," he scowled at her. "There is room in our kingdom for every Jew and for everyone who wants to be a Jew. It is a mighty kingdom."

"I'm afraid."

"No need to fear, my dear, we'll all be going soon."

36

Gerti stood aside as though she had no right to ask questions.

The town is empty; the light no longer flows. It seems to have frozen, listening intently. An alien orange shadow nibbles stealthily at the geranium leaves. Bitter damp seeps into the thatch of the creeping vines. Pappenheim worries about the musicians. He treats them to chocolate, cream cake. Such kindness makes them submissive. No more quarrels. Now the light filters through the thick drapery and illuminates the wide veranda. Dr. Schutz's love is not so easy as in days gone by. The orange shadow lingers upon him and his beloved. The high school girl burrows ever more deeply into his summer coat, as though afraid of a sudden parting.

The post office is shut down. A cold light falls on the smooth marble stairs. The gate with its Gothic relief conjures up a memorial in ruins. The night before, Pappenheim stood outside the post office and laughed. "Everything is closed."

As Pappenheim stood laughing on the stairs of the post office, a terrible struggle was in progress at the pharmacy. Two men from out of town grabbed the poison chest. Martin fought them, snatched the jars from their hands, and shouted after them, "I will not permit this." Those two skeletal men had arrived a few days before. Their faces were cold with desperation.

Mandelbaum and his trio arrived like thieves in the night. Pappenheim took them downstairs, and brought tea.

"What happened?"

"We got a transfer," said Mandelbaum.

"Did you ask for it?"

"Of course we asked for it. A young man, a junior officer, has already sent on the documents. We told him that we had to get to the festival. He laughed, and he gave us a transfer. What do you say? We're in for it."

"That's wonderful," said Pappenheim. "Oh, I can't believe it. You need to rest."

"No, dear friend. That's not why we're here. We didn't have a chance to prepare anything. We have to rehearse."

The tin sun was fixed on the cold horizon. "How far is it from here to Vienna?" asked someone adrift on his own limp thoughts. "I'd say—two hundred kilometers, no more." These words hung in the air like tired ravens. The old favorite, apple strudel, was baking down in the kitchen. The sweet smell wafted on to the veranda.

"Why don't we ask for a visa?" said a musician who had traveled in his youth.

"Say you had a visa—where would you go?" The man was struck dumb by the question. The conductor put his card down and said: "As for me, I'm willing to go anywhere."

Martin took the winter clothes out of storage, and the house smelled of naphthaline. The dream of Poland calmed Trudy. Martin sat down and assured her: "In Poland, everything will be right. That's where we came from, and that's where we're bound. Those who were there have got to go back." There was music in his voice—Trudy listened and didn't ask questions.

A group of angry people stood by the dead phone, cursing the bureaucracy that, suddenly and without warning, had cut them off from their loved ones. Order, they grumbled, order. An energetic few wrote long letters of complaint. They described all the hardships that came from being disconnected. They claimed compensation from their travel agents, from all the authorities responsible for their being here. Of course, this was all futile. All telephone lines were disconnected; the post office was shut down. Domestic servants fled as if from a fire. The town began to live in a state of siege.

"What will they do to us in Poland?" asked one of the musicians.

"What do you mean? You'll be a musician as you've always been," answered a friend who dozed nearby.

"Then why all this moving around?"

"The force of circumstance," was the reply.

"Kill me, I don't understand. My common sense doesn't grasp it."

"In that case, kill your common sense and you'll start to understand."

Silence envelops the houses. The withered vines grow wild. The acacia flourishes. It is autumn and spring in a strange coupling. At night there is no air to breathe. Semitzki is on the bottle. He drinks like a peasant, mixes Polish and Yiddish. Of all his languages, the language of his childhood seems to be the only one left.

"Why are you drinking so much, dear?" asks Frau Zauberblit tenderly.

"When a man goes home he ought to be happy."

"It's cold there, really cold."

"Yes, but it's a pure, healthy cold, a cold with hope."

The registrations are over. The clerks at the Sanitation Department sit around drinking tea. They've done their duty. Now they await orders.

But surprises never cease in the streets. Several days ago, a resident of Badenheim, who had been a major in the Great War, stood near the post office, and demanded to know why it was closed. Pappenheim, who had not given up his habit of a daily visit to the closed post office, answered, perhaps incautiously, that the town was cut off.

"I don't understand," said the major. "Is there a plague?"

"A Jewish plague."

"Are you trying to make fun of me?"

"No, I'm not. Try leaving." Turning his head, with the narrow, metallic gaze that was used to scanning maps and fields, the major now focused on the short figure of Dr. Pappenheim, and seemed about to reprimand him and send him away.

"Haven't you registered at the Sanitation Department?" Pappenheim continued to harass him.

For two days, the major fought the department. He cursed the Jews and he cursed the bureaucracy. He terrorized the deserted streets of town. Finally, he shot himself in the head. Dr. Langmann, who never left the window, said to himself, You must admit, the Jews are an ugly people. I find them useless.

Just then, the conductor put down his cards and asked, "Do you remember anything from home?"

"Which home?" asked Blumenthal the musician, a simple man whose life was a prolonged yawn. The conductor used to taunt him in the early days, but it was no use; he was wrapped up in his doze.

"From your Jewish home."

"Nothing."

"My parents converted, damn it."

"Then forget everything and go back to Vienna."

"My friend, I am in good standing at the Sanitation Department."

"What do they want of us?"

"It's hard to say," said the conductor, as though faced with a difficult musical score. "If there's truth in those rumors that we're going to Poland, then we'd better start learning. I don't know a thing."

"At our age, we're a little rusty in the head, wouldn't you say?"

"There's no choice. We'll have to learn Polish."

"Is that how you imagine it?"

Gray days stretched across the town. Meals were no longer being served at the hotel. People queued by the serving hatch for dinner—barley soup and dry bread. The musicians opened their bags. A whiff of dead leaves and of drafty roads blew down the long corridors.

Suddenly the old rabbi appeared in the street. Many years ago they'd brought him to Badenheim from the east. He had served as rabbi of the local synagogue, which was in fact an old age home, until the last members had died, leaving the place empty. The rabbi had been stricken with paralysis. It was generally believed that he had passed away with the others.

The proprietor of the hotel stood at the entrance and said, "Won't you come in, sir?"—more like a doorman than the proprietor of a hotel. Two musicians lifted the wheelchair. The rabbi shaded his eyes, and a blue vein throbbed on his white forehead.

"Jews?" asked the rabbi.

"Jews," said the proprietor.

"And who is your rabbi?"

"You are. You are our rabbi."

The rabbi's face expressed some astonishment. His feeble memory tried to discover if they were playing with him.

"Perhaps you will allow us to serve you a drink?"

The rabbi frowned. "Kosher?"

The proprietor lowered his eyes and did not answer.

"Everyone here is Jewish?" The rabbi recovered. There was a sudden gleam of cunning in his eyes.

"Everyone, I believe."

"And what do you do?"

"Nothing," said the proprietor of the hotel, and smiled.

Semitzki rushed to his aid, "We're planning to go back to Poland."

"What?" said the rabbi, straining to hear.

"To go back to Poland," repeated Semitzki.

The riddle was partially solved the next day. A kindly Christian woman had nursed the rabbi all these years; then, a few days before, she had suddenly abandoned the house. After days of trying to manipulate the wheelchair, the rabbi had finally succeeded.

The rabbi posed questions, and the people answered him. Many years of isolation had made him forget the language, and he spoke Yiddish sprinkled with the Holy Tongue. Some musicians appeared in the doorway carrying luggage.

"Who are they?" asked the rabbi.

"Musicians."

"Are they going to play?"

"No, they want to go home, but the roads are barricaded."

"Let them spend the Sabbath with us."

"What did he say?" asked the astonished musicians.

The autumnal light, the tin light, governs the town these days. The proprietor stands in the kitchen like one of the servants and ladles out soup. Supplies are not delivered. Provisions are running low. The dining room is like a soup kitchen. Long shadows crawl on the tables at night. There is a faltering look in the eyes of the musicians. A few days ago they were still grumbling. Now their hopes are dashed. They comprehend: there is no going back. Pappenheim's optimism has also dissolved. The owner of the pastry shop shakes a fist at the hotel, or, more accurately, at Pappenheim, whom he threatens to murder.

"What does the rabbi say?" asked Frau Zauberblit.

"He's sleeping," whispered the proprietor.

The musicians took no pity on the hotel and stuffed their bags with crockery and silverware. Semitzki took them to task: "What for? No one uses fancy dishes in Poland." "What harm are we doing?" said one of them, like an amateur thief. "If we come back, we'll return it."

The fleshy vines steal inside now, and spread over the veranda. This is their last burst of growth before winter. The forsaken chairs

41

stand oafishly in place. A thick shadow nests inside the geranium pot. The flowers redden like rotten beets.

"What ever happened to the major?" asks someone.

"He killed himself."

By the shuttered windows of the pastry shop stood Bertha Stummglanz. They brought her here last night. Her parents died some years ago, and the house was transferred to the local council.

"Do you remember me?" asked Sally.

"I think I do, I think we were schoolmates."

"No, dear. My name is Sally, and this is Gerti."

"Oh, I've made a mistake then, haven't I?" said Bertha apologetically.

"My name is Sally, and this is Gerti."

Bertha could not remember. Her memory was evidently deserting her. Her eyes wandered aimlessly.

"Why is everything closed?"

"The town is being transferred. Dr. Pappenheim says that everything is going to Poland, including us."

"Dr. Pappenheim?"

"The impresario, don't you remember him?"

Strangers are brought in from the gate. Dr. Pappenheim stands at the entrance of the hotel like a doorman.

"Why did you come here?" someone asked.

"They were born here, so they had to come back."

"It's a fine place," Dr. Pappenheim interjected. "Mandelbaum is with us; the twins are with us."

"The twins? Who are the twins?"

"Where are you from, Jews?" asked the rabbi. An ancient grief glazed his eyes.

"This is our rabbi," said Pappenheim proudly, "a real one of the old school."

The rabbi's questions never stop. The proprietor wears a skullcap, and serves him cold water.

No end to surprises. Last night Helena came home. Her husband the lieutenant threw her off the estate. She had the face of her ailing mother. Incredulous, Trudy stroked her hands like a blind woman. Martin was drunk with joy. "Now we can go. Together we can go anywhere."

42

Every day brought more newcomers, descendants of former Badenheimers. The town's curse had pursued them all these years, and now they were caught. Dr. Pappenheim received a letter from the Sanitation Department, instructing him to put his articles at its disposal. Pappenheim rejoiced—a grand tour awaits us!

Autumn turns to dust. The wind growls in the empty streets. Mandelbaum tortures the trio, polishes the music. The twins are cloistered again. An air of gravity pervades the hotel. Pappenheim walks on tiptoe, saying, "Hush, hush, you're disturbing the sound." The musicians quietly nibble their bread. "Practice won't do us any good. It's too late now for what you didn't accomplish when you were young." Pappenheim comforts them: "In the new place, there'll be time, you'll be able to practice. Where there's a will there's a way." He himself plans to take up research.

Dr. Pappenheim makes continuing efforts to talk to the owner of the pastry shop. "Why be angry with us? What have we done? We haven't committed a crime, after all. Tell us what our crime is. In Poland, you can open up a bigger shop. A person has to broaden his horizons." Wasted words. The owner of the shop stands at the window, raving: "If if weren't for this hotel, if it weren't for the corruption, they wouldn't have closed the town. It's all because of Pappenheim. He ought to be arrested." He only stops at night.

Mandelbaum looks happier. The trio inspires him. He is getting new tones from his violin.

"When do we set off?" he asks Pappenheim, the way he used to ask his agent.

"Soon," says Pappenheim, like the bearer of a secret.

"We're improving, we're improving."

It poured on Saturday night. The rabbi prayed loudly. People hugged the walls like shadows. The proprietor brought wine and candles, and the rabbi performed the Havdala service.

Immediately after the Havdala, the musicians went off to pack. Their bags were big and swollen. Dr. Pappenheim was surprised at the commotion, and said, "I'm going like this—empty-handed. If they want me, they'll take me like this—empty-handed."

The next day was bright and cold. Mandelbaum rose early and stood with the trio on the smooth steps of the hotel. The rehearsals had left their mark: his distinguished brow had turned white. Semitzki escorted Frau Zauberblit with a cumbersome elegance.

Professor Fusshalt stood in his bathrobe as if he'd been shaken out of a fitful sleep: "The proofs, what will happen to the proofs?" Zimbelmann the musician wrapped the rabbi in two velvet blankets and put him in his wheelchair. The proprietor said, "What must we bring?" "Nothing, don't worry," said Pappenheim. By the old ornamented gate, the clerk called the roll. The people answered their names as at a morning parade. A long journey stretched before them. At the familiar railway station there stood a hissing engine with many empty carriages. No one pushed. No one cried.

—*translated by Betsy Rosenberg*

They've moved the house
Yoram Kaniuk

Akhai hardly remembered his childhood among the prickly pears. There had been orange groves, & after the rains they had picked anemones. Once they found a blue one, which was put to dry in Carmela K.'s copy of *King Solomon's Mines,* where it thinned to a fine dust. In the vineyards he fell asleep from watch to watch. People said he would be an animal doctor some day, because he understood the laughter of the jackals at night. He argued when it was said they carried rabies; in their wails he heard hints of secret things. When his father drove them off with tin cans & fires, Akhai sat staring out into the darkness at their beautiful scared eyes.

Then came the war. In his unit they said that he killed his quota & fell asleep. He might as well have been fighting in a dream. But he knew that the land of the wailing jackals was being destroyed. He returned without a scratch because his grandmother—who sat by the window mooning at the flocks of south-winging birds—said psalms for him. He couldn't understand why God listened to her prayers more than to others for people worthier of compassion than himself.

Something of the beaten jackals had rubbed off on him. He only smiled at the irremediable hurts; they were like the spreading town

45

he'd grown up in that was corroding the enchanted wasteland. If only, he once thought, I could be someone who needs no one. He thought of the anemone in Carmela K.'s book, which was donated in the end to an immigrants' camp. The camp was beaten sodden by rain and snow, & the anemone, now dust, was reconverted to eternal energy, to the awesome orbit of the solar system, which spins once on its own axis every 240 million years. He didn't always understand the loser in him. I, Akhai, he thought, trying to smile, am not & never will be a prince. His insides were frozen with a kind of beat fatigue.

On his way to study veterinary medicine in Los Angeles, he passed through Tel Aviv. He drank coffee in a cafe & saw streets full of cars. Some men who were back from the war said there was a party in a loft on Reines Street—to which Akhai didn't go. A man with a concentration-camp face sold him a bargain watch. All night long he watched its hands moving to far places. He flew to Paris & waited while a warm breeze blew at Orly. He saw planes landing & taking off & didn't know if P.M. meant before or after lunch. There was no one to ask, so he ate the candy bar that his mother had given him, & a heavily rouged woman in red asked him the time. He didn't know what year it was, or what connection there might be between the handsome watch on his wrist & the ineluctable extinction of human life. Something in him was looking feverishly for the banality in the world's wonders. Cars crawled toward the airport & a man beside him said it must be a funeral. A light flashed on in his brain. If cars moving slowly meant a funeral, then fast meant life, the future, the tyranny of time. Slow meant the past, a flower's wilting. & so he saw funerals all the way out of town. Next came a forced landing & two days in London. & again cars moving slowly, & he said funeral to himself. It gave him something to think about & took his mind off what lay ahead. It had all already happened—in proof of which there were funerals. Lachrymose eyes in the headlights. The structure of grief broke down into pistons & cylinders & X number of strokes per second.

He fell asleep on the plane to America & failed to see the lamblike clouds below. A woman on the airplane fainted, & he awoke to give her artificial respiration. This was his first love. He rarely expressed an opinion about things that happened, because he was generally asleep at the crucial moment. So they escaped him. The resurrected woman sat beside him, trying to find out who & why he was. He fell asleep explaining, which made her laugh & get off in New York as though she hadn't loved him back. Only she had. But the words escaped him. It wasn't so much overcaution as an aversion to sentimentality, or what is commonly called impulsiveness, or a love of adventure. He grabbed at the straws of things & thought it felt peaceful to live in a world of uninterpreted clues. I've shot off my quota. Grandmother said psalms, blessed & exalted be His name.

In New York there were Coca Cola machines, & a passenger said, that lady who fainted got off to look for something, but that man has no sense of humor. He saw two blacks by a black car, which made him laugh; yet he knew he really had no sense of humor, since he couldn't step out onto life as though it were a carpet. He was looking for the doomed eyes of the jackal in a woman born with fur. New York was somewhere in the fog, but instead of going to see it he sat in the airport watching columns of cars & thinking funeral. He laughed. That's my humor, he thought—sad, like a moth by a candle.

Eventually he reached Los Angeles. A large flat city on a porcelain moon. A dream world in which naked girls leaped into swimming pools filled with artificial water. He stood holding his suitcase next to Jim Clinton's Pants Shop, with a million pairs of pants in different colors, across from a gas pump that went up & down, & watched a giant truck move a house. A whole house, with a roof & a television antenna & a garden of green plastic. A man sat smiling inside it. The truck was en route to La Cienaga, & Akhai thought it was weird to see a house out for a drive. A house was a house: it was a place to cook in, to be born & die in, a place with a yard & a donkey. Akhai's father slept in a house with a rackety old fan, not in a fine white house on a truck. A man with a praise-the-Lord face said to him, each time this pump goes down somebody makes a quarter, & each time it goes up again, somebody makes another. It's crazy to see a house move, said Akhai. Look how slowly it's going, said the man. It must be to a funeral, said Akhai, which made the man laugh. He introduced himself as Max. An Israeli & a future millionaire. Which was how Max & Akhai met & became roommates in a little apartment on Hollywood Boulevard.

He registered for the university & bought a used car & went on

47

living, as always, on the fringes of things. He drove down the long streets of the city as though they were a thin tissue of treachery, & Max laughed each time he said, look, they're going to a funeral. Whenever they couldn't find the address of some party, Akhai would say, they've moved the house, & would think of the house on the truck by the gas pump. When asked about himself, he would say forthrightly, that's how I am, Akhai, a real heavy. People laughed when he said in moments of high drama, they've moved the house, or they've moved the street. It was all in the timing; the laughter came by itself. After which he'd become his inscrutable self again. Before long, people stopped asking. He went on a field trip with a tall girl from the geology department to see the house of her mother, who had gone to London to consult her astrologist. Look what a big funeral, he said to her in the San Joaquin Valley, & when she laughed & he saw that she had gold teeth & a throat down which too many men had disappeared, he made his getaway, though not before giving her number to Brother Karamazov, who said he could tell any woman by the noise her ass made in a dress. Whatever he said kept him in a state of high tension, but not many people were interested in the sufferings of a young man who had last seen God in the gleaming eyes of a jackal.

Max was full of calling cards. He dreamed of building empires. In the meantime he was looking. Work didn't agree with him. His cards said: *Max D., Inc.; Max; Max & Sons, Indonesian Furniture; Max Japanese Industries; Max, Restaurateur; Max's Plastic Balloons; Max's Circular Houses.* He had hundreds of them, & had an old landlady who didn't like Akhai. He has a face like a jellyfish, she said. Who can figure him out? Fat, round Max, though, was the joy of her sixty-year-old life. Once a month she swallowed some pills, went to the electronic beauty parlor to have her hair done & her nails manicured purple, came home again, petted the cat, removed the plastic slipcovers from the sofas, put on a shocking pink slip, & said, come in. In came Max, circular, with flowers in one hand. I haven't a penny to pay the rent, he would say, getting into bed to knock her up. She cried & cried while he caressed her old eyelashes & told her how beautiful she was. Why doesn't Akhai ever pay it? she would ask. But Max stuck up for his friend & told her she had no idea how sad he was. Something terrible had once happened to him while artificially respirating a woman, from whom he caught cancer

48

of the breath, a disease as incurable as life. Mrs. Jones, however, was no intellectual whiz, & the pills only mixed her up more, though she could put away five Maxes for breakfast. & so she took things in the same spirit that Akhai did, which was to say with a fatigued sort of alertness. What Akhai liked best about Max was the consummate charm of his helplessness.

After several years, though, Max stopped laughing at Akhai's jokes. Which was strange, considering their close relationship & their near successes in business. Akhai changed his major from veterinary medicine to physics. Something was getting on his nerves. A woman died in his arms during a premature confession before he could learn her name. He was beginning to suspect that all his loves were doomed to be nameless, dead, or unconscious women. Physics is like anything else, he decided, & went to work washing windows in new houses. He and Max set up a chain of assembly shops for prefabricated furniture from Hong Kong, but the ship sank. They tried making nutcrackers from Israeli olive wood, but the wood arrived late. & then, when the cars were bumper to bumper on the freeway, & Akhai said it's a funeral, Max forgot to laugh.

The ghastliness of the flat-out city with its houses riding on trucks! Soon afterward Sonia came to live in the empty pigeon coop in Mrs. Jones's back yard, & Akhai saw her there, a strange bird, & was caught in her trap but said nothing. In the evenings One-Eyed Yoske and Brother Karamazov came to watch television. They sat while the rain fell outside & a girl in the house across from them sang as hard as she could through the window. The melancholy that descended on them then! Akhai looked out at Sonia, the pigeon coop, & the rain. The way life polished off the eternity of sadness that was built into it brick by brick! What next? Where to? Max couldn't stop vibrating. Once there was a gold rush in the Nevada desert, for uranium no one could find. Except for one woman who got a stroke from her Geiger counter when she came too near a real vein of the stuff. The federal government paid a pension to her heirs. How Max was dying to be an heir! He searched through every telephone book in the world for nonexistent uncles and cousins while One-Eyed Yoske sadly said that Brother Karamazov was going to commit suicide on account of all the asses he'd never heard. He and Karamazov opened an Israeli restaurant, with

Bedouin dancing and felafel, in order to have a hot meal every night. Max had a new card printed up: *Max, Akhai, Yoske A., & Mr. Karov (Karamazov): Foods of the Orient, Inc.* He hosted the customers in Arab dress & sang Hebrew songs about making the wilderness bloom.

One morning Akhai announced, I'm going to Guatemala. What on earth for? Max wanted to know. To make money, said Akhai. Max laughed & said, fat chance of you making money, & went off to pay his monthly respects to the landlady. When Akhai was gone, Sonia came to ask why he had never come to her or asked about her, & Max said, maybe because you're what he's looking for in Guatemala. She was awestruck by the thought, as though she knew that a man who traveled thousands of miles from where she was to look for her would have to be reckoned with.

Akhai bought a new car on time & drove off into the jungles & green mountains. It was hard to breathe in the mountains, where coffee grew in the hard gray fog. Little people wrapped in blankets smiled at him from the eternal cold. In Guatemala he met a Dutchman who knocked people off for one hundred dollars per head, & he sold him his car. The money was barely enough for the return ticket home, but Akhai was left with a feeling of great accomplishment. That Dutchman with his Italian dolls in his house full of rugs! Akhai drank strong booze & thought of Max with the landlady. Vaguely he began to remember things that had never happened. Could Sonia be more than just a bird living in Mrs. Jones's pigeon coop because Max couldn't pay the rent? Sometimes Akhai slipped money to her because he knew Mrs. Jones had no cash for her beauty parlor or her pills. He planned to buy special pills for her in Mexico. & he did, though he tricked them into thinking that they were for himself. In Mexico, en route to Guatemala, you could travel through the cactuses into the forgotten lands of the extinct coyotes. A black-eyed lioness nursed him with powdered milk, & there were two Americans, men after his own heart, who bought dear & sold cheap. They all had drinks together in a hacienda where a gold-braided lady served them almonds, herring, & tequila. Afterward among fruit trees Akhai said to himself, they've moved my life, & for the first time he laughed at one of his own jokes, perhaps because Max had stopped laughing. The thought of Max's not laughing gave him the sweet shivers, as though his grandmother had started praying for the enemy to plug him. Such treachery, like white water.

He had no visa, so he told the police at the border that he was born in Zichron Ya'akov, California, & they thought what the hell, another Swede. He looked like one too, except that his wrinkled forehead was receding fast. He drove through a town in the high mountains of Mexico whose map he knew by heart, as if he had been born there. It was then he realized that dying was the same as being born, because this city was his grave to which he'd return again & again until the end. The place to be born in, he told himself, is the place you die in.

Max was waiting for him at the airport. How was it among the savages? he asked as they drove back. How was it? repeated Akhai. A *fershtunkene* jungle! But in the market in Guatemala City, Mister, I saw the prettiest artificial flowers you could imagine, a nickel a dozen. At which point something happened to Max. His eyes dimmed & then opened wide like an adding machine, so that Akhai could see the jaded but inspiring power of the American dream with perfect clarity. (Why are they going so slowly? asked Akhai as they crawled along a huge road with plastic trees that slowly shook their limbs back and forth.) There was a dryness in the air. Children painted an empty swimming pool & birds flew wearily through a thick cloud of smog. Max was thinking out loud. At first he bought & sold dozens. Then hundreds. Then thousands. Then he took out a slide rule and arrived at the logical conclusion that the plastic flowers market in Guatemala City was the simple but ingenious bonanza he had been looking for all his life. In half an hour *Max & Akhai, Inc.*'s plastic flowers were crisscrossing America by train; boatloads of them, belonging to Max's *International Decorative Objects,* were circumnavigating the globe; supermarkets of flowers, the *Israel-American Max Corporation,* sold bouquets in all sizes and shapes; & hundreds of Japanese bouquet makers taught the world the art of plastic *ikebana.* Cities full of blooming plastic. *Max & Akhai Worldwide Plastics, Inc.* The billions flowed like water down a hill. What happened to the exit, asked Akhai, have they moved it too? But the schmuck didn't laugh. A howl faded inside him, like the laugh of a hyena he had once heard in the vineyards in his childhood that never was.

Max went to study plastics while Akhai sat looking at a book of

Fra Angelico reproductions that Sonia had bought him upon his return from Guatemala. That was how they met. What beautiful sugar angels, said Sonia, & Akhai told her of the terrible loneliness of the mountains of Guatemala. His eyes flashed when he described the jungles at high altitudes full of lost cities with red roofs. He finished his third year of physics & contemplated the terrible limitlessness teetering over the world, the helplessness of physics & of Max, the timeless, spaceless nature of a universe suspended above an abyss. He understood why he had been told by some Mexicans in a remote hacienda that it was possible to eat mushrooms & walk through the inwardly produced shadows of colors, without space, without time. Sonia came & went while Akhai studied with listless intensity, a bit taken in by it all, about distant things that Sonia refused to remember. Her crying at night was suffused with longing, yet Akhai couldn't remember ever having longed for anything—until he began to long for the eternally unfinished road that stretched from Mexico City to the high mountains of Guatemala. Among brown adobe huts, over a plate of chile & a glass of tequila, with salt on the back of his hand, he learned a prayer that was endlessly whispered like a joke. It was about a moved house that always came blankly back to its sender with some words stamped on it: *Received, read, & returned by God.* Sonia asked him if prayers were answered, but he knew that except for the prayers of his grandmother, who said psalms and had the keys to heaven, they returned untouched from the terrible galactic spaces. It's in nominal payment, he said to her, & so they merged in the beautiful paintings of Fra Angelico. He knew exactly which spiderwebs the angels used for weaving & on which you could walk when there was quiet inside you or madness was knocking at the gates. & so Akhai discovered his true mania—the face of the extinct jackal-god of his grandmother—on a round trip to distant places from which one returned unchanged.

He spent days behind the wheel overpowered by the desire to make a fortune & sell & return tired & bursting with money. But what he had was not legal tender & could not be deposited in any bank: the marvelously sublime void of an immense world that was nothing but windy spirit disguised as mountains, valleys, & men growing coffee at high altitudes.

Akhai noticed that the girl who once sang in the window had

grown up. That when Max dreamed of plastics his artificial eyes filled with yearning. That One-Eyed Yoske and Brother Kara-mazov were putting on weight & selling the Orient to bit actors waiting for a Hollywood miracle. That the same girl who had seemed so ethereal through the window (on whose frosty glass pane she had drawn a rabbit) had the breasts & body of a woman & would soon wear a fur coat & go on the prowl for prey—a painted doll thumbing through the slicks for an idol to love. . . . Once (after bringing the police commissioner regards from the Dutchman) Akhai flew in a helicopter belonging to the Los Angeles Police Department & saw how the cars on the freeways were moving side by side & toward each other with satanic speed. From the heli-copter window it seemed as though no more than a few inches miraculously separated them. People here passed one another without saying hello, while the good people of Mexico walked on moonbeams like sidewalks hung from above. Max was so set on plastics that he had even tired of giving himself each month to Mrs. Jones, who wasn't getting any younger. Max was ready for the trip to the flower market in Guatemala City, where he would at last make the move that would change his history.

Akhai tried to warn him off. First of all, he said, I'm taking Sonia, & the food along the way is only for hunger. It takes ten days to get there, & there are cannibal Indians & mountains in which you can't breathe. But Max wasn't listening. His ships were plowing the seas while his trains moved mountains of plastic, & there was no rerouting his dream to some more compassionate destination of mere desire. Akhai and Sonia had many beautiful & many awful times together. The bars of their cage filled Max with longing & made him want to come back a second time with a different face. He couldn't understand why Sonia didn't move in with them. But she said that it suited her more to be a bird in a coop. She was blue-eyed, open-faced, & white as death. Whoever looked into her eyes saw a duskiness there, as though all the caresses and sweet whisperings in the world could never assuage her pain. They bought a car & set out. What a funeral, said Akhai, & Max didn't laugh. Sonia laughed too much, & Max thought, when will that prick wise up and realize what castles I'll build in Cordoba or the Côte d'Azur.

Max stared incredulously out at what the books called the wonders of nature, which were like dull droppings across his life's path. He imagined God like that: old & disreputable, counting his wales & calluses & blowing soap bubbles at a rejoicing world, hallelujah. Sonia was mesmerized by the changing scenery. At night they slept in small inns & ate chile. Max was dehydrating & dwindling away. He turned red and dry from the heat &, later on, brown. A horrible curtain of fatigue covered his eyes & he kept having to puke. In a small city by a wide river where it was very dry they drank water from earthenware jugs. Max drank Vichy water that he found in a store. The bottle came wrapped in spiderwebs & the woman who sold it to him bared perfect black teeth when she laughed. A full moon was in the sky. It was hot, & Sonia took off her clothes & sat naked with her bird's body on the veranda, from which the silhouettes of the city looked like giant scarecrows, singing an old Scottish ballad. Akhai stared at the sky through the window with its pattern of lion heads while Max tried to sleep in the next room. Gargantuan mosquitoes kept attacking him in formation. He fought wearily for his life, then gave up & fell snoringly asleep.

The heat was as heavy as rocks & the black night sky choked back each breath of air. The natives came to look at Sonia on the veranda. A woman in black began to howl, her eyes shining out of the lunar-lit street. A man passed by with a silver tray on which lay a roast suckling pig with a red flower in its mouth. The tray gleamed pale in the lamplight, & they all stepped aside for its bearer, who climbed the steps & knocked. Akhai opened the door in his underpants. A down payment for all of us, said the man, for the beautiful señora, the she devil of love. Akhai slammed the door & Sonia burst into laughter that froze like wax on her snow-white skin. To her amazement she saw herself, *her*self, in all those glittering eyes. Now, more than ever before, she knew who she was & why she lived in a pigeon coop & loved a man with two sad jokes to his name & a past with no approach roads. & so she stopped singing & began to cry, not because she felt hurt, but because the world had no idea how much love was hidden in such remotenesses. The men below the moonlit veranda groaned *Sonia*. Thin and fragile, with sky-blue eyes & white skin, she seemed to them like the wounds of Jesus's hands on the gilded cross in the little church across the street. A gray-eyed priest emerged from it, cast a glance at the new Eve, saw hissing snakes of seduction, & crossed himself. There was

54

a heavy silence, as though salvation were nigh, until someone said, no prayer of no padre is going to bring that white devil to my bed tonight, & everyone laughed, even the padre, though he went on praying & fingering his beads. I love them as much as they love me, Sonia thought, feeling the loss of the impalpable charm hidden inside her & knowing that every bird found its mate in the end. Akhai would still belong to her even if he spent his life driving to Guatemala City or sailing paper ducks on a pond of mineral water. Beloved by those standing below, she would gladly have accepted goddesshood for their sake alone. She knew how much they needed a goddess to absolve them, & felt pitying contempt for the sinbilant priest who couldn't decide which was better, roast pig or white devil. All happily knew how sweet was the sinnable sin. & yet the town was six days from Mexico City, from whence the archbishop had yet to come to instruct his flock. The priest knew what Sonia knew—that each saint of his little church was a goddess like her, wilted to become one of these beautiful people with the oozing blood of Christ. Born among white & brown adobe, the priest knew too that Mary & Eve were one deity in two dresses. How sweet the wounded peace of God amid this pageant of cunning & profound gaiety! Such cunning, such temptation, as beautiful as moonlight. I'll be a wall around God's city, thought the padre, looking lovingly at his flock with eyes that longed for understanding. Sonia wept for them & they for her. Akhai thought that the priest was shocked, but he was mistaken. The tears rolling down Sonia's cheeks fell on the men below, who licked them & cried, the blood of sweet sin, the blood of sweet sin! They loved Sonia so much that they headed for home without having to be dragged by their wives. With the birth of their great love, the shock of her nudity lost all its value.

Akhai & Sonia could now eat the pig as a first, a last payment—a payment to end all payments. There was a sweetness in the air that rubbed off on them all. They cried & laughed & blew hidden kisses to the beautiful woman, making Akhai realize what depths there were in this lady of the dovecote, whose muffled pain was unveiled only slowly, like wine sipped, or blood oozed, or time passed. He remembered the watch he had bought from the concentration-camp man & he thought, I've killed to fill my quota, I've lived to fill my quota, & now I'm done with Grandmother at last. I've paid her vows to her God & now I'm free as a bird, which means Sonia & the open spaces of Guatemala & extinct cities lost in the rain forests. The moon drew a circle of light around Sonia's shoulders & lit up the night until distant clouds blotted it out. By the time Sonia's tears could stop flowing, she was drenched with them like a valley with rain. The river glistened in the distance with a magical light. Sonia went inside to get dressed & caressed Akhai's body as though he were someone she'd found in a heap of burning embers. Now I'll give birth to you, Akhai, she said, I'll squeeze you out of me, & she fell asleep with a smile on her lips.

After crossing the river on a ferry, they reached the high mountains. It was cold & damp, & gray men grew coffee in the clouds. Down below they saw the distant earth. Max was on edge & kept losing weight, while Akhai had all but stopped speaking. He held Sonia's hand & swallowed the marvelously clear distances with his eyes. Max asked how they'd get back from Guatemala City, because he'd noticed that they were traveling on a one-way road. The way there, Max, said Akhai, taking a long time to answer, is also the way back. In the long silence that followed you could hear Max's heart plunk. And what if we meet a car coming the other way? he asked from the floor of the car. That valley beneath the clouds, said Akhai, is called *el valle de las cruces*. On a clear day you can see the crosses of all the men who couldn't steer straight in the fog.

Then Sonia was laughing & singing a song into the cloud-stirred mountains. Max wept into the embroidered handkerchief he had bought in Mexico City. No more than half of him was left, Akhai saw, & wondered if by the time they arrived there would still be anyone to establish *Max & Akhai Artificial Flowers, Inc.* You couldn't say it saddened him & you couldn't say it didn't. A vague desire to go on forever howled inside him, for he had long since forgotten why he had started out. Only Max, fading out on the floor, still made him think of the bitterness of it. He no longer knew if he had come out of astonishment, jest, or suspicion, or maybe out of all three together. And Max couldn't help him to guess. He was lying unconscious on the floor of the car when the stately spires of Guatemala City hovered in sight.

The noon-napping city. The heavy, city-suspended noon. Narrow streets & baroque houses. They drove past drowsing

56

homes. A policeman saluted from his high barrel & gave them the wrong directions. Max came to & drank a bottle of juice. The idea of billions started coursing like blood through his veins again. Akhai wanted to go see the Dutchman, to rest, to drink tequila, but Max wanted only the market. The market! They drove on in circles in the rays of the setting sun, dusk breaking slowly through the wakening houses, until Max said, this town hall—that's what it is, isn't it? Yes!—we've already passed it five times, Akhai.

That's right. We have.

Five times?

I've lost count.

Why?

I'm looking for it.

What?

I'm looking for it, Max.

I thought you knew where it was.

I could have been wrong.

Sonia of the pigeon coop laughed. A wind riffled her hair. People left their sealed houses to walk in the cool evening breeze. Sonia said farewell to the devils in Akhai's heart. He wanted to forget. To forget. Why. Why. But Max wanted the marketplace. What marketplace? He couldn't remember. Once upon a time. His grandmother said psalms. So what if they moved the house? I shot my quota. My father hugged a donkey around the neck, he wanted to tell Sonia, but would she understand? A long time ago with Carmela K. in the vineyards. All forgotten. The market! Empty nights of Fra Angelico, cardboard dolls, sugar angels. Ah, somewhere it was lovely, was it not? The market! The market! What's your hurry? You're right, we've passed by here too. I've lost count. Maybe really six. So what. Aren't the churches superb?

I didn't come here to see any crummy churches!

So what did you come here to see?

The market.

Look, Max, said Akhai, maybe they've moved it.

The poor bastard laughed. His jaws sprang open & black blood sprang from his throat. Bile shot from his mouth, pasteurized, like life. Catching himself, he started to scream through the terrible laughter that distorted him unrecognizably. You got your laugh in the end, Akhai! What laugh? Akhai asked. At your shitty joke, Max said. Not at all, said Akhai, they really moved it. Max kept laughing without knowing why any more. Sonia knew but said nothing. Max threw his *Max & Akhai Flowers Inc.* cards into the air & the wind scattered them every which way. All his trains would travel empty. His ships wrecked forever, Max laughed & laughed & laughed.

—*translated by Hillel Halkin*

The orgy
Yehuda Amichai

Yesterday was Yom Kippur. Not that I fasted, not that I went to shul, but I did take a look in from the synagogue entrance. The entrance was narrow, but the splendor inside was expansive, its edges dissolved in an aura of light and talis-and-yarmulka whiteness. I stood next to the black doorman, who invited me to enter as you might invite some curious person to enter an expensive nightclub. The ache of living in a place far from my home stirred in me again. Or, more accurately, I should say an ache's approximation. The tortures of foreignness had been subdued in me for some time, only to become a scraping and tapping in my bowels—infiltrating even the joys of my dick on nights of love. Anyway, that organ began to be selfish. It kept the sweetness of its affairs to itself, without sharing that sweetness, as it did when I was younger, with the rest of my body.

It is written: "And you shall afflict your souls." It is *not* written: "And you shall afflict your bodies." As far as afflicting my soul was concerned, all year had been Yom Kippur for me. If I would afflict my body by fasting and standing all day in shul, I wouldn't be able to fulfill the commandment of afflicting my soul. Why? Because only food can strengthen the body for full sensual awareness of the affliction of its soul. A felon who is sick and wounded is always, first very diligently and mercifully, healed in a hospital before being tried and judged. I was already propounding these incisively logical arguments to myself as I walked back to my dark apartment on Seventy-sixth Street, which takes its darkness and sadness from Columbus Avenue and Amsterdam Avenue—lying between them.

These logical conversations are helpful exercises for my fatigued brain. My teachers at the university in Jerusalem promised me a great future that would begin the very moment I laid down my pen at the last stroke of the last word of my dissertation. I've dreamed about that elaborate flourish more than once. But this same passion for logic set itself like a golem against the completion of my doctorate. At that dangerous stage, my teachers turned into fathers and doctors and sent me to the United States for a "change of climate," as they put it so kindly. A person will do many things to pull himself out of a hole. My method is to say, This is not a dissertation I am writing, I'm not obligated to do it, this is not my city, not my apartment, and, in sum, this is not me. And as a result of all this, the not-I will be able to do the not-work.

I washed out a couple of my T shirts and shorts and hung them to dry in the narrow bathtub. He who does his laundry on Yom Kippur does an act of atonement. ("Though your sins be scarlet, they shall be white as snow.") Whenever my underwear is white, I reason, I'm pure as a babe. But now come women—and even men— wearing underwear blazing in all the colors of sin. And thus begins the destruction of the distinction between inner and outer, between soul and body. I well know that my generation is among the last to speak of them separately. It's a habit that's captured even distinguished physicists returning from their polished laboratories in the evening, who will see the sky and say, "The sun is setting." So I continue to talk about my body and about my soul: the former is tired while the latter is full of pep, or vice versa. My body refreshes itself with sleep, while my soul is awake being crushed in its factory of good and bad dreams. Another game.

Meanwhile my clothes were dripping into the tub, and the beats got fainter, as if they were so many hearts holding back my life. I sat in the red armchair. It didn't turn white. It was remembering all the dirty things I'd done in it and couldn't forget. Overhead, in the

60

apartment above me, they were moving the furniture around as usual. I listened to scraping and dragging and sweeping. Heavy things were being moved around light things, and the light things hid from them, with hovering, fluttering wings. This was my heaven: pounding steps engulfing soft steps. Bodies and souls in an eternal game of tag. The tittering of angels and the hoofing of goats.

In the early afternoon, about the time of Mincha, I went down to Lower Manhattan to see the ships. "Get ye to the harbor, sad one" (from my private book of proverbs). The ships stood dwarfed by the skyscrapers. I read their names like prayers; I forget my own name—one link in a chain of forgettings. Also, I couldn't tell you the names of places where I happen to be. As in a war when they designate a place by code, the place becomes a non-place, and life not-life. I walked from ship to ship. Some had the names of fruits. The bridges, taut and hovering over me, swelled a happiness in me to tears, and I felt comforted. I granted myself atonement. Ships are the angels in a generation that refuses to be either angels or prophets. The possibility of sailing out, and the sweet weakness of not-sailing, excited me, till I sang out, "Open us a gate even as the gate swings closed!" into the noise of the harbor.

With the coming of evening, I returned to my dim rooms. My underwear—that soul of my body—was already dry. I folded it with the attentiveness and precision of a solitary man. I was a proud exile, filled with grief. I prepared myself a big meal, proper for those afflicting themselves on the evening after Yom Kippur. I opened a can of pineapple and drank wine grown and bottled in Zichron Ya'akov.

That very evening the possibility of a real orgy became apparent. A telephone call and a visit from a friend or two brought the news.

But later on, hope of the event we all longed for again dimmed. For more than a few years we had been talking about it, but we had never managed to pull it off. At eleven o'clock, one of my friends quoted me some lines from a well-known poet over the phone:

A LAMENTATION ON THE ROYAL COMMISSIONER LAO-SOHN

The orgy went on, moving Eastward.
But we, unfortunately, moved on to the West.

The next morning the possibility again began to take shape. For a few days—from Yom Kippur to Hoshanah Rabba—hope thickened. Sam Abend, Steve, Maude, Maggie, Malkah, Janet, Bob, and Tim the architect almost achieved a close and facilitating contact. The need to pass through the shared carnal experience to something sublime and spiritual was so great that a heavy depression fell on all of us. We hoped secretly in our hearts that this depression was nothing other than the tight coils of our will that were destined to unspring and leap into act. The great possibility of realizing my terrible longing for a different life, to live with others, to be the others themselves, didn't stop troubling me. But by Simchas Torah the possibility of the orgy seemed to disperse like clouds that would never yield rain. Then suddenly, the day after Simchas Torah, our big chance came.

2

Those same autumn days all my friends were busy with the death of God—with His death and the chances of His living, with His existence and His nonexistence, with the invention of His being and the invention of His death. Many intellectuals were going around to different universities to debate publicly everything connected with the death of God. Steve, my intimate and enemy, was one of those actively involved. An orthodox rabbi turned professor of philosophy, he handled the discussions with great panache; and that evening after Simchas Torah, the hall in which he spoke was crowded and hot, while outside the cold had already emptied the streets. I still sat in the audience, but with little doubt that in a short time I would be sitting with the debaters on stage. The auditorium was paneled in expensive wood—the silent rustle of Canadian forests transmogrified to a lecture hall.

Steve sat behind a flashing pitcher of water, while his opponent, a Protestant theologian, spoke through the mike. His face was pink and his hair white; he spoke about the Lord, the incarnation of Love and the Good, Life Omnipresent, and about childhood. I loved the man because he had the audacity to be simple and warm. The good minister added that God sometimes hides Himself so that we shall have to seek Him. And I chimed in—in my heart because I never dared use my mouth: God shows a dead face so that we'll busy ourselves with His resurrection. And by all this wrenching of heart, and labor of soul, and anguished fussing around His bier, everyone will be busying himself with Him, so He'll live forever. He's a God who's inclined to regular dying, so the menace of His death perpetually hangs over us. By way of contrast to what I'd said in my heart, Maude, who was sitting next to me, answered in hers: I know He's dead. His death poisons the universe. His corpse is huge, and it's impossible to turn it away from the earth, and there isn't enough room in the ground to bury it. To this my hand remarked to hers, touching it: We are the honey in the carcass of the lion. Her knee, which pressed against my knee, continued on its own with the wisdom of knees: we live in a carcass like creeping worms. My tongue (now cleaving to my palate from all the honey) whispered: Life is like a giant cheese, a confusion of holes and tunnels and openings. With that we ended our body chat. The chairman of the panel, a Jew resembling a hawk, gave the floor to Steve. And Steve, my intimate and sweet enemy, looked even more handsome than usual. A big curl going a little silver made his face like a window from which his mischievous eyes looked out; his face was the face of a clever boy.

Maude sat tense and full of desire. Certainly her heart was torn between me and him. Certainly she was again making comparisons. It was a good thing she was dressed in a dark suit; otherwise you would have been able to see the marks of passion on her skin, and smell that smell of hers—of a waking animal.

Steve was dressed in the most elegant Madison Avenue fashion, his white hands shooting out of the sleeves of his blue velvet jacket. Without saying a word, he began to cover the blackboard behind the table with Latin and Greek letters and weird mathematical symbols: the Signs and Manifestations of men of science. Then he began to explain everything in a voice that still had something of Talmudic singsong in it. First he proved that God is alive and well. Using exactly the same symbols, he proved that He is dead. And with still the same symbols, he then proved that there is no contradiction between the two.

A great flame of envy rose from my neck at the thought that these were the same logical strategies with which he forestalled all possibility that Maude would object to taking her clothes off.

Being a logician herself, she couldn't help yielding to the same mode of argument. All women are naked under their clothes. Correct. If all women are, then you must be too. Ergo, a complete woman is a naked woman. Let us assign her the letter "a"; let all her articles of clothing be given other letters as needed. Granted. It is possible, then, to write thus: $a=a-(b+c+d)$. This equation is good only in the summer. In the wintertime you have to add letters for nylons, garter belts, undershirts, thermal underwear, and the like: $a=a-(b+c+d+e+f+g)$.

In the bedroom of Steve's apartment a blackboard is hanging over the bed. At the place on the wall where other people hang a romantic picture or a mirror so they can see themselves in their passion—and thus be objective observers of the subjective act— Steve has a schoolroom blackboard, and the multicolored chalk dust sometimes gets mixed with sweat and curly hairs. Steve's logical power is like the power of a vortex or a Moloch. In a strange way and despite myself, I am drawn to such types. That's how I lost Malkah, the Israeli gym teacher who's now attached herself to our group of intellectuals. That's also how my longing body lost Maude. They come back to me different and strange, as after some terrible process. Steve calls these round-robin swappings an orgy with a slow beat, a stuttering orgy, a crawling orgy.

Malkah sat four rows behind us. Maude spotted her and waved her hand in that intimate code that women have among themselves, especially women who've slept with the same man. And when I turned around to Malkah, I wasn't myself but an allusive wave, an incidental, a sad and gentle gesture. On stage, Steve was speaking about the concept of God's concealed face and the significance of its inherent death. There's a lot of face-concealing in my life—and it's like a solar eclipse. Malkah's eyes were calm and satisfied because she'd satisfied a lot of love; after intermission I sat down next to her. Her skin was still the skin she acquired on the beaches of Herzliah. She was a popular beach bunny in her time, and everyone who ran after her bruised first his feet and then his heart. The freckles on her face and body were red stars in the daytime and black at night. Malkah said whispered, pacifying things to me about faulty elevators that went up and down and skipped floors and got all messed up and that's why we didn't meet that night at the college when I got lost in the ballet department looking for her.

The hawk man on stage was erasing Steve's symbols with wide-arched, black strokes, like a boy sketching in the high heavens. He began his remarks by criticizing Steve, and the

64

theologian was happy, with a light in his eye. But suddenly that quick logical kink hit him, and in a few seconds the good man's plumes of childlikeness were plucked and all his sedating angels had flown. "This is like a rape with the tattered clothes flying all around," Malkah whispered to me. Then Maude got up, walked down the aisle, and very charmingly went up the wooden stairs at the side of the stage. She was wearing flared black pants and a black jacket that fanned out below the hips, like the costume of a lady lawyer in some ballet about a terrible trial: a high-styled Portia in *The Merchant of Venice*. She said wondrous things: All mankind but myself—*they* are God. They determine my destiny and my environment.

I said to Malkah, "All mankind but myself are objects of somebody's love. But not me." And I sang her my own "Adir Hu": "Mighty is He, sad is He, who shall establish His house soo-on." Here Malkah said, "That's you, all right. You're sad, and you'll build your house soon, but it won't be mighty. It'll be pretty sad." I continued my line: "Mighty is He, a woman is He." Malkah smiled: "Again you want to be me. You've already tried to switch with my body; you entered me—but only a little part of you penetrated. You'll never be able to be me or anybody else. And that's what so sad about you."

The symposium ended. It was cold outside. We stood around until the whole group got itself together. The cold cut like knives. The debate continued out on the sidewalk, and I heard two opinions on a cold night. While listening to one, I stuck my left hand in my left pants pocket. After that I listened to the rebuttal and stuck my other hand in my right pocket. Meanwhile the left one had warmed up and I could take it out, ready for the next opinion. Instead I gazed around. I watched the lighted windows hidden behind venetian blinds. The slits of light cut painfully into my aching heart. Steve said in his soft, lilting voice, "Coming up with three or four opinions after an evening's debate is absolute proof that a man needs three or four women." And he went on educing evidence from the second day of yontif in the Diaspora: "It was ancient *doubt* about fixing the precise time of a festival that led to the establishment of a second day. Similarly, doubt about fixing one precise love obligates a man to have a couple of lovers at the very same time." The others' voices hushed, and the possibility of an orgy reared itself again. The people standing out in the cold looked around at each other to see who was with them.

It was midnight. We made little progress, and didn't know where we were going. We found ourselves standing outside the women's detention center. A man stood next to us on the sidewalk and shouted something, his head raised like a wailing jackal. On the fifth floor, you could see the distant face of a woman behind the bars. The transfer of inmates from jail to jail was made in the early hours after midnight. It's the same with me. Whoever wants to love me will have to rescue me boldly, like in the Middle Ages. With my luck, who'd get the ransom money but that bitch Black Solitude! My past commandeers all the dazzling coins, and still can't get enough.

Meanwhile somebody brought out a couple of bottles of liquor. No one spoke for fear speech would make the orgy bloom. Maude had a place on a street in the Village that curved around like a ram's horn. Going up the wooden steps, we began to pair off. Redheaded Sam Abend—another enemy of Steve's and mine—attached himself to Malkah. It was as if his freckles were pulled, freckle to freckle, to those of Malkah, like bolts. I tried to displace their closeness but couldn't. Taking off our overcoats—some were wool, some of other animals' skins—turned into a strange rite of coupling and mixing; and the big soft pile on one of the beds was redolent of mixed human and animal smells. A black coat was entwined with the woolly sleeves of a white coat. There was a pause. It was as if our taking off our coats was a substitute for the expected orgy. Things didn't flow. If a couple of people had continued to take off the rest of their clothes, dream possessed, we would have been closer to our goal. Sam Abend tried to salvage what there was to salvage. He embraced Malkah the gym teacher and sat her on his lap, while we all sat around them. What is a Modern Woman? She's one who doesn't mind taking her clothes off in front of her friends. In the Garden of Eden they were ashamed because they ate from the Tree of Knowledge and were afraid of God. If God is dead, who's there to be embarrassed in front of? Anyway, some woman has to start it.

Malkah: "Why me?" "Because you were an officer in the Israeli Defense Forces and you were fearless and because you're strong and can use your powerful legs to kick anybody who comes near

66

you that you don't want." Maude tried to pull Malkah's dress off, but Malkah pushed her and she fell sprawling out on the carpet, to everyone's delight. What is a Modern Woman? She's dead, like God. Afterward, when all those assembled had despaired, Malkah started to take off her dress. She did it with an indifferent pull of her shoulders, her lips pursed in contempt and boredom. She finished, remaining dressed only in her black underwear, and when no man moved—the confusion and yearning were so great—she knelt like a bridge on the rug. And a perfect bridge it was; her phys ed teacher's body was perfect, and her thighs were brown and full. Everyone remarked on the bridge and on the beauty of her body, and she was in the center, her wonderful body taut with absolute contempt for all the orgiasts. Only Sam Abend tried to pick her up as she was, but couldn't make it. Someone asked, "What about everybody else?" Sam Abend knelt as if by a spring and kissed her navel. Then Malkah got up and the two of them disappeared into the bathroom, where they filled the tub with all the blankets and towels and dirty laundry and did their thing, privately. Maude gave me one of her lover's cigars and lit it with a lighter that another lover forgot behind the bed. Maude is rich. Her parents, who are separated, send her money. Their money's mingling in their daughter is the only connection left between the couple.

I smoked the cigar, trying to make clouds around my head. Maggie arrived. Maggie is pretty, with bright eyes. She's the assistant to the manager of an art gallery specializing in the trendy and wild, but her eyes remain calm. She lives in a small apartment designed like a toy train, with the toilet out on the landing; and whenever she goes out to answer the call of nature, the keys she uses to open the sky-blue door jingle. Somehow she was drawn into one of the maelstroms that Steve whips up in his life. After a time he invited her out to the lectures, where ideas and opinions heat up like a dust haze. Maggie was very pale—maybe from all the dust that had settled on her—but her eyes always stayed clean and bright. Before the discussions, or after them, Steve would whisper a few sweet nothings in her ear. Sometimes he even spoke to her during the lecture itself, looking at her from the stage while talking about the bearing of love on the death of God. He would say sentimental things to her, like "Someone like you makes lecturing all worth it," or "You alone are proof that God isn't dead." After the lecture she would come over to him to give her love to the man behind the eloquence. (Of an engineer, you'd say that she wanted to know the man behind the schematics; of a smoker, to know the man behind the smoke.)

Thus Steve seduced her: "You are an expert in artistic matters. Certainly you've seen the hands of Albrecht Dürer—the famous praying ones—many times." (With the next words he would place his own hands on her full thighs.) Dürer's hands are pressed against each other in the waste of self-love, but he, Steve, would pray in the spirit of communion with his fellowman. So his hands reach the baby folds of her buttocks, as he says things about the beginning being the end, and the end being the beginning, and buttocks being the projection of the thighs, and thighs being the inspiration of the ass (though it is plumper) and the nobility of the back (though it is more supple). And in his own inimitable way he asserts that neither the beginning nor the end is important—it's the middle that is the essence. Meanwhile his fingertips have made it to that mysterious place where three meet and nearly are one: smooth and tender skin, a band of panty, and curly hair. His hands cease being prayerful and become godly. And then the two of them stop talking to follow his handicraft with an almost scientific curiosity, as if Steve and Maggie were doing something to some third person. "Note here that what is subjective becomes objective—we are both acting and observing in one and the same moment. The eyes become pure instruments of perception, as if no brain were working behind them."

Once Steve told me that women in love in his bed resembled each other like airports all over the world. Everything beyond them— their cities, landscapes, clouds, their people living out their lives—is all only so much local dressing.

Maude was talking on the phone, a fact unimportant in itself if it weren't for the momentous subject of her conversation. She lifted the receiver from the phone's base, which was shaped like a white kitten, and stretched out on the bed letting the cord follow between her legs like a snake. The whole burden of the conversation seemed to lie on her; she fondled the receiver and drank from it and gushed her words into it. A few of the guests stood around her after having tired of looking at Malkah's new bridges. Maude undulated around and completed her striptease by shaking her shoes off her feet. Sam Abend said, "That's a pretty hot conversation." No doubt at the other end of the line was a man wriggling around just like her. You could probably arrange orgies-by-telephone, the way they set up chess matches long distance. It isn't God that's dead; feeling is dead, love is dead. "Because we wanted to live painlessly we killed Pain, like an old toothache—and with it, Love." These were Maude's last words into the phone. True to form, she then stood up and fell onto our group like an exploding shell. The room was witness: the closet door crashed open, spilling sweaters and linen and blouses like entrails. One of her shoes swung from the doorknob and the smack of the door dislodged and burst open an overnight case always kept packed and ready to go: "I was born in a suitcase."

Then the women pushed the men off the wide bed—the pile of coats with them—and a clowning female organism took their place on the bed. It was a sort of many-armed and -legged machine emitting cries and naughty whispers. The men stood around, wanting to fall on this pack and wreak design and devastation upon it. But even stronger was the desire to strike into that smooth-surfaced confused mass with a stick—like a naughty kid with a stick in his hand and the need to beat up whatever looks happy to him. It was a terrible Thing of female intrigue: a stratocumulus alive with naked leg lightning and shrill giggles. Beside this glob, all the male occupations, like trucking and driving tanks and airplanes, and building hundred-story buildings, all the affairs of microscopes and stock markets and soccer—each according to its kind—seemed insubstantial, purposeless, and without effect.

Even as the general passion of the orgy reached the boiling point, it was only a skittering grace too quickly slipping, and the bundle of girls scattered. I ended up half dozing in the armchair. Steve and Maude and Maggie lay side by side on the bed without touching each other. They were arguing among themselves, their faces turned toward the ceiling, their words rising from them in three vertical columns.

"The test is whether you can get along without him."

"I feel the same way about you."

"She wants 100 percent, but I can only give 72 percent."

"She doesn't look too good, but she's happy."

"That sweet ass throws him into a blue funk."

"Bondage . . . bondage . . ."

"His fat gut is an independent and humorous intellectual."

"All women want to get laid; all men want to get laid."

"Whoever doesn't want to get laid is neither a man nor a woman."

"And so forth, and so on, et cetera." (Gabbing)

"She looks good when she's depressed."

". . . to be a hero or a coward . . ."

"It's a question of responsibility."

"My mother's angry with me."

"Because of the Greek?"

"Yeah—the Greek professor who thought he was Jesus Christ one day and decided to walk on the reservoir in Central Park."

"They took him away."

"It was disgusting. There was half-eaten food all over the floor, like when dogs eat; and it stank."

"He's always threatening me that he'll change."

"Honey, if you don't do such and such, I *will* change."

Steve slid away, but the girls pulled him back to them. Maude placed a threatening hand where his pants bulged, but Maggie snatched her hand away like a spider. They let him get up, and he got up and left the room. Maude and Maggie continued the conversation—Maude submitting Maggie's love for Steve to logical exercise.

"Would you still love him if he had only one eye?"

"Yes."

"If he was missing a hand?"

"Yes."

"How about a leg?"

"Yes."

"Missing both legs? His penis? In a wheelchair? Without ears?"

"Yes yes yes yes."

And they continued this way till all that was left of Steve was a basketful of bone and flesh chunks. Then they laughed together and, as if spotting me, said in surprise, "You have to change him like a picture on the wall." Maggie laughed and slapped her chubby knees, which had dimples like the knots in the string around a stuffed roasted veal.

Maggie's father is a minister, and Steve's father is a rabbi, and

70

Maude's father is a dentist; and I fell into a really deep sleep. A light dream settled on me: I was on a small boat, and the boat had entered a narrow canal. Through openings in the canal's embankment, I could see a great and faraway sea between cliffs smoothly rounded like bald heads. The sea was very spread out, and there was a powerful flowing movement which couldn't be seen from north to south. And the whole current flowed through a huge gilded gate that was a glittering harp, dripping wires and swinging lightly back and forth in rhythm with the current's breathing.

When I woke up, Maude was talking about Steve's psychiatrist, who'd died two weeks ago. "I can fight an analyst who's living, but there's no remedy against a dead one."

The man who was at the other end of the telephone call came over. He was a young architect who came to rearrange Maude's furniture and hang new pictures on the walls.

Steve came back to the bed and the deliberations were resumed. Steve told a tale about a rabbi who presided over two villages and lived between them. People came to him with questions of halachah. But living between two villages, how could he give them answers?

Maude stretched out and fell asleep; her hair spilled down to the floor. The architect caressed Maggie's heavy thighs. Steve was trying again to convince her that there was nothing between him and Maude. Maggie maintained that he obviously loved her because of her fourth apartment, which was conveniently near Columbia. The architect said, "Angels don't have wings of feathers, but of plump white thighs." Maggie said, half asleep, "My time is your time." That was really a wonderful thing to say in love, and a sweet shiver covered my back. Steve said: "A woman always cares for her body with great concentration. Therefore there are no virgins. Every woman's already made love to herself."

3

From that night on, we were no longer just a group of people discussing the death of God. We included professional intellectuals like Sam Abend, Steve, Maude, and myself; and regular hangers-on like Maggie, Malkah, and the architect; and stray people who went with us from place to place, attaching themselves and falling away on the wide, smooth parkways between university and university.

After a while we bought two or three small buses for mass transit, and those times we'd come to the college towns from different directions, we'd coordinate our arrival like a guerrilla army. Brilliant guitarists or saxophonists or drummers would join us and disappear the next day at those same crossroads where angels with different missions formerly used to separate.

After the organized debates, there was always an hour of milling around and wandering off, until all of us found our way back together again at parties in apartment buildings with beautiful gardens. We also managed an orgy here and there. Good-looking young men and women—long-haired and tan—showed up and danced and then off took their clothes as in some lovely, delicate dream, and paired off before our sad eyes.

I especially loved the road trips. There was the first snow in the country, and the last snow before spring that froze yellowish around the awful factories. Once we were discussing orgy theory in a cafeteria while some trouble with our car was being repaired in a garage. One kind of orgy is to have everyone make love simultaneously in separate rooms. Sam Abend remarked that it was like a lot of bees making honey. Steve said it was more like a whorehouse. I said it was like the Septuagint translation of the Bible: seventy language experts sat in seventy rooms and all came up with exactly the same translation even though there was no contact between them. Similarly, all the lovers would love the same love in their separate sealed rooms ("I love you." "I love you back"). Maggie said that an orgy is a matter of mutual longing that has no culmination or satisfaction. There's contact—touching skin, and hair, and hands, and genitals—like the groping of blind people. And it's not important whose, so long as you don't feel lost. Desire becomes a constant touching toward only more intense desire, because we forget most of the words that are said. The first thing forgotten is the words; after that you can still feel the shape of the words, not as letters, but in their physicality as words—in the breath caught in your throat, in your heart, in your smile, in your mind. Someone'll say, "We had this profound conversation till two in the morning." Only he won't remember the words themselves, but their shape, like the shape of a corpse under a white sheet.

And that's how we traveled and talked and traveled. We put distance between ourselves and Yom Kippur, but, like the year, we approached it again. We explained that white Yom Kippur to Maude and Maggie, and the weakness that Steve and I still felt every day, three times a day, when the time came for praying. It's not a verbal thing, but a sensation of emptiness and dizziness from the hollow of a place reserved for something that's not there. That same weakness and that same disquiet attended our evening debates. Addendum to the evolution of prayer: Man has gone from sacrifice to full-throated prayer, from full-throated prayer to whispered prayer, from whispered prayer to silent prayer, from silent prayer to death.

So it happened that on one of the first days of spring we got to Princeton, city of the illustrious university. We unloaded our gear, which by that time included speaker systems, film clips, illustrations, blackboards, plastic concept models, and bizarre clothes in all the colors of the rainbow. The debate in the evening was a big success, but in comparison the orgy was a failure. Maybe it was the fatigue of spring.

I spent the night in the beautiful, spacious home of Brenda, a local intellectual, whose husband had left her to run off with some wild beauty queen from out west. A distinguished teacher of logic's canon, she hadn't had the strength to pursue the runaway couple. "I've grown used to hugging myself in my sleep." Her eyes were beautiful, her body supple, her skin dark brown and smooth as silk, even though she was already past forty. Her eyes were permanently sad. Everything symbolized distance for her: the tree outside the window, the window itself, and even the pile of her clothes on the chair by the bed. "The parts of my body," she said, "tire in different stages and my body isn't sensually coordinated. When my legs get tired, my mind is awake to its thoughts, and when my thinking tires, my belly and cunt want love." We lay down next to each other naked.

"See how the lantern light from the garden falls on the table." Brenda is known for her comments on falling light. Sunset rays and sunlight at noon, light filtered through curtains, and light broken by shadows. We talked a lot. The difference between us, we said, was the difference between going and not remaining. We are changing. We will change. After an hour, her thinking tired and her body woke up. I caressed her wonderful skin in a quiet frenzy and lay on her a long time after I had entered her. Desire takes many forms.

73

Brenda's silky brown skin is one of them. At long last, her entire body became aroused, and afterward we again lay side by side. "We're going to hurt each other." My voice failed me.

The next morning, the group got together again. As always, we were joined by a few newcomers whom the failed orgy and its desire had attracted to us. It was a sweet, cold spring day. Brenda's light was falling on half-frozen lakes. We all drove out to the bird sanctuary at the city limits. There we got down on our stomachs, each in his own recess, and were given binoculars. The bushes were full of birds—red ones called red cardinals, and blue ones called blue jays, and all kinds of ravens doing their high, worried, and measured business on the earth. Quick, excited cries broke from the people lying in ambush in the bird lookout. ("Stalking desire.") As I spoke, I got up unnoticed. I put distance between myself and them, till their voices were lost in the cool, clear air. I got to a hill and code-named it Spring's Fortress; and I crawled around between the trees and bushes and last fall's leaves like a soldier preparing to capture the hill. An advance-guard bird broke into a solitary warning chirrup. I continued to push forward stealthily, when suddenly from a nest in a tree overhead a bunch of them broke into an automatic chirping machine—tiki-tiki-tiki—like you hear at the beginning of a battle. I was heavy moving, and wounded from longing, and tired from a night of loving the falling light. I sought cover behind a tree stump and lay down. Behind my back, the shrill caw of a sniper bird finished me off.

I remained lying on my back like the war dead. Sunlight fell on me and illustrated me with its lovely golden designs. From the corner of my eye I saw an abandoned farmhouse that had been painted red. Below it the river flowed, released from the coast, as dead men are released from our frozen necessity to go on living. I heard my friends' voices from below. Apparently they'd got up from their lairs and scattered in all directions. They dispersed, going separate ways, and I don't know if they ever got together again and were one after that.

—*translated by Elinor Grumet*

Louidor Louidor
David Shahar

Early one morning, on the path leading up from Wadi Kelt to Nebi Mousa, Arab ruffians from Abu Isa's gang caught Louidor the Silent, tortured him, and cut off his penis. Two Arab goatherds from the village of Abu Dis who were on their way to the river tried to stop them, claiming that Louidor was a Jewish saint. To this the men replied, *"Hada mush wili yahudi, hada jasus sahyuni"* (meaning "He's no Jewish saint but a Zionist spy"), and warned them not to interfere in something that was none of their business. The goatherds escaped, and told the story to the Greek monk from the Greek church of El-Azariyeh, who was driving back to Jerusalem from a visit to the monasteries of the Jordan valley with several Catholic pilgrims. When their car reached the path, they found Louidor lying bleeding and unconscious with his amputated male member stuck in his mouth.

This happened not long before the outbreak of the Second World War, and I heard about it that same evening from Pesach the Fat, owner of the Cancan Café. Pesach the Fat was then living opposite the government hospital in the alleyway leading to Melissande Street—which is today called Queen Helleni Street—and when he left his house to go to the café that morning, he heard all the details

75

from the hospital doorman. When Pesach heard what had happened to Louidor he fainted, and the doorman dragged him into the hospital, where they treated him with valerian drops. As soon as he regained consciousness, Pesach the Fat got up and ran for his life; later he confessed that the moment he came to he felt that he was about to faint again, both from the smell of the hospital and from the thought that the castrated Louidor was lying somewhere in the same building. When he told us the story, he was leaning on the café counter. There was still a grayish pallor covering his usually red cheeks, and a masklike smile on his lips exposed his short, widely spaced teeth. He wasn't really smiling, of course; it was just that he always looked as if he was smiling when he spoke. "Imagine," he said to his partner Yomtov the Sad, who was standing next to him and drying the dishes very energetically while he listened with his mouth pursed and his eyes full of tears, "only yesterday Berl Raban met him at the Jaffa Gate." "I saw him yesterday too," I said to Pesach the Fat, but he paid no attention to me.

I saw Louidor when I ran into a strange gathering of people in the Old City, near the Jaffa Gate. A tall, gaunt Arab, dry as a branch blasted by the desert sun and wind, knelt and bowed down outside the Citadel Gates, and then he spoke in the name of Mohammed the prophet of God to the people gathered around him: city Arabs passing by, shopkeepers from the shops in the square, hawkers of mementos, Arab peasant women with baskets of vegetables on their heads, porters with harnesses on their backs, and *tamar hindi* sellers with burnished copper barrels strapped to their bellies. Two bespectacled old Englishwomen were standing on the steps of the Citadel, and one of them shouted into the ear of her companion, who was apparently a little deaf: "Oh, Doris, look! It's a dervish! A mad visionary. The Moslems think them saints—you know, holy men—and no one is allowed to harm a hair of their heads. What luck! Wait, wait—perhaps he'll have an attack and begin to dance. Two weeks ago in Nablus I saw a dervish whirling round like a top and making the most dreadful noises until he fell to the ground. You'll never believe it, but after he fell they brought him a live snake and he began to eat it, and somebody told me it was a poisonous snake, too!"

From this I learned that the European name for the prophetic madmen the Arabs called *wili* was "dervish." Mrs. Luria once told me, among her other recollections of Turkish times, about a *wili* who came to a grand reception given by the Turkish pasha who was the governor of Jerusalem. This same pasha, who thought nothing of hanging Arabs at the Jaffa Gate and delighted in having petty offenders whipped for their crimes, did not dare show his uninvited guest the door, even though the European consuls might consider his presence an affront to their dignity and take offense. With his wild hair, his crazy eyes, and his filthy robes full of lice and fleas, the *wili* seated himself among the decorated and perfumed guests at the pasha's right hand. The pasha not only allowed him to sit at his table, but showered him with gifts when he left.

The present *wili*—who was the only one I ever saw with my own eyes—did not grant the old Englishwoman's wish: he neither danced, nor spun, nor ate poisonous snakes. All he did was speak, in a deep rich voice, in literary Arabic. The little Arabic I knew was not enough for me to understand his discourse. All I understood was the beginning, which was none other than the opening verse of the Koran, which we were then beginning to study in our Arabic classes at school: "In the name of Allah, the compassionate, the merciful, Praise be to Allah, Lord of the Universe, the compassionate, the merciful, Master of the Judgment Day," as well as something about the "return to Medina the blessed city, and Mecca the holy city, and the broad and glorious lands of Arabia"—pious cant which awoke no interest in me at all. But so long as I was at the edge of the crowd, outside the circle, free to turn away and leave whenever I wished by any of the roads leading out of the walls, through the Jaffa Gate or the New Gate, I stood my ground and waited in case the *wili* started performing all kinds of amazing and wonderful tricks.

All of a sudden I felt that the human circle was closing in on me, that I was being crushed in the middle of the crowd, surrounded by the smell of the fellahin's robes and breath. And to add to my terror of suffocation I heard the fellah standing right behind me say something about the "Jewish *wili*" to his friend, and in my mind's eye I already saw the whole crowd of Arabs falling on me—the solitary Jewish child, the stranger in their midst who had dared to approach their holy man.

"If I don't get away at once they'll kill me," I said to myself and broke out of the circle of fellahin with unexpected ease, like a knife cutting through butter. They simply fell back, astonished at my sudden dash, and made way for me.

I was about to leave the Old City by the Jaffa Gate when I saw Berl Raban sitting outside a small café on the corner of Greek Patriarchate Street a few feet away, watching the *wili* and his audience.

"So you've come to listen to Louidor the Silent too?" he asked me in an amused, ironic tone. "What do you think of his original ideas?"

His astounding question made sense of what I had heard the Arab fellah saying a moment before about the "Jewish *wili*": this Moslem holy man, this dervish whose miraculous feats were eagerly awaited by the two old Englishwomen, was none other than Louidor the Silent! Louidor the Silent, who had vanished from my mind, and Jerusalem, and Yaeli Gutkin's life many years ago. I remembered that Haim Longlife, Berl's brother, once said he had seen Louidor wandering about the Ramleh marketplace in Bedouin robes, and Mrs. Luria listened to this tale—as she listened to all Haim Longlife's wild tales—with a scornful smile and a wave of her hand.

"I never imagined that that *wili* was Louidor the Silent," I said to Berl. "And I don't know Arabic very well either. I didn't understand exactly what he wanted of his audience."

"Sit down and I'll tell you exactly what Louidor the Silent wants," said Berl, who was in high good humor, grinning broadly under his mustache and motioning me to join him at his table. With Louidor the Silent, whose appearance wrung my heart, only a few feet away, Berl's jocularity hit me like a blast of cold air. This was the same Berl who had once remarked, on finding an old Arab beggar sleeping in the garbage shed behind the clinic kitchen on a winter's night, "What would his mother have said if she'd known her son would end up like this?" Now he not only did not pity his friend Louidor but, on the contrary, was full of a kind of glee. As for me, my heart was full, not just with pity (I pitied Louidor far more than the old Arab curled up among the garbage cans on that freezing winter night), but with an obscure fear as well. Suppose one of those two old Englishwomen—the one whose friend had just told her that the crazy dervish was about to start spinning like a top, and make awful noises, then fall and then eat a poisonous snake—suppose she had been Louidor the Silent's mother. What a terrible sharp pain would have pierced her heart at the sight of what had happened to him, to Louidor, her darling Louidor, her beloved son! That old Arab had been overcome with joy when Berl told the head nurse to let him sleep in the waiting room. With him, the problem was not how to make his accommodation for the night, or his life in general, more pleasant, but how to get rid of him. It turned out that he was an Arab from Bab-khan-el-zet, and his family, as well as all the muktars and sheiks and directors of Moslem charity funds, had washed their hands of him. But as for Louidor, his mother could have appeared with a bundle of fine clothes in one hand and a bag of gold coins in the other and said, "Here, take. These are for you. Come and wash yourself, and cut your hair, and dress yourself like a respectable human being and start to see life and enjoy the pleasures of this world!" And it was clear, from the faraway look in his eye, that he would have answered her, "Woman, what have I to do with you?" The fear that stirred in me, beneath the pain of my knowledge that this wild emaciated *wili* in his filthy ragged robes was none other than Louidor the Silent, came from that faraway look. His eyes were covered with a wet, reddish film, and he stared at the crowd as though from another world, seeing no one.

In light of this otherworldly expression—and of Louidor's bearing, dress, presence, and the literary Arabic bursting from his mouth in prolonged cries, punctuated by sudden pauses during which the crowd responded with a roar of *"Allah akbar"*—Berl's words sounded jarring and out of place. I sat down beside him to hear "exactly what it was that Louidor wanted." Instead of calming me, what he told me distressed me even more. It seemed to me that I was watching a man being roasted alive on burning coals, and even as the smell of his charred flesh rose in my nostrils, I was reading a newspaper article about him, this man who had set himself on fire for political reasons. The article exposed all the fundamental errors behind his political reasoning, and dismissed his self-immolation in one sentence. This trick, the reader learned, was well planned to stir the emotions of the mob, hence in fact deserved no more than a sneer.

"Louidor," said Berl, "is a rationalist, pacifist intellectual. When he arrived in Jaffa he suddenly realized that Eretz Yisrael is full of Arabs. We have no other country, and two peoples can't rule the same territory at the same time. And if in fact the land of Israel belongs to the people of Israel, the Arabs must leave. So what is to be done? Should we rise up and drive them away by force? God forbid. We aren't savages. The use of force is the root of all evil; no good ever comes of it, and no injustice can be remedied by it. So we have no alternative but to persuade them to go back of their own free will to the big, spacious Arab lands from which they came. But who's going to persuade them? A Jew has no moral right to decide what's good for an Arab or what road he should take. Only an Arab has the moral right to act as guide to the Arab people, and Louidor couldn't persuade the Arabs so long as he himself was a Jew. Now that he has learned their language and customs, converted to Islam, had himself circumcised again, gone on the pilgrimage to Mecca, and returned with the title of *haj*, he finally, thank God, has the moral right to persuade the Arabs to go back to the broad, blessed lands of Arabia."

What Berl Raban was actually doing was arguing with Louidor through me. Louidor would shout at the crowd in Arabic, and Berl, speaking through me, would answer him hoarsely in Hebrew. He did not say a single word about Louidor's ancient love for Yaeli Gutkin, didn't once mention the affair. On the other hand, he told me about something I had never heard of, something that had come long before the affair with Yaeli and was connected with Louidor's first appearance in Jerusalem.

When did Louidor first come to Jerusalem? He came sixteen years before I myself was born there—the same year that Lev Tolstoy died. If the Russian author had not died, Louidor would not have come to Jerusalem; and as far as Louidor Shatz was concerned, Tolstoy died twice.

Louidor, then a boy of seventeen, had decided to make a pilgrimage to Tolstoy, his revered teacher and guide, in order to enjoy the light of his countenance and obtain inspiration from his teachings. From his hometown of Zlatopol in the Ukraine, he walked for several weeks to Tolstoy's estate, Yasnaya Polyana, but when he arrived he was told that Tolstoy was dead. While Louidor was making his way on foot, Tolstoy had escaped by train from his estate and his wife Sophia and died in the home of the stationmaster in the village of Astapovo.

Louidor did not go home. Instead, he joined a group of Russian intellectuals who had founded an agricultural commune in a little village in the Ukrainian province of Yelizavetgrad. There he would live according to Tolstoy's teachings: his love of man, his renunciation of property, and his pacifism, even in the face of those who would kill. In that Russian commune, while Louidor was leafing casually through the pages of a journal which had published an old correspondence between Tolstoy and his friend the literary critic Strakhov, the name Konstantin Shapiro suddenly caught his eye, and Tolstoy died a second time. "That little Konstantin Shapiro killed the great Tolstoy!" In these words Berl Raban summed up how Louidor felt when he read the ancient letter. He got up and quit his commune, left the land of Tolstoy, and came to Jerusalem. Tolstoy died because of poor little Konstantin Shapiro—marginal, insignificant K. A. Shapiro, bowing and kneeling outside the gates, shut out of the circle of Tolstoy's life—not because of the big, important, obvious issues, the fundamental issues, like the huge Tolstoy estate or the affair of his illegitimate son. Contrary to all his feelings and beliefs and opinions and principles, and after all the struggles and wrestlings and commotion and uproar, Tolstoy did not divide his land among the peasants who worked it but bequeathed it all to his wife and children.

Nevertheless Louidor admired him. He continued to admire Tolstoy even after he found out about the scandal of his illegitimate son. Tolstoy had gone to bed with, among others, a certain peasant woman, the wife of one of his serfs, who bore him a son called Timothy. Later, when Timothy grew up, Tolstoy made him a coach driver for one of the younger legitimate sons borne him by his legal wife Sophia. And the popular saying "Like father like son" was true, Louidor discovered; for Lev Tolstoy's father, too, had had an illegitimate son who served one of the legitimate members of the family as a groom. Louidor asked himself how Tolstoy could have looked on without embarrassment as his son Timothy, in servant's livery, climbed onto the driver's seat and awaited the orders of his master, the legitimate son. Still, he admired the great moralist Tolstoy—until, as he was paging through that ancient correspondence, his attention was caught by the name Konstantin Shapiro.

In the course of this correspondence, Strakhov told Tolstoy about a certain Konstantin Shapiro who was considered an artist in the field of photography although he looked like a Jewboy. It came about that, in fact, he was a Jewboy, a *Zhid*. He was compiling a book of portraits of Russian writers, and had already photographed Dostoevski and Turgenev. Now he wanted to take Tolstoy's photograph, and he had approached Strakhov in order to obtain his recommendation. But Strakhov's recommendation didn't help the Jewboy. Tolstoy did not even trouble to remember Konstantin Shapiro's name. In his reply, Shapiro became "Pinaro," and Tolstoy refused to allow this "Pinaro" to photograph him.

As he read these words, Louidor's heart contracted with a painful childhood memory. One evening his father came home and said that the Hebrew poet Konstantin Shapiro was dead. Sitting by the window with his face to the setting sun, Louidor's father told him about the dead poet. As a child, he said, Konstantin Shapiro had loved reading Hebrew poetry. In a small room facing a dark alley that stank of sewage, the boy would sit and read the Hebrew poems which filled his heart with light and joy and the fragrance of spring blossoms. He saw himself in the streets of a reborn Jerusalem, standing between the pillars of the king's palace and singing the songs of Zion to his people. The crowd would cheer him and the daughters of Jerusalem bind garlands of flowers about his brow. But Konstantin's father was an Orthodox Jew who regarded the reading of secular Hebrew poetry as blasphemous, heretical. He beat his son, then tied him to the table and forced him to copy out page after page of the Jewish book of religious precepts called the *Shulchan Aruch*. From then on, Konstantin Shapiro was careful to read Hebrew poetry in secret, far from his father and everyone else in the Jewish quarter who believed as his father did. Once, far from home, he was sitting and reading a Hebrew poem on the river bank. He sat on the grass and ate a piece of bread as he read. On hearing a rustle in the reeds, he lifted his head. Someone had seen him, and ran quickly to inform on him. When he arrived home, his father greeted him with a furious glare. It was the fast of Tisha B'Av, and he had eaten in public. His father turned him out of the house, and in the whole village there was no one willing to take him in.

Konstantin ran away to the distant metropolis of Petrograd, but he discovered that a Jew needed a permit to live there. Since he had no such permit, he sent home an urgent request for his papers and a sum of money to tide him over until he found work. He waited and waited, but he heard nothing from home. Without a penny to his name and without a resident's permit, the boy wandered about the big, strange city, sleeping outdoors in outlying suburbs where there was less danger of being apprehended. To earn a few pennies for a hot meal, he would sweep snow from the pavements. One day he collapsed in a courtyard in a slum on the edge of town, a place called Peterburgskaya Storona. A Christian washerwoman who lived there took pity on him and brought him in. While she went out to work each day, her young daughter looked after him tenderly, and he fell in love with her.

When he recovered from his illness, Konstantin Shapiro married the washerwoman's daughter and became a Christian. He studied photography and in the course of time became a famous photographer. He was appointed court photographer to Prince Vladimir Alexandrovich and photographer of the Fine Arts Academy. After he was well established in his profession, he helped all the Hebrew poets and writers who approached him and gave them money.

Then the pogroms against the Jews broke out, and Konstantin Shapiro remembered his childhood dream of a kingdom of Israel in the land of Israel. He decided that the time had come to make it come true. He sent a large donation to a group of Jews who thought and felt as he did and had banded together in the "Lovers of Zion" movement. But the money was returned. The Lovers of Zion refused to accept money from a Jew who had abandoned his religion. It was like that slap in the face he'd received from his father, and his childhood dream turned into a recurrent nightmare. He would dream of standing between the giant pillars of the king's palace and singing the songs of Zion to his people. The crowd received him with cheers and the daughters of Jerusalem bound garlands of flowers about his brow. Suddenly he would hear a shout: "What are you to us? Get the hell out of here!" And his father turned him out of the house. . . . No, not his father—the young Lovers of Zion. They would tear the garlands of flowers from his head and trample them underfoot.

This nightmare would sometimes turn into another, even more terrible. The priests would be dragging him by the feet to the Christian cemetery while he tried with all his might to scream, "I'm alive! I'm alive!" But his voice would be inaudible. Three gravediggers dressed in black were digging a grave in the snow that covered the tombstones all around. Bells rang in his ears all the way to the grave, growing louder and louder. With a supreme effort he would manage to shout, "I'm alive!"—and at that moment he would wake up to the sound of bells in the Armenian church opposite the window of his room.

In fact, those bells of the Armenian church rang so loud in Konstantin Shapiro's ears that finally he could stand their persecution no longer. He gave up his apartment and moved to another, even though breaking his lease involved him in prolonged litigation and cost him much trouble and money. He resolved to leave Russia and emigrate to the land of his childhood dreams, but death overtook him. He was buried in the little village of Strylna on the Finnish bay, his wife's birthplace. Three young Hebrew students who were preparing themselves for immigration to Eretz Yisrael walked behind his coffin and lowered it into the earth while the first spring breezes fluttered in from the bay.

Louidor took the journal containing the ancient correspondence, bundled it into his haversack, and left the Russian commune without saying a word to anyone. But a shock hit him when he reached Jaffa. An Arab sailor took him from the steamer to a boat, and from the boat onto the soil of Eretz Yisrael. Jaffa was full of Arabs and Arab voices and an Arab uproar and Arab smells. He had never imagined—or dreamed in the worst of his dreams when he lay in his bed at night—that other people belonging to another nation had got there before him. He had heard of Arabs, of course, but he had imagined encountering them beyond the borders, on the desert trails leading to Egypt or on one of the roads leading to the Euphrates River. Like Konstantin Shapiro, these Arabs brought back a childhood memory, a verse he had learned: "In the ways hast thou sat for them, / As the Arabian in the wilderness . . ."

In the wilderness—but not in Eretz Yisrael. When he went up from Jaffa to Jerusalem and met Yaeli in the Cancan Café he told her with a smile (only with Yaeli was Louidor able to talk about himself with a smile, the easy, relaxed smile of a person at one and the same time inside and outside himself, above and beyond his thoughts and memories and ambitions and feelings and fears) that on his first night in the country, in the dirty little hotel in Jaffa, he had been unable to sleep—not because of the bedbugs or the oppressive heat and the rivers of sweat, but because of the Arab language. Prolonged cries of "*Yaalah yaalah yaalah yaalah yaalah*" rang in his

84

ears all night long, merging with Konstantin Shapiro's nightmares, which also began to haunt him. That whole sleepless night he wept aloud, wailing like a child of seven. Then, toward morning, he began to laugh as he had never laughed before. He laughed out loud; peals of laughter welled out of him; he writhed in laughter at the weeping of the night. He laughed when he opened his eyes in the first light of morning, because he suddenly saw that all night long he had wept for what would have happened to the dead man if, God forbid, he had remained alive and his dreams had come true. Louidor's heart broke with pity for Konstantin Shapiro, dead and buried beneath the earth by the Finnish bay, with the grass growing through his cheekbones spring after spring now for many a year. What would have happened to him if he had not died and if he had succeeded at last in reaching the land of his dreams? Here he is, standing between the giant pillars of the king's palace to sing the songs of Zion to his people, as the Levites had once sung the psalms of David on the temple steps. The murmuring of the crowd rises in his ears. In a moment they will begin to cheer and applaud and the daughters of Jerusalem will bind garlands of flowers about his brow. Then, lifting his eyes and looking about him, he sees a great crowd of Arabs in *abbayehs* and *keffiyehs* and tarbushes waving their arms in the air and shouting threateningly, "*Yaalah yaalah yaalah yaalah.*" "I must have taken the wrong road," says Konstantin Shapiro to the shrunken old man with piercing eyes and a wild beard standing next to him. "I've come to Baghdad instead of Jerusalem."

"No, you didn't take the wrong road," says Tolstoy. "This is Jerusalem, all right. But you don't belong here. Can't you see that nobody understands you and nobody wants you here?"

"In that case," says Konstantin Shapiro to Tolstoy, "if I don't belong here in Jerusalem, I'll go to Bethlehem in Judah and from there to Hebron."

"You go back home, and stop pushing yourself in where you're not wanted," says Tolstoy and slams the door shut in his face. The thunder of bells echoes in his ears and fills his head to bursting. He is afraid to turn around and see the three priests who are pursuing him, intent on dragging him to the graveyard. He hears their footsteps approaching, and with all his strength he knocks on the door locked against him, beats with his fists on the door of the house, and shouts so that someone will come and let him in. There are people inside, but nobody comes. There is a great crowd celebrating inside, and in the uproar no one can hear his knocking. He knocks and shouts and wakes up bathed in sweat to the noise of the Arab bazaar in the steaming heat of the morning.

Every morning Louidor would wake up to the noise of the Arab bazaar, and his heart would break for Konstantin Shapiro, because he himself had come to Jerusalem and succeeded in realizing his lifelong dream.

"What's his poetry like?" asked Yaeli.

"Whose poetry?" asked Louidor. He knew that Yaeli admired a modern Hebrew poet called Eshba'al Ashtaroth, and that she liked reading poetry in general.

"Konstantin Shapiro's poetry, your dybbuk's poetry," said Yaeli, and laughed. Her little snub nose, which peeled in the sun, wrinkled up as she laughed and her eyes glinted mischievously. "I've never heard of him." Louidor would have liked to take her head between his hands and kiss her again and again, her eyes, nose, mouth, cheeks, throat—she was so adorable—but he didn't dare. For a moment he sat in melancholy silence, and then he said: "I don't know. It never occurred to me to read his poetry. It never even occurred to me to read his biography. All these years I never thought of him at all. It was only when I read Strakhov's letter to Tolstoy that I suddenly remembered the story my father told me when I was seven years old. I don't even know if what I remember from my father's story is anything like what really happened to Konstantin Shapiro."

"In that case" said Yaeli, taking up the straw hat lying on the seat beside her, preparing to get up and leave, "I'll try to get hold of Konstantin Shapiro's poems and read them for you. I'll go to the B'nai Brith library and ask the librarian. Little Srulik knows exactly what he's got in his library."

When she got up and walked toward the café door, the anxiety which had been with him since his arrival in the country—from the moment the Arab sailor had lifted him onto the Jaffa shore—surged up again and spread to the tips of his fingers and toes. He felt an urge to run to his room and shut himself up, but he went on sitting where he was, trying to keep calm. Yomtov the Sad, the owner of the café, was drying dishes next to the counter, and his partner, Pesach the

Fat, was bent over the accounts at his side. Above the counter was a shelf laden with packets and bags and potbellied jars. To his dismay Louidor suddenly saw that the shelf, bowed beneath its load and resting on two shaky wooden supports joined to the wall with rusty nails, was trembling as a horse-drawn cart passed the café door. In another moment the shelf, with all its packets and jars, would crash down on Yomtov's and Pesach's heads. Louidor leaped from his chair, pointed to the shelf, and cried, "It's falling!" Pesach looked up from his accounts, smiled so that all his short, widely-spaced teeth showed, and said, "Don't worry, Louidor. That shelf has held firm up to now, and it'll hold firm for the next twenty years, too."

"But something must be done before it falls!" said Louidor, and went outside so as not to see the glass jars shattering on their heads. With extraordinary clarity he envisioned the moment of breaking in all its detail: the rusty nails bending, the supports splitting, the shelf breaking in half, the jars falling down with a tinkling of glass, and the blood spurting from the faces and heads of the two partners. How could Pesach smile so calmly when at any moment his skull might be smashed in?

"Right," said Louidor to himself as he conducted a silent argument with Pesach the Fat, "I'm tense. My nerves are on edge, and you're a calm, relaxed, easygoing man with strong nerves. But even if your nerves were made of blue steel, that wouldn't change the fact that the shelf above your head is shaky, that it's heavily laden, and resting on broken supports joined to the wall with rusty nails! You may argue that my morbid imagination is carrying me away, whereas you yourself are a practical man standing with both fat feet on the solid ground. If you really are a practical man who takes a practical view of things that have to be done in a world of action—why, all the more reason for you to take practical steps while there's still time. Throw out that whole shaky structure and build a new, steady one in its place. Don't wait until it breaks your head, or Yomtov's head, or someone else's head! Why is it that you practical people are always relying on miracles and never do anything until the blow falls?"

After he closed the door of his room behind him, he dropped onto his bed and fell into a deep sleep. Suddenly he woke and jumped up, determined to return to the Cancan at once and fix the shelf himself.

87

No, not fix it but build a new one instead. If the owners weren't prepared to do what had to be done—even though their criminal negligence might lead to the death of not only the two Arab maids who went in and out of the kitchen under the shelf, but also of Pesach's children, his own children, who came from time to time to play there—then it was up to him, Louidor, who saw the danger and was aware of it, to install a new shelf with his own hands. Where there are no men, you must try to be a man! The sight of himself standing there, pulling the rusty nails out of the wall, dismantling the broken supports, screwing in iron ones, and putting in a new, strong shelf filled him with pleasure.

But then he recalled the affair of the geranium pots, and his pleasure gave way to distress. One day he'd gone out onto the balcony of his room, and seen that the hotel chambermaid—the same foolish Arab woman who washed dishes at night in the Cancan—had placed a geranium pot right on the edge of the balustrade. Any little breeze could have blown it off onto the heads of the passersby in the street. He hurried to pull the flowerpot backward toward the balcony, and then he saw that the other flowerpots too, on both adjacent balconies, were about to fall into the street. He immediately knocked on the door of the neighboring room. The old half-deaf wool merchant from Germany who lived there was sitting with both feet in a basin of hot water. He looked blankly at Louidor and said in the end, "Take the flowerpot to your room. I don't like geraniums. I never liked that flower." So Louidor carried the geranium to his balcony with a joyful and unexpected feeling of relief. Since this flowerpot too would now be standing on the balustrade of his own balcony, he would always be able to move it backward after the maid was gone without having to bother the old man every day. At that moment the hotel owner himself appeared on the third balcony, and Louidor explained to him that he was ready, even eager, to take charge of the third flowerpot as well, thereby relieving the owner of the duty of looking after both the flowerpot and the heads of all the passersby. A look of fury appeared on the hotel owner's long face. He came running from the third room, grabbed the flowerpot out of Louidor's hands, and returned it to the wool merchant's balcony. After placing it on the balustrade at an even sharper angle than before, so that it was really teetering, ready at any moment to slip and shatter on the head of the first passerby, he yelled in the direction of Louidor's balcony, "You're not the boss here, to tell me what to do! I'm the owner of this hotel, and I'll decide where to put the flowerpots! It's not the flowerpots I'll get rid of, but you! You're only a guest here!"

At the memory of the rage contorting the hotel owner's long face, which was ugly enough anyway, and the words "It's not the flowerpots I'll get rid of, but you!" Louidor's heart contracted so painfully that he felt he could not stay in the alien room a moment longer. The very walls rejected him, and in his hurry to escape he ran to the balcony and thought of jumping down to the street. It was late at night. He did not know exactly what time it was, but he knew he must have been sleeping in his clothes for several hours since returning from the Cancan. In the silence of the night, the shops were shut and the houses, with the exception of a few lighted windows here and there, were lost in darkness. A black cat walked past, stopped in the middle of the street to scratch its ear with its back paw, tensed a moment, looked back, then, in two or three leaps, made its way to a garbage can. Louidor leaned over the balustrade and suddenly discovered, directly below him, the source of the black cat's tension. A boy and a girl were standing there, hugging and caressing each other in silence; a shudder passed through Louidor's body. "I could have become an unknowing murderer—and not just any murderer, but the murderer of a pair of lovers," he said to himself.

Then he remembered a story he had once read in the paper which had (from the "philosophic point of view") preoccupied him for a long time. A certain Frenchwoman had decided to commit suicide by jumping from the right-hand tower of Notre Dame Cathedral. She jumped, and landed on two young girls, American students who were touring Paris. Both were killed on the spot, while the woman herself survived with only two broken bones in one of her legs. Louidor thought about this story for a long time, and asked himself if there really was any connection between man and his fate. Two young Americans killed just because a woman in Paris decided to commit suicide! And now he himself had almost killed a pair of lovers just because he wanted to escape from the hatred of an alien landlord by the shortest possible route.

Louidor went back toward his room and turned in the direction of the stairs. He started to descend lightly, but halfway down he stopped, ran back up to the top, and burst onto the balcony again. He had remembered that in leaning over the balustrade he had moved the geranium pot and that it might fall onto the heads of the lovers. The flowerpot was in fact close to the edge, but the lovers were no longer there. Moving slowly along the sidewalk, stopping every few steps to hug and kiss in the darkness, they were now standing under the wool merchant's flowerpot. If he could have, Louidor would have gone into each of the rooms next to his own and moved the flowerpots back before making his escape. "And who knows how many flowerpots are still waiting to fall on them on their way?" he said to himself as, already on the sidewalk below, he walked behind the lovers. When they vanished beyond the turn in the road, Louidor was left in the empty street. The cat was rummaging in the garbage can, which gave off a sour, stale smell of rotten fruit. He lengthened his stride, but the more he hurried, the more the hostile street closed in on him. He felt oppressed by a suffocating sensation. "There's nowhere to escape," he said to himself, "except inward."

A piece of newspaper, which had apparently escaped from the garbage can in the night breeze, stuck to his shoe and fluttered about with every step he took. Bending down to remove it, he saw a picture of a deer standing on top of a hill and under it some words about a deer; he could not quite make them out in the dark—perhaps "Land of the Deer."* The suffocating oppressiveness vanished, and his heart expanded with a wild, pounding exhilaration. "It's now or never," he said aloud, and in a few minutes he reached the Russian compound at a run and turned down the path leading to Yaeli's room. Without a moment's hesitation, he knocked on her door three times. No reply. He went round to the dark window and knocked on it too. If she had been in her room, she would have awakened by now. He knocked and called, "Yaeli, Yaeli!" over and over, repeating to himself, "The high mountains for the deer, the high mountains for the deer." The sound of heavy, muffled footsteps came echoing from the direction of Meah Shearim and Musrara, and with them something that sounded like an angry exchange of words. Louidor was not deterred. On the contrary, to his surprise, he suddenly felt himself to be a mighty

*"Eretz Hazvi": "Land of the Deer," or "The Beautiful Land," an ancient term of endearment for Eretz Yisrael. The girl's name, "Yael," also means "deer" in Hebrew.

rock ready to smash anyone who dared approach Yaeli's window. At the same time, he giggled at a kind of pun which suddenly flashed across his mind: "And when the mountain finally came to the deer, the deer wasn't at home!" The footsteps came closer and two figures emerged from the darkness—Illya and Ivan, two Russian friends who lived in the basement of the hotel from which Louidor had just escaped. A furious rage, the like of which he had never known, flooded through him. He was certain that these two crooks were planning to enter Yaeli's room in the dead of night and exploit her kindheartedness, innocence, and compassion—for Yaeli would never shut her door against the weary, the hungry, the thirsty, or against this pair of wretched exiles. They would overcome her and rape her, both of them together and each of them in turn. "And she," he said to himself, "she would be too shy even to scream!" He knew in his heart that as soon as the two dared approach her window he would kill them with his bare hands. He would beat them both to death. Strangle them!

"But perhaps there won't be any need for them to rape her?" he suddenly asked himself. "Maybe she's waiting for them? And not only tonight! Who knows, maybe they come to her every night when they've finished their drinking and swilling." Louidor knew that the Russians were in the habit of getting drunk every night in Shmuel's wineshop in Meah Shearim, but it had never occurred to him to wonder what they did after they were drunk. Sweat burst from every pore of his skin, and his body collapsed weakly. Slowly he tottered weak-kneed toward the bench in the open square in the middle of the Russian compound. He turned his face away so that they would not recognize him. He did not even have the strength to greet them, but to his dismay they followed him and sat down on the bench beside him.

"What, is it you, Louidor?" cried Illya. Drunken tears were dripping from his eyes, and at the sight of Louidor he burst into loud weeping. "Stop it, stop it—stop crying!" cried Ivan. "You must pull yourself together!"

The weeping Illya was the master, and Ivan was his servant. Once Illya had apparently been a man of property, but since his arrival in Jerusalem—or at least since Louidor had met him at the hotel—he was as poor as Ivan. Although both of them lived in the basement, they didn't always have the money to pay the monthly rent on time. Sometimes they were even obliged to drink their vodka on credit.

Louidor wanted to get up, but Illya grabbed hold of his coat collar and with tears pouring from his eyes begged him not to abandon him and not to spit in his face, even though he, Illya, was vile. "Yes, yes," he wailed hoarsely, "I have a base soul—a mean, base soul!"

"No, your soul is not base, but noble!" said Ivan consolingly, "and now pull yourself together and stop crying."

"No, no," cried Illya vehemently, "I must tell Louidor the truth, the whole truth. I won't hide anything from him. Know then, Louidor, that this evening my soul was revealed in all its baseness. When we went into Shmuel's wineshop this evening to have a drink, Ivan saw that his glass was dirty, and it *was* dirty. Mr. Shmuel forgot to wash it before pouring Ivan's drink. 'Listen, Mr. Shmuel,' Ivan said to him, 'the glass is dirty. Please be so kind as to pour me another drink in its place.' Mr. Shmuel came up to have a look at the glass, and he was just about to exchange it for another one when I flew into a terrible rage. I raged at Ivan. How dare a man who was born in my father's stable, wallowing in filth until I raised him up from the dregs—how dare he suddenly demand another glass? My lord and master—an aristocrat all of a sudden! 'So,' I said to Ivan, 'you can't drink from that glass? That glass isn't clean enough to suit your tastes? All your life you've been drinking from spotless crystal glasses? If that's the way it is, if you don't want to drink from the glass, you'll drink from my shoe!' And on the spot I took off my left shoe, poured all the vodka into it, forced it into his mouth and said, 'Drink, you son of a bitch.' And what do you think, Louidor? He drank the vodka from my left shoe! Do you hear, Louidor? I myself couldn't stand the stink of that shoe. As soon as I took it off, a terrible stink filled the whole wineshop. I knew very well that Ivan would not disobey me. I knew that what I was doing was vile, vile! I knew that Ivan is ten times better than I, if only because he keeps me alive with his work. Am I able to earn my living? If it had not been for Ivan, I would have starved to death long ago. And not only that: despite the fact that he was born in a stable, Ivan is ten times better than I, because the good God gave him a great soul. And maybe that's why! I knew that I was not fit to kiss his feet, but nevertheless I forced him to drink out of my left shoe and enjoyed the sight of it! I was overcome with joy to see my good friend Ivan—my only friend in the whole world, the friend who saved my life—sitting and drinking his vodka out of my stinking shoe. In the whole world there is not so base and mean and vile a man as I!''

"Enough! Stop crying now and pull yourself together and get up!'' Ivan interrupted him and tried to lift him up, but Illya was too heavy for him and fell back onto the bench. Louidor hurried to help Ivan, and by a concerted effort they got him to his feet. Supported on either side by Ivan and Louidor, Illya reached his bed. But before collapsing onto it, he roused himself to thank Louidor and covered him with kisses. Before Louidor had time to draw back, Illya's tears and saliva were all over his face. Despite his weakness and drunkenness and general state of collapse, Illya was embracing Louidor with great strength. Louidor was obliged to wrestle with him, and it was only with a great effort and Ivan's help that he succeeded in freeing himself from the vise of those arms. He ran to the tap in the yard and stood there a long time, letting the water run over his head and face and neck, before going to his room and shutting himself in. At first he thought he would fall asleep the moment his head touched the pillow, but then he jumped up, overcome by nausea. Now the room seemed not only alien, but as revolting as Illya's stinking breath and slimy saliva. He grabbed the haversack lying in the corner by the head of his bed and rushed outside. All Louidor possessed was bundled up in that haversack, and he knew he would never return.

On his second journey through the night streets he had somewhere to go. He hurried toward Yaeli's room, and when he reached the bench on the corner of the path he sat down and placed his haversack at his feet. He rummaged in it and found a pencil, but no paper. He dug about in the depths of the haversack and in the end impatiently tore the last blank page out of the ancient journal which had published the correspondence between Tolstoy and Strakhov. He went over to the solitary lamp post standing in the middle of the Russian compound— next to the giant column which had been lying there on its side since the days of King Herod; apparently the stonecutters had abandoned it half-finished, having discovered a deep, irreparable crack in the stone. Louidor placed the sheet of paper on the column and began to write rapidly in a small, cramped hand. He decided to tell Yaeli everything, and then push the paper through the crack under her door. Then "It's her," he said to himself at the sound of a woman's steps approaching from behind. He turned his head and saw her hurrying along at the top of the compound. So great was his emotion that he began to tremble all over; he was shaking as violently as when he had had malaria on the plain of Jericho. "It's the hand of God—now or never!" He took one step toward her but felt that his shivering knees were about to give way beneath him. He pushed the piece of paper into his pocket and fell back onto the bench next to his haversack. At this moment Yaeli reached him and looked at him apprehensively. As soon as she recognized him, her eyes lit up and she said gently, "What's the matter, Louidor? Why don't you go home to bed?" He said to himself that one such moment was worth the suffering of a lifetime. He wanted to tell her the things that were written in the letter pushed into his pocket, but he couldn't speak. Nothing came out of his mouth but the sound of his chattering teeth. "Aren't you feeling well? Are you ill? Come with me. I live here, in the lane on the other side of the gate." As though in a dream too good to be true, as though in paradise, he stood up and followed her, repeating to himself, "It's the hand of God, the hand of God!" Hand in hand they went into her room. Pointing to her bed, she told him to undress and get into it; in the meantime she would make him something hot to drink. While he was sipping the hot tea, she drew the curtain on the other side of the table and began to undress behind it. As she was doing so, she smiled at him warmly—which calmed him down at once. He got up, clasped her to him with a strong embrace, and covered the nape of her neck with feverish kisses. "What's the matter with you? Have you gone mad?" cried Yaeli and shook him off. "Go right back to bed and stop this nonsense!" No longer did she look at him with love and warmth, but with a terrible contempt, a kind of ridicule and disgust—as if it was not he, her desired and beloved who embraced her to enter her, but a repulsive frog. This look seemed to split his soul in two, to sever his penis from his body and fling it out of the window like some loathsome insect. On trembling legs Louidor went back to bed and turned his face to the wall. She covered him with the blanket and said, "And now good night, and pleasant dreams."

And indeed, as soon as Yaeli lay down on the couch, she fell fast asleep, but Louidor the Silent lay wide awake, cowering beneath a terrible fear: it was not the hand of God but the hand of Satan that had brought him here to torture him! He choked back his groans and suddenly stood up, determined to rape her in her sleep. Here she was, sprawled out in front of him with nothing covering her but a nightgown. He could do whatever he liked to her, whatever he had imagined in the best of his daydreams; but when he went up to her, the memory of her look of contempt and disgust cut her off from him and made him go limp. The whole world had become too hard and bleak to bear. He went back to bed, but tossed and turned and could not sleep. He stood up, walked around the room, and fell back on the bed. He stood up again, went to the window, and drew back the curtain, but no abyss gaped before him, only the nearby gravel of the path. With the first light, he could no longer endure her deep sleep and heavy, rhythmic breathing. So he ran outside and began running around in the streets, that seemed petrified by the dreams of dawn that come just before waking. At the same time, Pesach the Fat, one of the two owners of the Cancan Café, came out to prepare breakfast for the first workers of the morning. Walking with his measured tread down the lane past the Russian compound, on his way to the corner of Melissande Street, he saw the door of Yaeli's room opening quietly and Louidor the Silent emerging from it, "as flustered as the saintly Joseph fleeing from Potiphar's wife." Thus he told the story later, to all the habitués of the Cancan Café, rolling his bulging eyes with a conspiratorial air and smiling slyly. That same day Louidor disappeared from Jerusalem. Only long afterward Haim Longlife, Berl's brother, told us that he had seen Louidor the Silent wandering about the marketplace in Ramleh in Bedouin robes. Mrs. Luria, however, did not believe him and dismissed his story with a scornful smile.

—*translated by Dalya Bilu*

Chapter from a novel
A. B. Yehoshua

The philanderer

But I did get to the front. Barely twenty-four hours after you sent me away I was there in the desert. They bundled me off in short order, and not because I was needed but because they wanted to kill me. They wanted to kill me, I tell you—wantonly, nothing to do with the war. And they did kill me too; it is someone else you see here before you.

At first things just crept along. It took me until noon to find the camp. I left the car at the parking lot and went looking for a gate, but there wasn't any—just a torn and trampled fence and a great commotion. People milling about among the barracks, military vehicles tearing along; but under this guise of frenzied activity you could already detect a new, unfamiliar lassitude, like a slow poison. The spine had cracked. You would ask the office girls something and realize they weren't taking it in. A kind of general absentmindedness. And wherever you went, you were pursued by the sound of transistor radios. They bore no tidings, though, and you'd had your fill of those everlasting old marching songs too. The senselessness of it, all of a sudden.

And before long I realize that of course they don't know what to do with me. Because except for a passport I've got no document to give them a lead. They hand me on from one barrack to the next, dispatch me to the computer to see if it will produce something, and sure enough, it does. It isn't me, though, but someone else with the same name, a man of fifty-five from Dimona, perhaps a relation.

Eventually I ended up at a small, remote barracks where they were herding all their doubtful cases—mainly people just come back from abroad and still toting their bright traveling bags. They were sprawling about on the faded lawn, and a girl soldier, a squat and unlovely redhead, was collecting everybody's passport, and took mine as I came.

We waited—

The majority were returning Israelis. When they heard I'd been away for ten years, their eyes lit up. They assumed I had come back especially for the war, and I didn't trouble to disabuse them. If it boosted their morale to think that, lo and behold, even at such times an Israeli doesn't get lost—then let them.

Every now and again the redhead would emerge, call out a name, and admit its owner into the barracks—and after a while he'd come out with a call-up order. At first they treated us as a nuisance, as if they were doing us a favor by drafting us at all, taking the trouble to hunt up our units for us; as if this entire call-up was hardly worth it because the war was bound to be over any moment now. But as time wore on, as the day faded, their attitude began to change, and the drafting process picked up pace.

Suddenly people are becoming important. Every man will be needed. The ranks are thinning. The transistor reeks of death. Between the lines, through the coded call-ups and the ambiguous news reports, it becomes apparent that something has gone wrong.

Gradually the crowd around me is thinning. People who have arrived after me are called into the office and swiftly dispatched, and still there is no sign that they have come up with anything about me. I am famished by now. I've had nothing to eat all day but that sandwich you gave me in the morning. All at once I'm tired of this hanging about, go into the office, ask the redhead, "And what about me?"

98

And she says: "You'll have to wait. They can't get hold of anything about you."

"Then what if I came back tomorrow?"

"No, don't go."

"Where's my passport?"

"What d'you want it for?"

"Just let me go and get something to eat, then . . ."

"No, stay here. . . . Please don't make trouble now."

At dusk a fresh batch of officers arrives at the camp. I never knew we even had any that old. Gray-haired, balding, in their fifties and sixties, turned out in uniforms of all periods, sporting chestfuls of ribbons. A few are limping, or walk with sticks. Captains, majors, and colonels. Relics of an era, springing into the breach, come to augment the blundering office personnel who are at their wits' end.

They disperse about the barracks, and meanwhile night has descended and all the windows have been blacked out with army blankets. Suddenly I find myself alone in a far corner of the camp. Even the transistor voices are gone, and the scent of orange groves rises in the air. I wanted to call you then, but the public telephone which had been in constant use had gone dead, and it seemed as if all this vast darkness had fallen silent. Even the drone of aircraft and helicopters had faded, and only the sound of a distant siren, perhaps from Jerusalem, passed overhead like a soft moan.

At last, about nine in the evening or later, the little redhead appears, calls me, and I follow her to an inner room of the barracks and find a lanky major awaiting me. He is about fifty and completely bald, with a red paratrooper's beret tucked under his shoulder strap; he looks fresh in his smartly pressed uniform, in his aura of after-shave lotion.

He stands leaning against a chair, one hand in a pocket, the other holding my passport. The girl, already gray with fatigue, sits down behind a desk. For some reason, the officer's presence in the room seems to confuse her.

"You came back four months ago?"

"Yes."

His voice is hard, forceful, his speech savagely clipped.

"You know you should have reported within fourteen days."

"Yes . . ."

"Why didn't you?"

"I didn't really mean to stay. . . . I was only delayed by chance. . . ."

"By chance?"

He takes a small step toward me and retreats again. Now I see that he keeps a tiny transistor in his shirt pocket, with a thin white wire running to his ear. He talks to me and listens to the news at the same time.

"How long have you been away?"

"Ten years or so."

"And never came back once in all that time?"

"No . . ."

"You mean you didn't care what was happening here?"

I smile. What can you say to a funny question like that?

"I read the papers . . ."

"The papers . . ." He sniffs contemptuously, and I see he is working up some obscure, dangerous rage.

"Bolting, were you?"

"No . . ." I am beginning to stammer, thrown off by these wild questions. "It's just that I couldn't come back . . ." I pause, then add, can't think why, in a low voice, "I was ill too . . ."

"What with?"—cutting me short rudely, with inexplicable venom.

"The name won't tell you anything."

He pauses, looks me over sternly, casts an irritable glance at the girl, who sits staring at the blank form before her, not knowing what she's supposed to write. And all the while he's listening to the voices from the transistor. Important news. His face darkens.

"You all right now?"

"Yes."

"And why didn't you report on time?"

"I told you. I didn't intend to stay."

"But you did."

"Yes . . ."

"Found something to your liking all of a sudden?"

There was a curious undertone to his questions, a kind of nagging provocation.

100

"No . . . I mean . . . it's not . . . I was just waiting for my grandmother to die."

"You were *what?*"

He moves closer as if unable to believe his ears. Now I notice the ugly reddish scar running down his neck. And the hand that lies inert in his pocket is paralyzed, or dead, or maybe it is an artificial hand.

"My grandmother had a stroke . . . went into coma . . . that's why I came back."

Suddenly this is a full-blown interrogation—it's as though he wants to prepare a charge against me without knowing my crime, but feels his way, casting about in every direction. We stand facing each other, and he is like a savage cat, tensing himself for the spring and giving way at the last minute. The girl listens hypnotized, scribbling with a pencil on an army form a mass of personal, intimate details which have nothing to do with the army.

But he is remarkably alert in the stifling, airless room, the worn blankets on the window sealing out the world. He continues with his cross-examination while he listens to the news flowing straight to his head, prying facts out of me which only aggravate his fury as they blend with the grim bulletins. He learns, for instance, that I'm a tenth-generation Israeli. I go on talking about myself, about the years in Paris, about the years before, the broken home, the father who disappeared; my attempts at studying—a year here, a course there, nothing settled, nothing followed through to the end. All at once my loneliness, my muddled life, lay exposed to the core. I even let on about the car, without meaning to. I didn't mention you, though, didn't once mention you, as if you didn't exist, as if you were unimportant. Not that I would have minded delivering you into his hands as well.

He drank it all in, missing nothing, tense, greedily worming every detail out of me, as though he was obsessed—but with a different sort of obsession, quite unlike my own.

At last the interrogation was over. I felt strangely serene. He gathered up the pages filled with the girl's round, childish script, read it all through from the beginning.

"As a matter of fact, I should have you court-martialed, but we mustn't waste time. We'll settle accounts after the war, after victory. What we've got to do now is to get you drafted in a hurry. It's because of people like you that we've been left with so few in the field. . . ."

I thought he was joking, but the girl had already begun to fill in the blanks: a mobilization order, Q.M. and armory forms.

"Whom to inform in case of fatality?" she asked.

I hesitated, then gave the address of my concierge in Paris.

Now I'll be free of him at last, I said to myself, but he showed no sign of letting me go. He gathered up my forms and personally escorted me to the Q.M.'s. It was nearly eleven o'clock, and the base was fairly quiet. We found the stores closed and in darkness. I thought, at least it's been put off till tomorrow, but he didn't mean to give up. He set out on a search for the quartermaster, went from one place to another, with me tagging along. I discovered in the process that he was high-handed with others as well, that he ordered everybody about. He finally ran the quartermaster to earth in the clubroom, sitting in the dark and watching television. He plucked him up—a swarthy, short, rather stupid-looking soldier—and for a start took his particulars in order to lodge a complaint against him. The soldier appeared stunned, tried to remonstrate, but was brutally silenced.

We return to the depot. The soldier—sullen, upset by the thought of the officer's complaint hanging over him—starts tossing out equipment.

"I'll show you what's-the-hurry," the major snarls, still seething, and meanwhile takes good care to see that no item is left out. Cartridge belt, straps, pouches, three knapsacks, a pup tent, pole and pegs, five blankets. I stand there dumbfounded, watching the huge pile of stuff I'd never want mounting up on the dirty floor. And he looks on, grave, stiff as a poker, the feeble lamplight on his bald skull.

I am seized with despair—

"I don't need five blankets . . . two's enough. It's summer now . . . autumn . . . whatever. It's not cold."

"And what'll you do in winter?"

"In winter?" I grin. "What do you mean winter? I won't be here in winter."

"That's what you think," he sneers, not even looking at me, scornful, as though constantly gathering evidence against me.

Meanwhile the soldier throws down cutlery, a dusty, greasy mess tin, a bayonet. He is morosely silent.

"A bayonet? What for?"—with an edge of hysteria to my laughter. "There's a ballistic war going on down there, and you give me a bayonet!"

But he doesn't answer, just bends and picks up the bayonet, places it between his thighs, unsheathes it, runs a long thin finger over the blade collecting black grease as he goes, sniffs at it with a wry face, then wipes it off on a blanket, returns the bayonet to its scabbard, and wordlessly tosses it on the pile of gear.

I sign my name to a list two or three pages long, constantly forgetting my serial number, obliged to refer to my call-up order again and again. But he already knows my number by heart and mockingly corrects me.

In the end, I lump all the equipment in one enormous bundle, the soldier helping me knot the corners of the blanket, while the major stands over us offering advice. Then the soldier heaves the bundle onto my back, and we set out into the darkness once more. It is nearly midnight, and I totter about under my oppressive load, with him marching ahead—bald, thin, upright, his dead hand in his pocket, a small map case slung over his shoulder, the transistor broadcasting into his ear—with his own personal soldier in tow.

He takes me to the armory. I am on the verge of collapse, my hunger turning to nausea, a desire to vomit something I haven't eaten, my mouth filling with the acrid taste of my illness. I feel the bundle coming apart on my back, and suddenly realize I am close to tears. In front of the armory I slump to the ground with my scattering equipment.

The armory is open and lit, and people are lined up in front of it, most of them officers who are taking out revolvers or small submachine guns. He circumvents the queue, walks straight in, inspects the rows of rifles and machine guns as if they were his private property. After a while he beckons me over to sign for a bazooka and two rocket launchers.

"I've never used this weapon . . ." I tell him in a low voice, afraid of incurring his wrath.

"I know," he answers, suddenly gentle, smiling to himself, pleased with his brainstorm: attaching me to a bazooka.

Now I was burdened with such quantities of stuff that I couldn't

103

move a step, but he had no plans for taking me anywhere.

"Get your kit into shape fast. I'm going to find transport to get us down south, to the front."

Suddenly I understand, in despair, in the darkness; something about this aging officer, who still moves in a thin cloud of after-shave, seems clear.

"You've made up your mind to kill me," I whisper.

And he smiles.

"You haven't heard a shot yet, and already you're thinking of death."

But stubborn and passionate, I repeat my words:

"You want to kill me."

And he, no longer smiling, curtly:

"Get your stuff into shape."

I make no move. Something has snapped in me, a kind of mutinous urge has seized me.

"I've had nothing to eat all day. If I don't get something I'll go to pieces completely. I'm already seeing double."

He keeps silent, not the flicker of an eyelid, still the same vacant, haughty stare. And then he puts his single hand to his map case, takes out two hard-boiled eggs, and offers them to me.

An hour after midnight, already in uniform and heavy boots, I lie dozing outside in the fast-cooling night air, my head heavy on the largest of the knapsacks—a bulge of army blankets and my old clothes—my feet propped up on bazooka and rockets, white splinters of eggshell scattered about me. I would never have managed the stiff, blood-encrusted straps of my pack without the help of the quiet redhead, who has taken pity on me. She, too, has been hounded by the officer, who has been snapping out orders at her, has sent her scurrying all over the camp. And presently he himself flits by, like a phantom, as in a dream. Now he is searching in vain for some vehicle to take me south, to the desert.

At two A.M., having despaired of finding anything that will do, he remembers my car and decides to press it into service as well.

I jump up at once, stung.

"But the car isn't mine . . . "

"So why should you care?"

And he sends the girl off at once to fetch new forms. I've noticed it before—the way he assumes authority without a moment's hesitation, signs any document with a confident flourish. Now he thrusts a piece of paper at me and takes the keys.

"If you come back after the war, you'll get what's left of it."

He goes to the parking lot to fetch the car himself. Old as it is, it pleases him on sight, and he promptly takes control; he raises the hood, checks oil and water, kicks at the tires, quick as a devil. He sends the girl, already hunched over with fatigue, to find paint and brush for blacking out the headlights, and she, ever efficient, returns with a big tin of black paint. He slaps it on with evident relish, front and rear, pads the driver's seat, and adjusts it to make room for his long legs; then watches in silence as I stack my equipment on the back seat. We set out.

He drives with one hand, but with accomplished skill. I've never seen such a voracious driver—as if he were raping the car, the road, and every other vehicle in sight. He overtakes left and right, maneuvering deftly, in the dark, the feeble headlights, no more than a token glimmer, weaving in and out of the endless convoys of tank carriers and ammunition trucks. The Morris grows bold under his hands.

I sit by his side, spent, as if I've already been through days and days of war; I look at his cucumber-shaped skull, at my personal major forever absorbing his newscasts, his face occasionally twisting in a grimace.

"But what's going on?"

"They fight," he replies laconically.

"But how's it go?"

"Tough, very tough."

"But what's happening exactly?"

"You'll soon see for yourself"—already trying to shake me off.

"They slipped one over on us? . . . ."

"You whining already? Better go to sleep."

And he turns his back on me.

Suddenly alone, on my way to the war, I rest my head on the windowsill, watch the parched, sun-seared fields, let the sweat dry on my face, breathe the cool autumn wind, and slowly drift off. And with the sound of the rattling engine, dreams come and presently lead me to Paris, home, walking late at night through the bustling streets, along the Seine, across little alleys, past the bright cafés, the chestnut vendors, down the steps of the metro at the Odéon. The distinct subway-station smell, a mixture of the sweetish smell of electricity and the breath of the crowds who have passed through these tunnels by day. I wander about the bare neon-lit platform and hear the roar of trains from distant stations approach and recede. My own train arrives, and I leap headlong into the red first-class carriage as though pushed from behind, and among the few passengers I immediately spot Grandmother sitting in a corner, a small basket with freshly baked, crumbly golden *croissants* in her lap. She is nibbling one daintily, picking the crumbs off her gingham dress, her old Sunday dress. I am filled with a great joy, the joy of reunion. So she has finally come out of her coma. I sit down beside her at once, knowing she won't recognize me at first, and therefore gently, in a soft voice so as not to startle her, I smile and say, "Hi, Grandma." She stops eating, turns to look at me, smiles back absently. Suddenly, intuitively, I realize she has shared out the inheritance already; now she's running away, traveling incognito around Paris. "Hi, Grandma," I say again, and she, from her seat, a little anxious, mutters *"Pardon?"* as though she doesn't understand Hebrew. I decide to speak French, and find I've forgotten, can't think of the simplest word in that language. I am longing to take one golden *croissant,* and again I say, almost desperately, "Hi, Grandma, don't you remember me? I'm Gabriel." She stops chewing, faintly alarmed, but it's obvious that she just doesn't understand what I'm saying. My Hebrew is utterly foreign to her. Now the train slows down for its next stop, and I glance at the signs. We are back at the Odéon, our point of departure.

She rises quickly, covers up the *croissants.* The doors slide open and she steps out onto the platform, tries to evade me, but there's only a sprinkling of people about and I walk by her side, staying close, waiting patiently for my French to come back. I open the glass doors before her, mount the stairs, push the barrier for her, and she smiles to herself, an old woman's smile of forbearance, keeps muttering *"Merci, merci,"* wondering what this strange young man can want with her. We come out into the street at daybreak. Paris at dawn, damp and nebulous, as though we had been riding the metro all night.

The blue Morris stands there on the pavement, just as it is, blacked-out lights and all, except that the Israeli license plate has been changed for a French one. Grandmother rummages in her handbag for the keys, and I stand before her, still waiting for my French to return, grasping for some first word, very hungry now, licking my lips. She unlocks the car, places the *croissant* basket on the passenger seat, settles herself behind the wheel, plainly eager to shake me off as fast as possible. She smiles, the smile now of a young girl being waylaid in the street, says *"Merci"* again, and starts the engine. And I cling to the slowly moving car, seized with the panic of losing her, thrust my head in, lean on the window, say— But no . . . wait . . . —and it is as if my head were beginning to move off on its own.

My head is slumped against the car door, half in, half out of the window. The sky is aglow with dawn light. The fields have given way to dunes, palm trees, and white Arab houses. We are standing still, with silent engine, stuck in a huge double traffic column. Vans, armored tracks, jeeps, command cars, civilian vehicles, and a great humming and milling about. My officer is outside, wiping the dew off the windshield. He doesn't appear tired after his night's driving; only a faint reddish glint shows in his eye. I want to get out, but something holds me back. I discover that he has tied me to the seat in my sleep, fastened the seatbelt. He comes around to release me.

"The way you carry on in your sleep . . . You kept dropping over the wheel."

I tumble out, bedraggled, shivering with the cold, and stand beside him. I feel sick with hunger. This is the third day of the war, and I don't know what is happening. It's over ten hours since I last listened to the news. I glance at the button still plugged into his ear.

He keeps even the news to himself.

"What're they saying now?"

"Nothing, playing music."

"Where are we?"

"Near Raffah."

"What's going on? What's new?"

"Nothing."

"What's the outlook?"

107

"We'll smash them."

These brief, self-assured replies, the lofty glance raised at the horizon, surveying the column twisting out of sight as if it were under his personal command. Now that I was in his hands I wanted some clue to him.

"Excuse me"—with a faint smile—"I still don't know your name. . . ."

He glares at me.

"Why do you want to know?"

"Well . . ."

"Call me Shahar."

"Shahar. . . . What do you do, Shahar? . . . I mean, in private life . . ."

He was beginning to fret.

"Why?"

"Dunno. I just wondered."

"I work at education."

You could have knocked me down with a feather.

"Education? What sort of education?"

"Special education. At a detention home."

"You don't say! Sounds like an interesting job."

But he seemed disinclined to carry on the conversation. And right there by my side, the words still faltering on my lips, he opens his trousers, whips out his penis, and urinates on the barren soil, holding himself erect as ever, feet planted wide, drops spattering my shoes.

Several soldiers in the truck ahead of us catch sight of him. He's drawn their attention as well. They laugh, shout their wisecracks at him; and he, not put out, his member still boldly prominent, meets the challenge, raises his hand at them as though blessing a congregation.

In the big canteen at Raffah I fainted without warning, without so much as a hint of foreboding, just like that—lined up in the crowd bearing down upon the counters, amid the buzz of transistor radios, the fast-emptying sandwich trays and the small bags of cocoa, the smell of food; first the bazooka slipped to the ground, then I. And he, no doubt afraid they'd snatch me away from him, detached himself from the party of officers he'd been lecturing at, hurried over and dragged me out, shoved me under a tap, my head in a pool

108

of mud, and turned on the water. I hear him telling the soldiers gathered round us, "It's fear"—and trying to shoo them away.

But it was hunger. "I'm so hungry"—in a throaty whisper, coming to, sitting up on the ground, pale, mud in my hair. "I keep telling you. Ever since last night I've been trying to explain."

Once again he takes two hard-boiled eggs out of his map case and gives them to me.

By midday he had taken me to the heart of Sinai. I never believed we'd get there. The little Morris was as good as gold. She forgot all her troubles, didn't overheat, not once, and started immediately. She obeyed him, that battered old wreck; he'd mesmerized even her, made her do as much as seventy miles an hour.

They had put up roadblocks along the way, of course, with the military police trying to keep back all sorts of adventurers drawn to the war. But the major outwitted them all, would pretend not to see them, sneak by, even simply fail to stop. And if they persisted and gave chase, he'd pull up some way ahead, shoot out of the little Morris like some long, thin rapier, stand there waiting—in his red paratrooper's beret and his other-war campaign ribbons—for the puffing and swearing M.P.'s to catch up with him. Then he'd say quietly:

"Yes? Anything on your mind?"

And they'd beat a retreat.

But at Refidim we came to a halt. They let no one through. You could already hear the boom of distant shelling, the sound of the muffled explosions seeming to come from the bowels of the earth. And overhead the whine of aircraft. We were directed to a large area with row upon row of civilian cars, like the parking lot of some concert hall or football field. People were thronging to the war as to a gigantic spectacle. The major told me to remove my equipment, and I strapped myself in, donned the helmet, picked up the bazooka, and set out after him, in search of a unit that would take me in.

We marched in a cloud of dust, tanks and armored tracks careening about us, and people in the sand. A people sinking in the sands. Here they were born and here they would perish. And in all that tumult we nevertheless attracted attention. The one-handed major, flushed with heat, sweat glistening on his bald crown, leading me, his personal soldier, along as if I were a full regiment; and I, loaded with gear, trailing him as if tied by an invisible rope. People would stand still for a moment to watch us.

At last he stopped near several armored tracks parked at the roadside, facing west. He inquired after the officer in charge, and they pointed out some boy, a short, skinny lad who was making coffee over a small campfire.

"When are you off?"

"Soon."

"Need a bazooka man?"

The boy looked up in surprise.

"Bazooka? I don't think so."

But the major stood his ground.

"You mean to tell me you've got your full complement?"

"In what way?" The kid was utterly bewildered.

"Then take him on," indicating me.

"But . . . who's he . . . ?"

"No buts—this is an order," cutting him short, motioning to me to get up on the nearest track.

I started unloading my equipment and passing it on to the young soldiers on the track, who were joking about the quantities of stuff I had been lugging about with me. At last they pulled me up, too, their steel contraption red hot after its long wait in the sun. Meanwhile my major was busy scribbling in a notebook—taking down the C.O.'s name, the number of the unit, even walking round to the front of the track to check the license plate number, making quite sure that I had been sucked up into the system, that all my escape routes were sealed off. In the end, he even made the kid sign a receipt for me as though I were a batch of supplies.

The men were watching in amazement.

"Just see that he does his bit," he called up at them. "He's been away from the country ten years. Meant to escape for good."

They eyed me.

"You nut," one of them whispered. "*Now* you come back?"

But I did not answer, just asked softly if anyone could spare me a piece of bread or something, and one of them held out a big slice of sweet, delicious-looking sponge cake. I bit into it at once, devoured it greedily, tears welling up into my eyes. Suddenly I felt relieved. Perhaps it was the cake, its homemade taste in my mouth; perhaps it

110

was having really got rid of him at last. And so, standing on the track as part of a crew, leaning against the hot steel frame, and swallowing cake, I gazed at the bald, erect officer who was still throwing his weight around, cross-examining the kid about the plan of attack—and the kid, quite flustered, not knowing what to say. At last, unsatisfied, he let the kid go. Still he lingered, as though he couldn't bear to part with me, stood there forlorn, gazing about him with that vacant, haughty stare of his. And in a flash I perceived the pathos of his madness and smiled at him from above, from the heights of my track—now that I was beyond his grasp.

Suddenly he shook himself and turned to go. And I called out to him, "Hey, Shahar, so long!" He turned his head at me for a final look, his eyes still smoldering with resentment, lifted his one hand at last in a weary gesture, a kind of aborted salute, mumbled, "Ah, goodbye . . . goodbye to you." and set out along the dusty tank-beaten track leading to command quarters. For a while I still watched his slow, steady, brash stride, and the tanks maneuvering carefully around him to the right and left.

Now I was surrounded by young, boyish faces, a close-knit crowd of regulars who seemed quite merry, keyed up for their fire dip, laughing at private jokes, talking about people I didn't know. Their presence had a calming effect on me. Then the boy officer called me over to his jeep in order to find out at his leisure just who I was and how the major had got hold of me. And so, in the middle of the desert, through the buzz of field telephones and the hum of crowds, I went over the whole story again, adding unnecessary facts, becoming embroiled in a strange confession about Grandmother, about the inheritance—a man standing before a silent boy, blurting out intimate details of his life. But I was thinking that perhaps he'd dispense with me, let me go. I also told him I hadn't the faintest idea of how to handle a bazooka, and that in any case war wasn't exactly my sort of thing. But I could tell that he wasn't going to give me up, that as long as I had been dumped on him he'd find some use for me. He heard me out, not saying a word himself, only smiling faintly now and then. In the end, he summoned a soldier, a bespectacled highbrow type, and told him to give me a crash course in bazooka operation.

Immediately the fellow put me down flat on the ground, stuck the

111

bazooka in my arms, and started lecturing me about sights and ranges and rocket types, and about a closed electric circuit. I kept nodding my head, though only half listening, taking in just one lesson—about keeping one's face clear of the backflash. Over and over, the bespectacled soldier repeated his grim warning about backflash, presumably having been burned himself at some time. In the middle of this curious private lesson they called us to come and get our food. They were opening a pile of tins, though I was the only one who had any appetite left. My ravenous hunger struck them as rather funny. They would open tin after tin, try a few mouthfuls, and pass it on to me. They watched amused as I, spoon in hand, would polish off at random whatever came my way: tins of beans, grapefruit slices, meat, halvah, sardines, and rounding it off with pickled cucumbers. I devoured everything.

Meanwhile the transistor rattles on amid the empty tins, and at last I hear all the news that has been kept from me for the past twenty-four hours—grim, somber news coming cloaked in unfamiliar terms: position warfare, crunching tactics, holding tactics, screening, retrooping—a whole new glossary striving to temper the blazing reality in which I am already deeply immersed.

All at once I am lonely, very lonely, and feel a kind of void inside. Can you see me in all that commotion, legions about me, and I, seated by the treads of an armored track, sheltering in a patch of torrid shade, in the sickening smell of burned gasoline, my clothes already filthy as though I had gone through two wars, sitting and watching how everything is being lined up for my death? Troops flow about us constantly, encircle us. Tanks and armored tracks, jeeps and cannon. And the beeps of the transmitters and the whoops of soldiers hailing their friends. It dawns on me that whatever happens, I won't come out of this alive. They are closing in on all sides. This people is itself a trap. I felt a sudden urge to write you a postcard, but just then we were hastily summoned, told to pack up and move.

We advanced, strung out in horizontal formation, and after a mile or two we were brought to a halt again. And thus we stood, in all our gear, helmets on our heads, drivers at their wheels, for a full four hours—staring at the blurred, ominous horizon where a soundless war was going on, eyes following mushrooms of dust unfurling in the distance, and smoke plumes of faraway fires—signs which the

112

men around me interpreted with much excitement. Slowly the desert grew red about us, and in an instant the sun blossomed up on the skyline as though someone had raised it over the burning canal, a sort of war prop playing its part in the battle. Toward dusk, the sun began to spill and ooze as though it too had been bombed and our faces, the track, and the weapons in our hands were stained scarlet.

In that same place, still fanned out horizontally, we waited for two days as though frozen to the spot. Personal, linear time broke up, splintered, and a different, collective time involved us in a sticky mess. Everything was going on simultaneously—eating and sleeping, listening to the radio and urinating, cleaning weapons and attending a lecture by some oddball who showed up with a small tape recorder and illustrated his talk with modern music. People played backgammon, went round in a constricted circle, leaped up on the track at a false alarm, squinted at the aircraft overhead; and somewhere else, beyond us, without meaning, there were sunrises and sunsets, twilights and dark nights, blazing noons and cool mornings. We were being crowded out of the world to make it easier for them to kill us. And I, an alien twice over, "the repatriate," as they dubbed me, would move among these boys, listen to their silly jokes, their childish, virginal daydreams. And they, not quite knowing how to handle me, still recalling my huge hunger of the first day, would offer me slices of cake, biscuits, chocolate, which I mechanically accepted and chewed morosely among the tracks. Once in the middle of the night the idea of escape occurred to me. I picked up some toilet paper and wandered off into the hills, which I took to be deserted till I discovered that our forces were encamped there as well. The desert was swarming with people.

At last we moved off, slowly at first, as though emerging from a heavy bog. Worn out, stubble cheeked, moving forward some distance and coming to a stop, moving and stopping; turning south and then to the north, veering east and forward again along the line of advance, as though remotely controlled by some delirious general. And suddenly, without warning, the first shells were falling on us and someone was killed. So the fighting began for us. On our bellies, scratching the earth, then up on the vehicles and on the move, now and again opening fire with everything at hand upon yellow targets, which were also swarming in a sort of delirium on the dusty horizon. I did not fire. The bazooka was slung at my shoulder, all right, but the rockets were buried deep under a bench on the track. I would crouch low, helmet over my face, turn myself into a thing, a mindless object, a dead weight, only now and then casting a swift glance at the nearby scene, the endless and unchanging desert.

Our unit changed all the time, breaking up and re-forming, switching command. We had lost the boy officer in the course of time and a new, older one had replaced him. Our track had broken down and they had transferred us to another. And through it all we would keep changing hands, would be turned over to someone and taken away again. From time to time we would run into a barrage of shellfire and bury our heads in the sand. Yet we were making headway; that much was evident. People tried to stir up some excitement: victory, breakthrough at last. But a hard, bitter victory. One evening we reached an important field-command post, were to guard some brigadier who sat, ringed by a dozen radio operators, amid a tangle of wires and receivers. A tired man, his eyes become slits from lack of sleep, he squatted on the ground, picked up one receiver after another, and with infinite patience, with horrible slowness, in a drowsy voice, sent out commands into space. All night we stayed by his side, and I listened, tried to follow him, understand the course of action, but it all just seemed more and more involved to me. Toward daybreak, during a brief lull, I ventured to approach him, asked when he thought the war would end. He looked at me with a fatherly smile and, in the same drowsy voice, with the same terrible deliberation, started talking about a protracted war, a matter of months, perhaps even years, and then he took up a receiver and in his weary voice ordered up some minor assault.

All the boys around me are already beginning to look like me—aging men, heads gone gray with the floury soil, beards grown wild, faces lined, eyes hollow with lack of sleep, here and there bandages wound around filthy heads. In the distance we can see the water of the canal. We are ordered off the tracks and told to dig in—each his own personal grave.

And then I hear the chanting. Voices chanting, praying. Live voices, not from the radio. It isn't light yet. We wake up trembling

114

with the cold, wrapped in our blankets, wet with dew, to find three men dressed in black, wearing beards and sidelocks, jumping about, swaying, singing, and clapping their hands. Like some pop group going through its routine. They come over to touch us with light, warm hands, shake us out of our sleep. They have come to cheer us up, restore our faith. Their *yeshiva* has sent them to circulate among the troops, distribute small prayer books, skullcaps, and fringed garments, put the boys in phylacteries.

A few of us already cling to them, enter into conversation. Sleepy, disheveled soldiers bare their arms to receive the phylacteries, repeat the words of the prayer with a sheepish grin. And they confer praise and blessings on us. A great victory, they say, another great miracle. Divine grace. But you can tell they aren't quite sure, their hearts aren't quite in it. We have disappointed them a little this time.

Morning breaks, and soon the air grows torrid. Preparations for breakfast are started, smoke rises from a cooking-fire, and the transistors intone the morning news. Their revivalist mission accomplished, they have packed up their equipment, phylacteries and all; they have installed themselves on a little hillock, removed small, battered cardboard cases from their command car, and produced their breakfast. We invite them to share ours, but they refuse politely, heads bowed, smiling to themselves, no thanks, they have brought their own. They won't even touch our water canteens for fear of abomination. I stroll over to them. From among the sacred articles, the prayer books, and fringed garments, they draw out bread, hard-boiled eggs, enormous tomatoes and cucumbers to which they add a pinch of salt and eat them, skin and all. They pour a yellowish liquid from a big red vacuum flask—stale tea, apparently brewed at home and carried all the way. I stand and watch them in mounting fascination. I had forgotten that Jews like these existed. The black hats, the beards and sidelocks. They have removed their caftans and sit there in their white shirts, splashes of an otherworldly color. Two of them are older men, forty or so, and between them sits an exquisite youth with a wispy beard and very long sidelocks. He seems shy and a bit scared by all the bustle around him, his white hand picking daintily at the food laid out on an old religious newspaper.

I hovered nearby, and as they became aware of my presence,

they smiled kindly at me. I took one of their fringed garments and put it in my pocket, and still I did not move away. They ate and swayed and chattered in Yiddish, which I did not understand. I gathered they were talking politics. I just stood there before them—a dirty, bedraggled soldier with a ten days' growth of beard, his eyes riveted on them. They were growing uneasy under my stare.

Suddenly I made a move—asked if I could have a tomato. They were startled, thought I must have gone out of my mind, but the oldest collected himself at once, picked up a tomato, and held it out to me. I sprinkled salt over it, sat down beside them, and began asking questions. Where were they from? What did they do? How did they live? Where would they go from here? And they answered—the two older men speaking, swaying all the time as though their replies were some sort of prayer, too. And in a flash it struck me. Their freedom. Their not really belonging to us. Their liberty to come and go, owing nothing, moving like black beetles among the troops in the desert. Metaphysical creatures. I couldn't let go of them.

But then the chaplain, a sergeant who was acting as a sort of impresario to them, came and urged them to hurry up; a shelling was expected soon, he said, and they had better clear out. They roused themselves at once, packed the leftover food, tied their cases with rope, and began to say grace, rattling on at incredible speed while clambering onto the command car and driving away.

Then I discovered the black caftan that one of them—the younger one, I assumed—had left on a rock. I picked it up. It was made of good solid material and bore the label of a tailor from Geulah Street in Jerusalem, attesting to the fact that this was a kosher garment, not woven "of divers sorts." It smelled faintly of sweat, not the smell of the sweating humanity about me but a sweetish smell, like incense or tobacco, an old-books sort of smell. I was about to throw it down again, and then suddenly, unthinkingly, I put it on. It was my size. "How do I look?" I asked a soldier hurrying past. He stopped and threw me an astonished glance, and I saw he didn't recognize me. He smiled and began to run.

Then we were hit by a barrage that was worse than anything we had known. We dropped to the ground, coiled up like fetuses, nails gripping the hard soil, helpless. The barrage, a blind force groping for us, slammed, fierce and accurate, into a crossroads some hundred yards off. A tiny mistake. And then hour after hour, in the dust, the whine and crash, eyes shut, mouths fill with grit, and nearby a track goes up in flames.

Toward evening quiet returned, as though nothing had happened. A profound hush. They shifted us some four miles on, under the flank of a hill, and again we spread blankets for the night.

At the crack of dawn, as if time had moved backward, we were once again wakened by the chanting and praying voices, the rhythmic handclapping. The three of them were back, as if they'd popped out of the ground, trying to rouse us.

"You've been here already! You've been here! You gave us prayer books!"

Angry voices shout them down. Dismayed, they fall silent, retreat in confusion, muttering to themselves in Yiddish. But then one little soldier lurches out of his blankets and mutely pushes up his left sleeve, a tormented look on his face as though awaiting the jab of the needle. The three of them take heart, start winding the phylacteries around his arm, open the prayer book before him, and show him what to read, fuss about him as if he were a sick patient. They lead him a few steps forward, a few steps back, swaying along with him, turning him around to the east, to the rising sun. We sprawl in our blankets and watch; from a distance it looks as though they are worshipping the sun.

Afterward they settle down to eat as on the first morning, dipping into their cardboard cases and coming out with more eggs, cucumbers, green peppers, and tomatoes—looking for all the world as if they gathered them in the desert. No soldiers stand around them this time, however. The men have lost interest, are still downcast after yesterday's shelling. Slowly I draw near, glance into the open cases. The religious articles are gone. They handed them out the day before, and picked up some loot of their own: army belts, cartridge cases, colored pictures of Sadat—take-home souvenirs.

Once again I marvel at their freedom.

"How's things? How're you?" I smile at them, trying to strike up a conversation.

"The Lord be praised," they reply at once, and I see they don't recognize me.

"Where will you go from here?"

"Back home, God willing. To tell of His miracles."

117

"What miracles? Don't you realize what's happening here?"

But they stand their ground.

"God willing. A great miracle."

"Are you guys married?"

They smile, nonplused.

"Thank God."

"Thank God yes or no?"

"Thank God . . . certainly . . ."

All at once they recognize me.

"Haven't we seen you before?"

"Uh-huh. Yesterday morning. Before the bombardment."

"And how have you been?"

"More or less."

I plumped down among them, in my hand a bag containing the young one's caftan. They recoiled slightly.

"Have you lost your coat?" I asked the young man, who had not uttered a word yet. He was wearing an Egyptian army tunic which he had presumably found lying about somewhere.

"Yes," with a tremulous, ravishing smile, "have you found it?"

"No."

"No matter, no matter, God will provide," the older man consoled him.

All the while they were eating with such airy ease, such confidence. Something about them disturbed me.

That exquisite youth, delicately munching his bread, holding it in his teeth, ignoring me, picking up crumbs with limpid fingers, still reading the same old religious paper spread out before him. They had run out of tea and were passing around a bottle filled with murky water—manna or dew gathered by the wayside. Their needs were evidently few. Again I felt like taking something from them, some vegetable or a slice of bread, but in the end, not asking permission, I picked up the young man's hat from the sand beside him and placed it on my head, began to rock back and forth to some obscure rhythm. They smiled, terribly embarrassed, turned red. I had noticed it before: we frighten them a little, repel them.

"Aren't you people hot with these things on your heads?"

"The Lord be praised."

118

"How do I look?"

I'm like a child.

"God willing . . . God willing . . ."—they force a grin.

The incomprehensibility of it all—

"What if we swap hats?" I said to the young one. "Give me something to remember you by?"

He was utterly bewildered; first he loses his coat, now they want to take his hat. But the oldest of the lot looked me full in the face, his eyes shrewd and penetrating, seeming to grasp my intention before I myself knew what I wanted.

"Let him take it. May it bring him luck . . . restore him unharmed to wife and children."

"I'm a bachelor, though. A philanderer, sort of . . ." I taunt them brazenly. "Carrying on with married women."

The man is not to be shaken, studies me as though only now really seeing me.

"You'll find a good wife, God willing . . . return home unharmed . . ."

Mushrooms of dust spring up on the skyline, followed with some delay, as though without connection, by the thunder of cannon. The day's work has begun. People start running. And once again the shells are groping for me, are out to destroy me. The chaplain rushes over to bundle off his flock, get them away to safety. The entire camp folds up, starts to dig itself in, returns to sand. I haven't even had time to say goodbye to them.

Now I knew: I needed only escape. I could do it too. It was all I thought of that day, squeezed in my corner deep in the track, silent, avoiding unnecessary contact with people, seeking to obscure myself. It was a sweltering day—the sky blanketed with a thick haze, the sun gone, visibility down to zero. Units kept trying to locate one another, to orient themselves; field radios chattered desperately. And over all, swirls of ominous dirty-yellow dust. We were pushing closer and closer to the canal. The breakthrough to the other side had already been made, and we were to join the forces now streaming across the water line. Toward evening we dipped our hands in the water, which heaved with exploding shells. New officers came and spoke eagerly of plans for the next day.

119

But my plot was ripe. This was a war without end, wasn't it, and anyhow what business did I have on the western bank of the canal? Or, for that matter, on the eastern?

Furtively I made my arrangements. I packed the sacred articles collected over the past two days—hat, black caftan, fringed garment—prepared some meat and cheese sandwiches, filled a couple of canteens with water. At night, when I got up to take the last watch, I gathered the stuff, crossed the encampment, and slipped behind the nearest hill. I removed my gear and covered it with stones, dug a small hole and buried my bazooka, doffed my khakis, cut them up with the bayonet, and scattered the strips to the wind. I took my civilian white shirt and my black cotton trousers out of the knapsack, pulled the fringed garment over my head, donned the stolen caftan, laid the hat on the ground beside me. I had a fortnight's beard and enough tousled hair on my head to pull two budding sidelocks over my temples.

And thus I sat in a crevice, within sight of the canal, shivering with cold, gazing at the sky—its darkness relieved from time to time by the flash of an exploding shell—waiting for the dawn, hearing the men of my unit being roused, moving off. I listened carefully for sounds of a search, someone calling my name, but heard nothing except the roar of engines revving up. Afterward a soft silence fell. No one had noticed my absence.

For a moment I felt amazed at having been thus swiftly obliterated.

I stayed where I was, not moving, waiting for signs of day, and in my excitement ate up my whole supply of sandwiches. At last I could see light, rising like a mist and spreading about me: a bleak, almost European dawn.

I bury the final relics of my military existence, my knapsack, shake the dust and sand out of my clothes, try to smooth them, pull them into shape. Then I stick the hat on my head and start walking out of history. I turn east.

Before I have done much walking I come across a road, and soon I hear the hum of a vehicle behind me, a bullet-riddled water tanker with thin trickles of water still spilling out of the bullet holes. I am debating with myself whether to lift my hand or not when the tanker pulls up beside me and I climb in. The driver, a little skinny Yemenite, doesn't appear surprised by the black-clad creature settling beside him, as though the desert were full of black *chasids* popping casually out of the hills.

Strange, but he did not talk to me, did not say a word. Perhaps he was running away himself; perhaps he had only just been shot at and was turning back, agitatedly humming some tune under his breath. I believe he never even realized whom he'd picked up by the roadside.

The barriers swung up readily before us, the military policemen not even sparing us a glance, preoccupied with the press of traffic going the other way. People could hardly wait to charge through to the war, to the western bank.

At Refidim I got off, and the little Yemenite was gone before I could thank him. And once again confusion, increasing by the minute: people milling about, vehicles driving every which way. Buoyant in my new clothes, almost floating on air, I could already feel the caress of liberty. I wandered about the camp, quietly searching for the northern exit. Yet I was aware of people turning, watching me. Even in this turmoil I excited attention. There must have been something not quite religious in my bearing, perhaps in the way I wore my hat. I became more and more apprehensive, began skirting roads, trying to make myself small, hiding, dodging between barracks, lingering beside tank shelters. Then, coming straight at me as though in a nightmare, the tall, bald major, very red in the face, very sunburned, still with that vain vacant look in his eyes. I nearly collapsed at his feet, but he swept past me without a sign of recognition, walking on with that slow, arrogant swagger.

So I had really undergone a change, some tangible change which I had not grasped yet. Now I was hugging a wall, shaken, stunned, watching him make his way toward a shelter. My eye caught a glint of blue. Grandmother's car. I had almost forgotten it.

Suddenly I made up my mind to redeem the car, too—why not?—to wait for darkness and then take it. I looked around, marked the spot, and went off in search of a synagogue where I could hole up until nightfall.

The synagogue was deserted and filthy. It had evidently housed some military contingent during the great confusion of the first days, for the floor was littered with empty cartridges. The Holy Ark was locked, but the shelves contained prayer books and in one small recess I discovered a few bottles of ceremonial wine.

121

Thus I sat by myself in a corner all day, slowly drinking the sweet, warm wine and browsing a little through a prayer book to obtain some rudimentary knowledge of the service. I was becoming groggy, but dared not sleep for fear someone should come and catch me by surprise. About midnight I left, taking along a plastic bag with a dozen prayer books, so that if anyone asked I could always say I had come to distribute prayer books to the men. The camp had quieted down somewhat; people were moving about less frenziedly. I even ran into a soldier and his girl kissing as if there were no war.

The Morris squatted, thick with dust, between a couple of smashed-up tanks. The doors were locked, but I remembered that one of the windows was loose and soon managed to break in. My hands shook as I touched the wheel. I laid my head on it. It seemed an eternity since I had left her, not just a few days of war.

I had come provided with a strip of tinfoil from a cigarette pack, and just as I used to, years ago, when I would take the car behind Grandmother's back, I crouched under the wheel and quickly crossed the ignition wires. The car started at once.

I set out—northward, eastward, God knows, I never had a sense of direction. I just looked at road signs, or stopped to ask the way home.

"What home?" the military policemen would ask me, grinning.

"Never mind, so long as it's out of the desert."

All the traffic was coming the other way. Tanks, guns, and huge ammunition trucks—a drab stream of khaki rumbling along with dimmed lights; and I in my little car traveling in the opposite direction, edging off onto the shoulder, nevertheless interfering with the smooth flow of the convoys. I caught streams of abuse: religious bugger, couldn't pick some other time to go bloody sightseeing in the Sinai? But I did not react, just smiled pleasantly, threading in and out of the convoys, not stopping, driving on and on as if possessed, flitting over the battered roads, pressing on to escape the desert.

By morning I reached the large military canteen at Raffah, worn out, aching from my night's drive, but already drunk with liberty. I went in to buy food, skipping from one counter to the next, swallowing soup, sausage, munching chocolate and sweets—until I spotted a bevy of orthodox men in the crowd, black counterparts of

122

myself, who eyed me curiously, confounded by my savage glut-tony, my lack of restraint, my indiscriminate back-and-forth tour between meat and milk counters. I decided to clear out at once, but by the exit one of them checks me, seizes my arm.

"Wait a minute, we're getting up a quorum for the morning prayer . . ."

"I prayed yesterday . . ." And I freed myself from his grip, jumped into the Morris, and took off, leaving them to their bewilder-ment.

A few miles farther on, the desert finally peters out, palm trees line the road, white houses, soft dunes dotted with tiny orchards. *Terra cognita.* Eretz Israel. And a marvelous smell of sea. Gradual-ly I slow down, stop. I've made it, then. I'm safe. Only now do I realize how tired I am, head swimming, eyelids heavy. I leave the car and sniff the morning air, and am drawn by the smell of the sea. Where is it, though? All at once I need the sea, must touch it. How does one get to the sea here? I flag down the grand limousine of a high officer speeding toward me. Where's the sea? I ask, and he flies into a rage, is ready to hit me, but points out the direction.

I arrive at a creamy beach, and it is as quiet as though I had stepped out of the world, as though there were no state, no war, nothing, nothing but the whisper of the waves.

I stretched out under a palm, facing the water, and fell asleep at once, as though someone had placed a chloroformed rag over my face. I could have lain like that for many days, except that the setting sun began to flicker through my sleep, and I awoke em-bedded in the sand—a small dune had drifted over me. The silky warmth of it. And I dozed on, basking in the sea breeze, wallowing in my sand cocoon; then I began to strip off my clothes—black caftan, fringed garment, pants, underwear, shoes, socks—and lay naked in the sand until at last I roused myself and walked down to the water to bathe.

What made it so wonderful was the sheer solitude. After spending all those days hemmed in by a mass of humanity, being alone again without a living soul in sight, I felt a deep serenity. Even the roar of aircraft was absorbed by the sound of the waves. And as for the Arabs living nearby, the war seemed to have deterred them from wandering out of doors. I got back into my underwear, strolled about as if this were my private beach. Time was coming back to me. Everything was gathering itself for the close of day. The sun, cyclops-eye resting on the water's edge, quietly watched me.

I go to the Morris, standing quietly with her nose to the sea, and discover to my surprise that the major has turned her into a kind of cupboard for himself. A few folded blankets and a pup tent are piled on the back seat; even the mysterious map case is there. I open it with frantic fingers and discover that it contains, to be sure, a set of large-scale maps of the Middle East, Libya, Sudan, Tunisia. It also contains a small box with a pair of brand-new lieutenant colonel's insignia (all set for promotion, is he?) and a white linen bag which still contains two old, partially crushed hard-boiled eggs, their shells a discolored pink. Without thinking, I peel and eat them with great relish. At the same time I study an interesting document that has turned up among his things—a sort of testament addressed to his wife and two sons. What it amounts to is a pompous and flowery declaration, a curious hodgepodge about himself and the Nation, Destiny, Vocation, History, Fate, Endurance. A bombastic effusion replete with cant and self-pity. A shiver runs down my back when I think of the fit he'll throw when he finds the car gone. He'll never rest till he's found it. For all I know, he's in pursuit now, perhaps even close on my heels. Come to think of it, he never seemed particularly engaged in this war.

I collect all the papers and maps, tear them up into small pieces and bury them in the sand, fling the empty case into the water, comb the car for any vestiges of his person. In the trunk I find the tin of paint and a brush he'd used to black out the headlights.

An idea strikes me—

Paint the car black, camouflage it.

I set to work right away. I stir the paint to revive it somewhat, and by the gray crepuscular light I cover the car in ebony black with broad strokes of my brush. I stand in my underwear, and in the last lingering light turn the Morris into a hearse. As I hum an old French chanson and apply the finishing touches, I become aware of someone watching me. I turn to look, and discover a few dark shapes on one of the dunes. A small party of cloaked Bedouins sit watching me at my work. They have come out of nowhere, unnoticed. When? Who knows? The brush drops from my hand. Fool that I am, I have thrown away my bazooka. Now all the weapon I have is the bayonet.

124

They observe me with rapt attention. I must be a real event to them. Possibly they are discussing my fate. I offer such easy prey.

But then, evidently sensing my alarm, some of them raise one hand slowly in a kind of greeting or brief salute.

I smile, bow slightly, then turn to my pile of clothes and dress rapidly: shirt, garment, pants, caftan, even the black hat. I suddenly feel that it may be precisely this garb which will protect me from them. They follow my every movement with their eyes, very likely astonished, no doubt astonished. I see them stand up to get a better view. Swiftly I gather my remaining paraphernalia, hide it in the sand, in the darkness, knowing full well that everything I have buried will be uncovered again as soon as I am gone, get into the car and try to start it. I fumble for the wires, but, flustered as I am, I fail and the car only splutters. After some minutes and a few more vain attempts, I see them approach within a pace or two of the car, where they form a circle to watch me fidgeting under the steering wheel. They must be sure of at least one thing now: I am making off with a stolen car. I keep grinning at the dark faces around me, grope feverishly for the blasted wires. And at long last I succeed, start the engine and break the spell of silence, switch on the lights—two beams cast on the black water—inch forward, try to turn, and promptly get stuck in the sand, wheels floundering.

Meanwhile the crowd around me swells and swells, like a flock of birds gathering in the darkness. Children, young boys, old men spring up from the ridges of dune. I squat by the wheels to clear away sand, get back into the car, try again. The engine stalls; I start it once more and only sink in deeper.

And then I turn to the silent silhouettes and wordlessly beg for help. This is the sign they have been waiting for. Promptly they hurl themselves at the car; dozens of hands cling to the fresh paint. I feel the car virtually floating on air, as we are borne to the road, and the moment the wheels touch ground I shoot forward, drive a short distance and stop, get out, look back at the dim, silent band huddled in the road, lift my hat and wave my thanks. I hear the buzzing of their voices as they murmur in Arabic, presumably bidding me farewell.

I return to the car and drive off.

To Jerusalem.

Yes, to Jerusalem. Why Jerusalem, of all places? Ah, but did I have any choice? Where else could I go? Where could I hide, wait out the storm? Me, with all my personal data recorded in the redhead's files, with the one-handed major in pursuit of the car? Could I show up at Grandmother's—a deserter, one who'd abandoned his weapons, a fugitive from justice?

Or did you imagine I could have returned to you? Lived with you, become more than a lover, become a member of the household? Was that even thinkable?

And why not pursue this destiny chosen for me? Especially since the best part of it had already been accomplished. I had escaped from the desert, crossed the border into Eretz Israel. I was dressed in black—hat, fringed garment, and all. I had got used to the smell of my predecessor's sweat. My beard was growing, and nursing a sidelock or two did not deter me. The Morris, a turncoat too, was perfectly disguised under the black paint. So why not carry on with my adventure?

My money was running out, too. I had to get through this difficult period somehow, hold on till the war should end or fizzle out. Why shouldn't the orthodox take me in? They seemed capable enough, at least to judge by their emissaries going round the desert. They appeared to be well taken care of.

These were the thoughts going through my mind on that nocturnal trip, under the pale light of the waning moon, as I crossed the southern villages and reached the plain, driving slowly to save fuel. I did not even know the date, let alone what was happening in the world.

And so, warily, through the dark countryside, at three o'clock in the morning, I started the ascent to Jerusalem. From time to time I would leave the highway and turn into side roads to wait, to confound a persistent pursuer; I would look at the dim mountain shapes, listen to the crickets. I hadn't been to Jerusalem since coming back from abroad, had been too busy with Grandmother, with the inheritance, and with the lawyers. When I entered the city at first light, I was overwhelmed—never mind how dirty and forlorn it looked, with sandbags heaped against walls and frazzled civil defense workers roaming its streets—I was shaken by its harsh beauty. On the outskirts of town, like a sign from heaven, my last drop of fuel gave out. I abandoned the car in an alley and went to look for them.

Finding them wasn't difficult; they stick to their own neighborhoods on the fringes of the city. Even at this hour they were already out and about, men and women, toting bags for early morning shopping. A light drizzle fell, and brought with it a smell of autumn. A different world. Shops opening, business as usual, the aroma of freshly baked bread. Here and there a cluster of men in close, heated conversation. Queer placards stuck up on walls, some of them torn.

I followed their trail, watching single black figures join a stream of others in black, scurrying along deeper and deeper into the heart of the orthodox quarters. When I saw the broad-brimmed *shtreimels*, the rusty fox fur trimmings, I knew I had reached my journey's end. No one would find me here.

A number of them stood talking on a street corner. I approached to establish contact.

They spotted me for an outsider at once—perhaps by the shape of my beard, the cut of my hair, perhaps by some more intimate sign. I could not fool them. At first they were overcome by the presence of a man dressed in their own image turning up among them in the middle of the war. Softly I asked them, "Can I stay with you a while?" I did not tell them I was coming from the desert, but said I had just arrived from Paris. They stared at the dust and sand on my clothes, at my dirty boots, and said nothing, listening in silence to my rambling speech. No doubt they took me for a madman or a crank. Yet I will say one thing for them—they didn't try to get rid of me but took me by the arm and gently, compassionately led me through alleys, across courtyards—I was still talking all the time, explaining myself—to a large stone building, a sort of *yeshiva* or school, which was swarming with people. They led me up to a room and said:

"Now start from the beginning."

At first I mixed things up, confused dates, switched from one point to another, telling them about Grandmother lying in a coma and about the car I would place at their disposal. Then, gradually, a coherent tale began to emerge out of my fatigue, and from then on I stuck to it. But just as at the major's cross-examination that first night, I did not once mention you. I saw again how easily I could wipe you out of my past.

They fetched a blond-curly fellow who looked every inch a gentile done up in beard and sidelocks. Addressing me in French with a faultless Parisian accent, he began to check up on the French details of my story, asking about streets in Paris, cafés, brands of wine and cheese, names of newspapers. Inspired, I replied in fluent French and in minute detail.

Seeing how well I knew Paris, it occurred to them briefly that I might not even be a Jew at all, and they asked me to strip. They were utterly perplexed, couldn't conceive why on earth I had come to them and what I really wanted. They began to question me again, tried a different approach, but by now I wouldn't change my story no matter what happened.

At last they went into a huddle, conferring in whispers, afraid to decide on their own. One of their number was sent to check something and came back nodding his head in confirmation. In the end they took me to their rabbi. I found myself in a sort of study, before a big old man who was sitting in a cloud of tobacco smoke and reading a newspaper. They told him my story, and he listened attentively, his eyes on my face, regarding me with a cordial, benevolent mien. When he heard about the car I would place at their disposal, he turned to me directly and questioned me in Hebrew: its year of make, engine capacity, number of seats, color, and, in conclusion, where I had parked it. The idea of my bringing them a car as my dowry, so to speak, seemed to please him immensely.

All at once he began to scold his people:

"He wants rest . . . can't you see he's tired . . . he's come from afar . . . all the way from Paris (with a tiny wink at me). Let him get some sleep first . . . you heartless fellows."

And he smiled gaily at me.

Their minds finally at ease, they took me down to the *yeshiva* courtyard, under the curious stares of a few hundred *yeshiva* students who again instinctively recognized me as a dissembler— and up to a bedroom which doubled as the *yeshiva* guestroom. It was equipped with old furniture and was quite plain, but pleasant and fairly clean. I was getting used to the faint religious odor clinging

128

to everything about me—a blend of musty old books, fried onions, and the faint reek of drains.

They made up one of the beds for me and trooped out, obedient to the rabbi's order to let me sleep. The time was eleven o'clock in the morning, and the world was bathed in a pearly gray light. Through the rather majestic lace curtains covering the window, the Old City I had never seen before appeared within grasp.

Before me lay a vast, breathtaking view of the city wall in all its splendor. I could see the spires of churches, minarets, small squares of cobbled courtyards, and olive groves on the mountains beyond. I stood at the window for a long time. Then I took my shoes off and lay down on the bed in my clothes. Something in the air of Jerusalem roused me, even though inwardly I was exhausted, almost feverish.

It took me a long time to get to sleep. I felt dirty, my hands were smeared with black paint, and there was sand in my hair and beard. It had been an eternity since I'd last felt a bed under me. I began to doze; the drone of the *yeshiva* boys at their study, their sudden shouts, gradually mingled with the murmur of the waves, the din of armored tracks and field radios.

Presently, still only half asleep, I heard a fellow guest enter the room. A short, sumptuously decked-out old man with a red silk skullcap on his head approached the bed and stood looking at me. When he saw I was only napping, he brightened and at once began chattering happily in Yiddish, determined to strike up an acquaintance with me. He refused to believe I knew no Yiddish and regaled me with a long story about himself; the substance of it, as far as I could make out, was that he had come to be matched to some girl, that he was to take her abroad, and that for the present he was undergoing a series of examinations—whether physical, spiritual, or both I couldn't tell.

He moved about the room, rattling on exuberantly, cracking jokes, as though there were no war in the world, no reality but his own. For some reason or other, he had convinced himself that I, too, had come for a wife, and he tried to advise me on the matter. I remember the whole conversation with him as through a fog. Sometimes I think it may only have been part of a dream, since after he took off his clothes and wandered about in his splendid underwear, spraying himself with a scent, he donned a black suit and disappeared, and I never saw him again.

Little by little I sank into a feverish, bitter sleep.

I woke up to a dark room at nine in the evening. Through the regal curtain stirring faintly in the evening breeze, the Old City lay wrapped in darkness, too. I heard no sound. I still felt as weak and exhausted as if I hadn't slept at all. Strangely, all at once, I was struck by a yearning for the desert, for some of the faces of the boys in my track who were fighting on the other bank of the canal now. I opened the window to the rare, alien, heady Jerusalem air. My head was throbbing. Now I know that I was burning with a high fever, that the disease had erupted, but at the time I imagined my headache was due to hunger, to my raging, ravaging hunger. I put on my boots, fumbled weakly with the laces, gave up, and went in search of food.

The *yeshiva* was silent and pitch-dark. I drifted between landings, over long corridors, and finally opened a door at random. In a small cubicle filled with cigarette smoke, its blinds down, two students in thin shirts with rolled-up sleeves were sitting bent over huge volumes of the Talmud and debating in whispers.

Evidently disturbed by my intrusion, they showed me the way to the dining hall and resumed their studies at once. The dining hall was empty, its benches turned up on the tables. A young woman in a gray dress and headkerchief was mopping the floors.

She stifled a scream at the sight of me as though she were seeing a ghost.

"I'm new here . . ." I stammered. "Please . . . d'you have any supper left?"

My sleep-rumpled state, my unlaced army boots, my hybrid of worldly and religious apparel, my bare head were enough to startle her, but she collected herself, laid a place at the table, produced a large spoon and a plateful of sliced bread, discreetly and wordlessly placed a black skullcap nearby, and at last brought an enormous bowl of creamy soup, thick with vegetables, dumplings, and bits of meat. A steaming spicy dish, my first proper hot meal in a fortnight.

Tears sprang to my eyes as I gulped the soup in great scalding spoonfuls. It was wonderfully tasty. And she, going about her work at the other end of the room, watching me stealthily, coming softly

130

to remove the empty bowl and bring it back filled again, smiling quietly to herself at my effusive gratitude—a handsome woman, though it was hard to tell, with all but her face and hands covered.

At last I rise, staggering after my heavy, hasty meal, leave without saying goodbye, grope my way up to bed, enter my room and stop, surprised to see the Old City, which I had left in darkness, now completely lit up. And in the *yeshiva* shutter after shutter is opened wide, lights go on.

Excited voices speak of a cease-fire, and disheveled men emerge from every room, move in a flurry about the courtyard below as though having concluded a battle. So I escaped prematurely and the war is over.

A kind of inner peace settles over me. I undress, tear back the bedclothes, go around plucking the blankets off the other beds, wrapping myself up, burning now, my head one lump of pounding pain.

I stayed in bed for two weeks, suffering from a curious disease—high temperature, piercing headaches, and a kidney infection. The doctor who treated me diagnosed Malta fever, which I'd caught, apparently, from the cattle droppings on the beach. They nursed me with great devotion, mysterious stranger though I was to them. At one point they considered moving me to a hospital, but I begged them to let me stay and they gave in, even though I was causing them a lot of trouble and considerable medical expense. At night they would post watches by my bedside—*yeshiva* boys studying the scriptures and reciting psalms for my benefit.

It was my illness which smoothed the transition from my secular existence to their way of life, and exempted me from unnecessary questions. Physical contact humanized them for me. When, after two weeks, I rose from my sickbed, shaky but cured, my beard grown heavy and close, I joined them without undue ceremony. They gave me a spare set of black clothes, used but in good repair, pajamas, and some linen; showed me how to use the prayer book; and taught me a passage or two of Mishna. In the meantime they had fitted keys to the Morris. Indeed, I had noticed as much before: that they were efficient and well organized, and above all disciplined.

Thus, I became the *yeshiva* chauffeur, meaning chauffeur to the old rabbi who had taken me in that first day. But I would also make the rounds of synagogues delivering tins of oil for memorial lamps, take small sidelocked orphans to pray at the Wailing Wall, drive a *mohel* out to one of the new suburbs to circumcise an infant born into their sect, or creep slowly in the long funeral procession of one or another prominent rabbi whose body had been shipped from overseas. Once in a while they would send me to the plain to take one of their group, on his way to raise funds among the faithful abroad, to the airport. Sometimes, in the small hours of the night, quietly and with dimmed headlights, I would convey the zealous bill posters and the slogan painters denouncing unchastity and wantonness.

I was getting to know all their little affairs. They maintain an isolated existence in this country, live in a closed system of their own. Sometimes I would wonder if they didn't even supply their own electricity and water, generated by private kosher plants.

I settled smoothly into my niche with them. They knew as well as I did that I might leave at any moment and vanish as I had come; nevertheless they treated me affably and did not question what was beyond them. They never gave me money, and I even bought gasoline with coupons they supplied, but all my other needs were taken care of. My clothes were washed and mended, my worn army boots replaced by a more suitable pair, and food—above all I was given plenty of food. That same hot fatty soup I had taken such a fancy to on my first night was still set before me every evening, though not by the same woman. The women of the community took turns serving the *yeshiva* students.

In time my sidelocks lengthened as well; not that I made any special effort—they simply grew, and the barber who came once a month to give the *yeshiva* students a haircut, and who cut my hair at the same time, simply did not dare touch them. At first I would hide the sidelocks behind my ears, but eventually I gave up. I would look in the mirror and be amazed to see how much I had come to resemble them, and was pleased to note that it gratified them too.

But this much and no more. In the deeper, spiritual sense, they had small success with me. I did not believe in God, and their various spiritual pursuits seemed pointless to me. What did strike me was that they instinctively realized as much and nevertheless did not bother me, or cherish undue hope for me. At first I asked questions that would make them jump to their feet and blanch, but not wishing to offend them, I stopped.

One way or another I'd generally manage to get out of the morning prayers, but I would join them for the evening service. With the prayer book lowered in my hands, my lips moving, I would watch them sway and sigh or beat their breasts at sundown, acting as if they felt some grief or want for God knows what, the dispersion, the Messiah, whatever. And yet, for all that, they were far from miserable. On the contrary—as free men, exempt from army service and civic obligations, they moved at their own sweet will about Jerusalem, looking with disdain upon the nonreligious, who served them as a sort of framework and instrument for their wily transactions. Frugal as they were by nature, and well organized within a disciplined and remarkably solid community, none of them wanted for anything, even though they produced nothing essential themselves but only supplied each other with services.

Winter had set in and there was plenty of work to be done. The old rabbi was always on the move, delighting in his car and chauffeur. And I would drive him from one place to the next—to preach sermons, to eulogize at funerals, to visit the sick, or to meet some of his flock at the airport. Crisscrossing Jerusalem, west to east, north to south, I came to know its every alley, was more and more drawn to this strange, marvelous city, could never get enough of it.

Whenever I took him to a *yeshiva* for a sermon, I wouldn't stay to listen. I could never catch the drift of his words anyway, and I always felt he was stirring up imaginary problems. Instead I would take the car and drive to a spot I had grown increasingly fond of: the top of Mount Scopus, near the Russian convent at a'Tur, with the city spread at my feet on one side, the display of Dead Sea and desert skyline on the other. There I had my observation point, supreme and absolute.

I would sit in the little car, which still bore the palm prints of the Bedouin from Raffah, and with the rain tapping on the roof, I would skim the pages of *Hamodeah,* a newspaper which was always flopping about the car since it was distributed free at the *yeshiva*; and so I would get a picture—even if only from a religious viewpoint, and rather garbled—of what was going on, would learn about the continuous sniping, the dubious agreements, the whines and lamentations, the fury and the recriminations, as if the war which had ended was still oozing and festering and out of its putrid dregs a new war was already being born.

So what was my hurry?

Presently the rain would stop, the skies would clear. I would drop the paper and leave the car, stroll along the convent wall, over puddles, through the lane of cypresses, my black desert-day hat cocked on my head, the fringes of my garment fluttering in the wind. I would gaze at the shreds of fog floating over the city, nod lightly at the Arabs peering at me from their dim shop interiors. I had already noticed that, oddly enough, they appeared less hostile in their attitude toward us, the black Jews, as though they deemed us natural to their landscape, or possibly less dangerous.

Bells start ringing. Monks pass me, nod in greeting. They imagine that I, too, am a servant of God in my way.

Arab children start following me, tickled by my black dress. There is silence all around. The wet, gray town lies at my feet. The black car sits like a faithful dog by the roadside.

So where should I hurry? To the redhead holding the list of equipment that I signed for and scattered in the desert? To the major who in his fearful obstinacy is doubtless still looking for me? To Grandmother lying unconscious? (I called the hospital several times to ask whether there was any change in her condition.) Or to you perhaps? To hide at your place, not as a lover but as a member of the household, at your mercy, at the mercy of mounting desire?

Yes, my desire has not waned. I have even had a few rather nasty days. Nor have I missed the covert glances of the chaste community maidens. I knew that I had only to drop a hint to the old rabbi for him to find me a match. They are only waiting for me to give them some explicit sign that I have indeed thrown in my lot with them.

A sign which I withhold, however.

—translated by Miriam Arad

134

from The crazy book
Haim Gouri

Arab Halva—moist, sticky, fibrous. The taste tears across my lips
like a memory. Within me Jaffa stirs, wakens from sleep; eyes and
faces of Jaffa.

I am there, it is afternoon, a city half-awake, swept by sea wind.
Jaffa arises from sleep domed and spired, shadowy orchards beneath a lilac sky, an ebbing sea like metal.

Evening. This is her silence. The boats return now to the wet
salty wharf, except one or two which remain out at sea, white sail on
dark water, touched by the sun's crimson. Smell of oranges, fish,
seaweed.

No wave washes up now on the jutting rocks south of the harbor.
No specter fleets of ships, wrecked or lost forever in weariness,
flicker now in the twilight.

Only the sea. Only the sea.

I walk in a city of low wintry skies, between tall Cypriot donkeys
in heat, and caravans of camels continuing the Bible, from Da-
mascus jangling their way south. I walk between black carriages
and red horses as if at the edge of a crumbling kingdom. I go to
Hassan Bek, an adulterer from another city, very near and very far
away. I walk and walk, trying to touch things.

135

Heavy gold. Shamuti oranges. A wintry, slaty sea wind lightly whips abayahs and dresses, washing and sails. Goats on the sandy caravan track between the orchards and the dunes. Bells. A woman. A jar. Imitating pictures immemorially familiar. Soon the dew will fall on the cannon of Ramadan. Houses with long memories. The southern neighbor, enchanting and sluttish, of my native town, scattered as if by chance upon these sands. Different. Not mine.

Spring. Noon at the market, disemboweled slit sheep at the sun-drenched, flyblown butcher stall; the potters' market, the alleys of ironworkers, labyrinths of silversmiths, light and shade of niche and arch and glimmer of gold. Farther on, legendary perfumes, spices borrowed from a past which has forgotten its beginnings. And bananas, onions, oranges.

Labyrinths. Alley upon alley, passages with no name, tunnels of light which disappear into cool darkness, vanishing faces. The sun picks its way westward over gramophoned restaurants choking forth the beseechings of Um Kultum and the consoling response, Egyptian, Abdul Wahab. Florentine walls. Porches with delicate iron trellises and geraniums in pots. I see women watching me from arched windows. Dark skinned women. Mouths reddening like ovens. Silent as concubines in dreams. Within, the blue of Islam. Of Isfahan.

Streets of the setting sun. Streets of flies, of traders, of shouts and shops and shops and stalls and cafés taking out backgammon tables and stools to the cooling pavement. For the coastal merchants, stout and beturbaned. Leisure. Haste is the work of the devil. Small cups of coffee. Narghiles. Amber beads. I walk past ragged children harvesting squashed cigarette butts from the gutters in the weakening sunlight. Hourani vagrants dozing on the pavements, dead to the world, wrapped in sacks, the soles of their feet like leather. And sea between the houses.

Not far from here, my mother and father must have stood after they disembarked from the *Ruslan* with their bundles, in front of Haim Baruch's hostel or some other.

I walk in yesterday's Jaffa, by its pure blue sea and its golden sands. Seeking footprints and loyalties.

Sunlight on the house of Haim Baruch.

Sunlight on the blood of Joseph Haim.

136

I am going to the Jaffa of clubs and knives and the insanity of preachers in mosques. I'm going to Jaffa. Don't go to Jaffa! Don't go to Jaffa! I am going to Jaffa, to Sheik el Farouki, to the "United Islam," to the mufti's Jaffa, dense, yelling, hoarse, pouring out of her mosques, brandishing green flags and sword hands, aflame with red Ottoman fez.

Sunlight on the house of Bluma.

Sunlight on the blood of Joseph Haim.

On gramophones tearing the sky.

I am going to Jaffa, to the tunes that have no end but much patience, to the white ice cream, the oily cakes on round copper trays, the semolina and sesame seeds and peanuts and coconut, to the green-almonded baklava, the oven-hot ring rolls, the mint leaves redolent with the smell of the hills at summer's end, to brown hard-boiled eggs, hummus and bean paste in their heavy pools of olive oil, to kebab on glowing coals, grilled tomatoes, charred slices of onion, to the remembered women who never move from their geranium windows, to the cool rooms, the chiaroscuro, the silence. I am going to Jaffa, seagirt, minaretted, and whored. Don't go to Jaffa! Don't go to Jaffa! You're crazy! They're killers, don't you know? You're crazy! Jaffa of the 1921 and 1929 riots. I am going to my forefathers, turbaned, panama-ed, felt-hatted, worker-capped, to my forefathers burning with the fiery love of Zion. To my fragile mothers, scorched by the pitiless sun, getting lost in these shifting dunes. I'm going to Jaffa. Don't go, you're crazy. All the shutters are closing. I'm going, to Manshieh, to Ajami, to Abu Kebir, to Brenner's blood, to the madly barking dogs, to the blue police light, to the black-furred turbans of the Palestine police, the steel-tipped batons and Colts and the rearing horses and the songs of the Haganah. I am going, I am going to Jaffa. Don't go!

—*translated by Ruth Nevo*

The gazelle hunt
Yitzhak Orpaz

The man raised his head and looked at the sky. A hawk of some kind, alone, with cleft wings, made wide circles above. The man blinked in the strong light.

"She's here," murmured the man, compressing his lips. His eyes combed the bare hills, gleaming brown and orange, rimmed with cliffs and stone boulders, which rose up from both sides of the ravine.

A white cap with a visor, a seaman's cap belonging to the man driving the jeep, made a quarter turn backward.

"Think we'll find anything here?" asked the driver. His arms rested on the steering wheel, calm and strong-looking as if they absorbed all the jolts of the jeep. The woman was looking at them. From the back seat, the man could see her profile, her eyelashes caressing the lenses of her dark glasses. Her head and knees were quiet, but everything else about her danced: the straw hat (the man's), the wide skirt, the thin, orange blouse over her small breasts. Her thighs were slim and long. From the back seat, the man could not see the tops of her thighs.

"She's here," said the man, whispering as if to himself. "The highest of the Eilat mountains begins here—from that dark cliff at

139

the turn in the wadi. The mountain is made of shelf upon shelf of primeval granite. You put your hand on one and it peels off; you put your foot on another and it peels off. You find yourself slipping down when you want to climb up."

The man tightened his hand on the black barrel of the hunting rifle. His fingers whitened. His shoulders were a mosaic of white and red. His face was a mosaic of white and red. White, alien skin, struck by the sun.

"And what if we don't find them?" asked the driver. He turned his head slightly, so that he seemed to be talking to the woman. "What if night comes and we don't find them? Will we go to Ein-Netafim for them? The deer go there for water. How about going after them at night?"

The woman turned her face suddenly, as if excited—or perhaps it only seemed so. As the jeep bumped along, the three heads bounced up and down, and this sometimes made them look excited.

"We won't go for them in the dark," said the man.

The woman fumbled in her fringed leather bag. Her shoulders were an orange-peach color. The driver's bare shoulders and back were the smoldering color of the cliffs in the sun; when he moved, the muscles in his back clamped together like copper braids. At times he moved his shoulder, and then it would almost touch the woman's slightly raised left shoulder.

They drove in silence. The woman took a thermos flask out of her bag, poured some water into a plastic cup, and handed it to the man. He rinsed his mouth and sprayed the water out in a jet. He didn't even gargle. He just sprayed the water out in a jet and looked at the mountain. The driver emptied the cup into his mouth, swallowing silently. The woman drank slowly, gulping the water, and when she finished, her lips were slightly parted and moist. The man and the driver both wore shorts; all three wore sandals. The driver had a scout's knife hanging from the belt of his shorts; the man held a single-barreled 16mm. hunting rifle. The woman fumbled inside her leather bag.

"Those hunters from the north slaughtered the lot. They probably didn't leave much alive around here."

"I guess not," said the man. "At any rate, ours is here." He made an arc with his hand, as if pointing to the ridge of the big

140

mountain, which was hidden behind the near hills. But the man knew where it was.

The sweat burned his eyes. After all, there was still life here: the hawk above, a few lizards down below—soundless life. Only the jeep broke the silence; its roar was hard and alien.

The driver laughed; his lips hardly moved. The way his upper teeth rested on his lower lip made him look as if he were always laughing. His laugh was brief. It was hard to tell whom it was meant for. The woman's laugh was thin, almost imperceptible. A thin line at the corner of her mouth, too sharp to be a dimple, too pretty to be just a wrinkle, marked her laughter. A line like a hidden arrow. And then the driver drew out his scout's knife and described in detail how he would skin the gazelle. "The gazelle's skin is white and soft on the inside," he said.

The man shoved a cartridge into the rifle and closed the safety catch. At that moment the driver put his knife back into its leather sheath, and the woman, her lips parted, voicelessly followed his movements as if hypnotized.

The hawk swooped down for about a hundred meters, and when it straightened out, powerful wings outstretched, it remained suspended like a bronze monument between heaven and earth. First, it was transparent, then glittering like mercury—about a hundred meters, perhaps more, above the heart of the big mountain, hidden behind the cape of granite boulders whose lowest slope cascaded down to the ravine. The gazelle stood looking at him.

She stood at a distance of about fifteen meters from the man, and at a man's height above him; stood on her four long, pale, stemlike legs which huddled together in fear, their small black hooves clutching, or perhaps caught in, the granite. Her dark-golden body tensed in an arc, her small pointed head and cleft oval buttocks straining toward the man.

"I knew I'd find you here," the man said to himself, lifting the hunting rifle slowly to his shoulder. The gazelle stood motionless. Her neck was long, snail-like, infinite. It sprouted directly from her stomach, from her breast, curved like the neck of a vase, like a stem, like an ornamental bow. She didn't stand comfortably. She looked as if she'd been surprised in mid-movement, as if she'd been surprised and had frozen in mid-movement. Her skin trembled in ripples, horizontally from her neck to her thighs and vertically from

her thighs down to the rock of the cliff. The trembling came in waves, or not in waves but short, quiet ripples in which reddish brown hues predominated. Like the water in a bay when the wind blows. But it was hot, and no wind blew.

She looks like a toy in a child's room, the man thought, smiling to himself. Except that she was alive. Her ears were like small funnels which had been glued to the sides of her head. But the gazelle looked at him.

The man steadied the rifle against his shoulder, took aim, and looked into the eyes of the gazelle, who was looking into his eyes. There was no haste in her look, no fright. "If I aim at her like this, forever, without pressing the trigger, she will stand like this forever, looking at me," the man said to himself. Her eyes were big and round. At first it was impossible to say what was in those eyes. Perhaps it was wonder. A liquid the color of coffee, the color of hot orange, the color of melted gold circled around her large pupils, flooding them. The hot color flowed into the eyes of the man. The man and the gazelle looked at each other. The man raised the rifle some twenty degrees above her noble head, above the great hypnotized eyes washed in brown gold, and fired.

The woman cried out in fright. Her face was frozen and her neck was slender. Perhaps she had wanted to cry out. Perhaps she had wanted to. The man driving the jeep said something about blood, or about a lack of blood, and squashed a huge green fly on the windshield of the jeep. That was when the woman gave her startled cry. She stamped her feet and crossed her hands over her heart. The driver's Adam's apple bobbed up and down. After the shot was fired, they both turned their heads to the smoking barrel, and then to the gazelle, fleeing for her life with graceful strides. At this moment, the man's head touched, or, to be exact, almost touched, the brim of the straw hat, his own hat, now on the woman's head. That was the moment when the man driving the jeep squashed the fly on the jeep window with his huge flat palm, saying something about people and about blood.

They drove quickly, as quickly as was possible in this winding wadi strewn with stones. "Run to the mountain, flee for your life to the heart of the mountain, gazelle," said the man to himself.

He unloaded the smoking cartridge, then cleaned the barrel with a stick padded with oiled wool. "You waited for me and I drove you away, gazelle," he said to himself. "But I couldn't take the look in your eyes." The man looked at the woman, at the contours of her face, at the sensitive line beyond the corner of her mouth which now dimpled with laughter or some other response.

"You're tired," said the woman, and passed him the straw hat. Her hair tumbled free to the hills. Fire caught at the grimacing cliffs, the capering rock giants, and the spilled intestines of the earth— cold, scarlet fire, fire dust, cold ashes which flared up—climbing from the bay to the ravines, from the ravines to the low hills and from the low hills through granite to the mountain. And the mountain burned noiselessly.

Perhaps he would come upon her now. If he came upon her now her neck would be ruddy, as if wine-soaked, and the skin of her body like a cloak of scarlet.

"They slaughtered the lot, those hunters from the north," said the driver. "Do you believe they left anything alive here?"

"I guess not," the other man said. "At any rate, mine's here. . . ." He made an arc with his hand, pointing at the big mountain, which was out of sight, hidden by the near hills. But the man knew where it was. The driver rested his arms on the steering wheel, calm and strong arms looking as if they absorbed all the jolts of the jeep. The woman was looking at them.

"To be strong, strong," the man said to himself. "The big mountain—where does it begin? Here's where it begins—in the dark rock at the turn in the wadi. The mountain is made of shelf upon shelf of primeval granite. You put your hand on a shelf and it peels off. You put your foot on a shelf and it peels off. And one doesn't slide upward."

The hawk rose from the heart of the mountain, its wing tips scorched, and soared away. The man watched its broad flight for a while, musing; the woman and the driver watched a giant lizard as it crossed the ravine. It moved slowly, almost leisurely, nobly curving its tail left and right. The woman laughed. Then the jeep driver laughed.

"At any rate, there's still something alive here," thought the man. "There's the hawk and there's a lizard. And of course," he said out loud, "there's the gazelle." The woman did not hear. Just then the driver told her about his fisherman friend who had hooked

144

a woman on his line. Now the two of them laughed, imagining the caress of water on their flesh.

The driver drew out his scout's knife, holding it between his teeth. "That's how he dives into the sea, the knife between his teeth, to cut coral." Then he waved the knife in the air and put it back in its sheath. "Look, this is how he'd skin the gazelle. Carefully he'd pass the blade over her stomach, from neck to thigh. Her skin would split, opening like lips, and then he'd strip off the lips with long strokes of his blade. The skin would come off the soft white flesh, up to the head and down from the thighs. He'd cut off the head and the small cleft hooves and throw them away." The woman tapped her feet. Like the drumming of distant hooves.

"It's cruel," said the woman, and her voice trembled. So did her breasts and her rounded knees. Her lips were parted and moist. The man felt the gazelle's eyes upon him. "Stop!" he called.

For a moment it was as if the mountain had risen before him. It emerged from the fog, and the reddish fog, the reddish dust, lit by the sun, shrouded it on all sides, crawling up to cover it; at its heart the tall granite boulders, and at its feet, in the turning of the wadi, the sloping hill, creviced like the skin of a lizard, torn into rocks and stones. There stood the gazelle.

"I knew I'd find you here, gazelle," said the man to himself.

At a distance of about fifteen meters from the man, and at a man's height above him, she stood on her four slender, stemlike limbs, on small, black hooves, her legs, huddled together in fear, caught in the granite rock. Her head slanted toward the man, as did her small, oval cleft buttocks—her dark-golden body arched backward.

"How beautiful you are," the man said to himself. Slowly he lifted the hunting rifle to his shoulder and his eyes. The gazelle stood motionless. Her neck was long, snail-like, infinite. It sprouted directly from her breast, curved like the neck of a vase, like a stem, like an ornamental bow.

She didn't stand comfortably. She looked as if she'd been surprised in mid-movement. As if she'd been surprised and had frozen in mid-movement. But her skin trembled in ripples, horizontally from neck to thigh, and vertically from her thighs down to the rock of the cliff. The trembling came in waves, or not in waves but short, quiet ripples in which reddish brown hues predominated.

145

Like the water in a bay when the wind blows. But it was hot, and no wind blew.

She looks like a toy in a child's room, the man thought, smiling to himself. Except that she was alive. Her ears looked like small funnels which had been glued to the sides of her head. But the gazelle looked at him.

"I'm sorry, but I have to take you with me. I have to shoot you so I can take you with me," said the man to himself. He steadied the rifle against his shoulder, took aim, and looked into the eyes of the gazelle, who was looking into his eyes. There was no haste in her look.

"If I aim at her like this, forever, without pressing the trigger, she will stand like this forever, looking at me," the man said to himself.

Her eyes were big and round. At first it was impossible to say what was in those eyes. Perhaps it was wonder, what you see in eyes when you don't know what's in them. There was no terror in her look. But terror lay around her large pupils. They were the color of coffee. They were soaked in this color, floating in it. And the eyes of the gazelle gazed at him.

"Maybe I shouldn't have come to you, gazelle. Maybe it would have been better if each of us had stayed put, I in my house in the north and you in the heart of the big mountain. But now that I'm here, I have to kill you."

They looked at each other, the man and the gazelle—he at her and she at him. Maybe it wasn't her skin that rippled. Maybe she was trembling beneath her skin. If he grabbed her small tail and pulled, the gazelle would be stripped of her skin. She'd come out of her skin as if it were a piece of clothing. She'd tremble for joy. And the driver of the jeep would tear her flesh into strips.

"I'll shoot you in the head, gazelle," said the man, frightened. "Between the eyes so you'll die quickly. That way you won't suffer." He pressed the butt of the rifle against his shoulder and sighted at a point between the gazelle's eyes. This way he saw her eyes clearly. The orange-brown flooded them. From her eyelids the hot orange flowed to her pupils, and from her pupils to his own eyes. His eyes dimmed. The drumming of the little hooves pounded in his knees, in his blood. His eyes stung with heat and sweat, entranced.

The woman cried out in fright. Her face froze and her neck was slender. The man driving the jeep said something about the blood of fish and squashed a huge green fly on the windshield of the jeep. It was at this moment that the woman gave her startled cry. The driver's Adam's apple bobbed up and down. The woman stamped her feet and crossed her hands over her heart. When the shot was fired they both turned their heads to the smoking barrel. Just then the man's head touched, or, to be exact, almost touched, the brim of the straw hat, his own hat, now on the woman's head. That was the moment when the woman cried out and the man driving the jeep said something about people and about blood.

The sky hung heavy, smoking. Eyes exhausted by light—what do they see? Reddish fog, burning cities in the distance, beyond the mountains. What did the hawk see when he swooped down and soared up again? The mountains crouching, innards exposed to the terrible light, to the blaze. Death had no dominion here. Nothing here was softer than a grain of stone.

"My hands trembled, gazelle. Believe me, I really wanted to kill you, but my hands trembled and the bullet got away from me."

The man opened the breech of the rifle and very cautiously laid the hot cartridge on the floor of the jeep, as if something alive might yet burst from it. He poked a wooden stick padded with oil-soaked wool into the barrel and meticulously passed it through several times. "It was your gaze that took my strength away, gazelle. You shouldn't have looked at me like that."

They drove quickly. The jeep bounced like crazy. The ridge of the large mountain vanished before the man's burning eyes, and from the voice murmuring inside him.

The driver lit himself a cigarette. He offered the man a cigarette. The man didn't smoke. He offered one to the woman. As the driver's arms encircled the steering wheel, the muscles in his back expanded, and the woman's narrow shoulders contracted. The driver lit his cigarette. He looked at the woman, stuck the cigarette into a long, thin ivory cigarette holder, and said nothing.

She had wonderful fingers. They grew marvelously long and delicate, as they slipped toward his broad, stocky fingers and almost covered them, so as to take the ivory cigarette holder. Her fingers were also very efficient, as when she poured water from the thermos into cups, or offered one of the men a sandwich, or

147

smoothed her fine, light hair, which had more life than silk, calm and fine. That was the moment when she took off the straw hat and gave it back to the man. "You must be suffering from the heat, my dear," she said, "and your skin is so white." Her sensitive lips passed slowly over the ivory of the cigarette holder. Her eyelashes caressed the lenses of her dark glasses. When her glasses glinted in the sun, her eyes seemed mocking.

The man put a rock into the jeep—a large chunk of granite with one corner serrated like a saw. He couldn't say what he wanted it for. The rock was very big and left him only a little room for his feet. The woman fumbled for a while in her fringed leather bag, took out a thermos flask, and poured cold water, first for the man, then for the driver, and finally for herself. The man just rinsed his mouth and sprayed out the water in a jet. He didn't even gargle. The driver didn't gargle either. He just poured the water down, holding the cup a bit above his mouth, and swallowed it without gulping. The woman drank slowly, gulp by gulp, sparingly, with an even rhythm; and when she'd finished drinking, the water was gone—not a drop had been wasted. Now she licked her moist and slightly parted lips with the tip of her tongue.

"Think they left anything alive around here?" asked the driver.

"I guess not," said the man. "At any rate, mine's here." The woman turned to look at the man. His skin was white. The sun had made a mess of him. His white body was patched with burns. The man did not look at her, but he saw her proud, flexible neck. Her neck was very flexible. She could turn her head as though it were hinged. The man driving the jeep had a thick, broad neck under his seaman's cap, but she, of course, could not see the back of his neck.

But she could see his arms and his hands. They lay heavy on the steering wheel, absorbing all the jolts of the jeep. The woman sat relaxed—her hands resting on her knees, her small breasts wriggling inside her blouse like fish caught in a net. Down below crouched the sea like a crocodile which had broken through the mountain and fallen asleep. The driver suggested that they lie in wait for the gazelle in Ein-Netafim that night. He suggested that meanwhile they go down to the sea for some underwater fishing.

148

Now. The ripple of the water whispered in their ears, and on their backs they felt the lashing of the water in the bay.

The man driving the jeep grew silent. When the jeep bounced, the woman sometimes grabbed the back of the driver's seat. But even then her hand did not really touch his shoulder. His shoulders and his hands were both well tanned; her hands were golden and his shoulders were the color of burning embers. At a curve in the wadi he would incline his shoulder—or it would be inclined by the momentum—so that it brushed her shoulder, or, to be more exact, her hair which fell over her shoulder, touching, caressing, for that is what smooth silken hair does when it brushes your shoulder. At any rate it was amazing, the harmony of color between her hair and the skin of his shoulder. Of course, you can't make comparisons between the hair of the head and the skin of the shoulder. And the nostrils of the woman's small nose were trembling.

It was hard to say who saw whom first. He smelled her with his eyes; but he saw her even before that, with his fingertips, with his ears, through the thirst-parched capillaries of his skin.

The jeep parked at the foot of the mountain. And the mountain smoked. The mountain was very high, hidden in smoke, distant, reddish. Behind it, a chasm. Before it, leading to it, an infinity of granite steps. The elbow of the boulder beside which they were parked was but the first of the granite steps.

"I knew I'd find you here, gazelle," said the man to himself.

At a distance of about fifteen meters, and at a man's height above him, she stood on her four slender, stemlike limbs, on small black hooves, her legs huddled together in fear, caught in the granite rock.

She stood tense as a bow, facing the man's gaze, her head and buttocks inclined toward the man and her body arched backward— her scarlet body spotted with gold, arched like a bow. A man's height above him.

"How beautiful you are," said the man. "At this moment you should be leaping light-footed in the heart of the high mountain. Actually I should let you go. But I can't let you go."

The man raised the hunting rifle, slowly, to his shoulder, and sighted along the barrel. The gazelle stood motionless. Her neck was long, snail-like, infinite. It sprouted directly from her breast, curved like the neck of a vase, like a stem, like an ornamental bow.

"If I only knew how to preserve that proud neck of yours, gazelle. But I don't know how to shoot you and preserve your proud neck at the same time."

She didn't stand comfortably. She looked as if she'd been surprised in mid-movement. But her skin trembled in ripples, horizontally from neck to thigh and vertically from her thighs down to the rock of the cliff. And between the ripples, shorter ripples in which scarlet hues predominated. Like the water of the bay when the wind blows. And no wind blew.

"I'm sorry, but I have to take you with me. I have to shoot you so I can take you with me," said the man to himself. He steadied the rifle against his shoulder, took aim, and looked into the eyes of the gazelle, who was looking into his eyes. There was no haste in her look.

"If I aim at her like this, forever, without pressing the trigger, she will stand like this forever, looking at me," said the man to himself.

Her eyes were big and round. At first it was impossible to say what was in those eyes. Perhaps it was wonder, what you see in eyes when you don't know what's in them. There was no terror in her look. But terror lay around her large pupils. They were the color of coffee. They were soaked in this color, floating in it. And the eyes of the gazelle gazed at him.

"Maybe I shouldn't have come to you, gazelle. Maybe it would have been better if each of us had stayed put, I in my house in the north, and you in the heart of the big mountain. But now that I'm here, I have to kill you."

They looked at each other, the man and the gazelle—he at her and she at him.

"I don't want your flesh, gazelle. I don't believe your meat will taste good after you're dead. I'd like to know the taste of your live flesh. I long to know the taste of your live flesh. But I don't know any way of preserving your live flesh, gazelle."

The gazelle trembled under her skin. If he grabbed her small tail and pulled, she would be stripped of her skin. She'd come out of her skin as if it were a piece of clothing. She'd tremble for joy. And the man driving the jeep would tear her flesh into strips.

150

"I'll shoot you in the head, gazelle," said the man, frightened. "Between the eyes, so you'll die quickly. That way neither of us will suffer."

The man planted his feet firmly on the granite, pressed the butt of his rifle against his shoulder, and sighted at a point between the gazelle's eyes. This way he saw her eyes clearly. The hot orange flooded them. From her eyelids, or perhaps from red rocks in the heart of the mountain, the orange-brown flowed to her pupils, and from her pupils to his own eyes.

"I must be strong, gazelle, so that I can shoot you, when you look at me and my heart lies in your eyes."

You climb the mountain. You could have climbed from the east, from the easy side. But you climb from the west, where the mountain exposes its innards—boulders of granite. You come to its innards, you strive for its peak. The granite stone is the hue of tempered steel—in the noon sun, bluish; in the setting sun, kindled, red, dripping blood. The granite stone peels away under your feet. It peels away under your hands. You slip, you wound your hands and your knees. You climb the mountain for an hour, two hours, three years, four eternities. You keep slipping and you feel, suddenly, that you're slipping upward. You don't see the peak—it is hidden by the cliff before you. And the cliff before you is made of steep, jutting steps. You trick the steps and go around them. Your walk is snail-like. You've left the lizards behind. No living thing crosses your path. You climb the last cliff. A square rock hangs over your head. And beyond the square rock—this you know for certain—soars the highest ridge of the mountain. You reach upward with your hands but there is no shelf to grasp. You reach down with your feet, and they slip. And you know that here a meeting waits for you. Having no choice, you lean your head on the rock. And in the bowels of the mountain you hear a roar and the sound of thunder breaking. You are sure: here a meeting is destined for you. Just raise your eyes.

The woman and the man driving the jeep laughed. It was at this moment that the driver told her about his fisherman friend who had hooked a mermaid on his line. And they felt the glee of water on their flesh. The man planted his feet firmly on the rock, pressed the

151

butt of the rifle to his shoulder, and sighted at a point between the gazelle's eyes. This way, he saw the gazelle's eyes clearly. The hot orange flooded them. From her eyelids, or perhaps from red rocks in the heart of the mountain, the hot orange flowed to her pupils, and from her pupils to his own eyes.

"I must be strong, gazelle, so that I can shoot you when you look at me, and my heart lies in your eyes."

The woman cried out in fright. Her face was frozen and her neck was slender as the gazelle's. The driver said something about people and about blood, and squashed a huge green fly on the windshield. It was at this moment that the woman gave her startled cry. The driver's Adam's apple bobbed up and down. The woman stamped her feet and crossed her hands over her heart. When the shot was fired they both turned their heads toward the smoking barrel and then to the gazelle, who was fleeing for her life. Just then the man's head touched, or, to be exact, almost touched, the brim of the straw hat, his own hat, now on the woman's head. That was the moment when the woman cried out and the man driving the jeep said something about people and about blood.

The sky hung heavy, smoking. Eyes exhausted by light—what do they see? Reddish fog, burning cities, in the distance, beyond the mountains. What did the hawk see when he swooped down and soared up again? The mountains crouching, innards exposed to the blaze, to the terrible light. Death had no dominion here. Nothing here was softer than a grain of stone, to grind with your teeth, to scrape with your nails, to smash on the rock.

The man lowered the rifle, laying it on the seat, then bent over the red granite rock and lifted it. He grasped the rock with both hands, so that the serrated head faced downward. And below him, some thirty centimeters beneath the serrated rock-head, was the driver's head and the thick, fleshy nape of his neck.

The woman and the driver laughed. It was at this moment that he told her about his friend the fisherman, who had hooked a woman on his line. One day, on his way home, he had seen through a window the buttocks of a woman making love. He had aimed his underwater gun and had shot a hook into her. Caught by the hook, the woman followed the man, and the man led the woman behind him, with the hook stuck in the flesh of her buttocks, until they reached home. And yes, the woman was his wife. This was the moment that the woman and the man driving the jeep laughed. They saw many fish and heard the gurgle and murmur of the water in their ears.

The water in the thermos flask was cold. The man only rinsed his mouth, he didn't even gargle; the man driving the jeep finished the cup in one swallow. The woman drank slowly, gulp by gulp, sparingly, in an even rhythm, and when she'd finished drinking all the water in the cup—she didn't waste a single drop—she licked her moist and slightly parted lips with the tip of her tongue.

"The hunters from the north slaughtered them all," said the man driving the jeep. "Do you think they left anything alive here?"

"I guess not," said the man. "At any rate, mine's here." As he spoke he drew an arc with his hand in the direction of the high mountain, which was hidden behind the hill of granite boulders.

—translated by Richard Flantz

Like salt on birds' tails
Uri Orlev

Somebody was trying to steal his motorcycle. Arik walked faster. He was in the nick of time. Another minute and he'd have had to start searching for it all over, to run lost-and-found ads in the papers. Had a sixth sense warned him? A telepathic link with one's possessions, he thought. Thought waves going out and bouncing back from them like radar. He pictured himself wrestling the thief into submission and dragging him off to the police. The type to watch out for was the skinny-looking one who could flatten you with a karate chop. His heart pounded as he neared the motorcycle. He had a sudden urge to walk past it as though it wasn't his. The thief, he saw to his astonishment, wore an air force uniform with lieutenant's bars and pilot's wings.

"You should be ashamed of yourself!" he scolded. "I could have you busted for this." Just then he recognized Daniel, who was busy making believe that he had mistaken Arik's cycle for his own. Unfortunately, it was the only one among the cars parked on the street. Daniel was about to mutter some excuse when he looked up and saw Arik.

"I didn't know you lived in Jerusalem," he said lamely.

"You didn't know I owned a motorcycle either," Arik said.

A happy ending! Not only did he not have to grapple with the thief, but it was a chance to renew an old acquaintance.

"Where were you off to?" he asked matter-of-factly. He would be sporting but cool.

"Forget it," said Daniel. "I'll manage."

"What for?" Arik answered. "If it's not far, I'll take you."

"Don't bother."

"You'd rather steal a ride from someone else?"

"That's my problem."

"You're not very considerate of others' property."

"And you always are?"

"At least I try to be."

Daniel had been a boarding student at the kibbutz school prior to his expulsion. Arik had been somehow fond of him, though he'd never stuck up for him publicly. Their unexpected encounter pleased him.

"Let's find a place to talk," he said with a conciliatory smile.

"I can't get over how you caught me in the act," said Daniel, helping to wheel the motorcycle into the street.

"Do you make a professional habit of this?"

"Only when I don't have my jeep."

"You haven't changed much," Arik laughed. He glanced admiringly at Daniel's bars and wings. "How does a young punk like you get to be a pilot?"

"It's the young punks who make the best pilots."

Arik kicked over the motor and slapped Daniel on the back.

"Hop on!"

It was Daniel who had masterminded the daring raid on the kibbutz canteen by slipping into the bakery and screaming his head off as though he were being tortured. When the kitchen staff ran in to investigate, he slipped back out again and locked the heavy metal door behind them. Then the children burst forth from their hiding place and looted the open shelves. When other kibbutzniks came from the dining room, alarmed by the kitchen staff's shouts, the children bombarded them with candies.

The case was brought to trial at children's court. The teachers arraigned Daniel one by one until he rose and said that if it weren't

156

for them the children would never convict him, since the break-in had been their great dream. "You're hypocrites!" he shouted. "The teachers run everything and the rest of you all lick their asses."

"Toady up to them," corrected the Hebrew teacher.

"What are you doing these days?" asked Daniel behind him as they rode.

"Learning to be average!" he shouted back.

"Are you married?"

"Yes!"

"How long?"

"Three years!"

They sat at the counter of a gas station diner. The conversation stalled and Arik began to regret the whole thing. It often happened that he tried to be nice and later felt sorry. His mood changed, though, once they started to reminisce. Once or twice Daniel laughed loudly in a voice that made people stare. Arik had never noticed before how the arrogant mask on Daniel's face concealed a sad plea for help. Perhaps that was why he had liked him then too.

"Where were you going?" he asked.

"On your cycle? To Motsa."

"It's really not far. I'll take you. Just a minute, I'd better call Nurit."

He phoned home. His wife answered with a mixture of anger, worry, and suspicion.

"If you're up to your old tricks again, Arik . . ."

He didn't let her finish. "No," he said. "Honestly. I'm with an old school friend. A pilot."

"Where are you?"

"At a gas station. I've promised him a ride out to Motsa."

"I'm going to bed," she announced. "Don't expect me to stay up for you."

They climbed back on the cycle.

"Come visit us some time!" Arik shouted over his shoulder. "I'd like you to meet Nurit."

"I will!" Daniel shouted back.

157

"Do you have a date with someone now?"

"Yes." Daniel laughed. "With an animal. I try to come late so as to skip the introductions."

They passed the city limits. A strong, damp wind blew in their faces. Arik put on his goggles and Daniel ducked his head. "I'd have left a message for you with the police," he said when they got there. "I'd have told them where it was."

The Animal was asleep. Or at least it seemed so when Daniel entered the house. He locked the door behind him as usual and undressed in the hall before tiptoeing barefoot to her room and groping his way to her bed. Under the blanket his hand touched a man's hairy chest. What a fuck-up of an evening! First the motorcycle and now this. He'd make the bitch pay for it yet. He slipped out again with his clothes in his arms and dressed in the bushes outside. Waiting to hitch a ride on the road, he laughed at the thought of how the story would sound when he told it back on the base.

2

Except for the small lamp in Dafna's room, the house was dark when Arik returned. He knew without looking, though, where every book and possession of his was, all the objects he loved or had simply collected to take up room and push back the borders of the void. Even everyday things had their battle stations in the strict regime of order he had imposed on the house. Each time he came home, peace descended on him only after careful scrutiny assured him that all was in place.

"Because I want to save time and not spend it on foolishness," he angrily explained to Nurit. "Do you know how much time you waste each time you have to go looking for your comb or your shoe? Or for that damned pot you can never find! When a thing has its place, you just stick out your hand and it's there. Even in the dark. Even if you're blind."

It took a supreme effort on his part to control himself with his two-year-old daughter, who spared nothing and moved, threw, and tore whatever she could. Sometimes he simply left the house and waited for her bedtime so that he could quickly, efficiently put everything back where it belonged.

158

He pulled back the blanket from Nurit, sat on the bed, and slowly massaged her back and breasts. He knew she would be annoyed when she awoke. But she didn't awake. Or else she was pretending still to sleep.

"Leave me alone," she groaned. "I told you on the telephone I wasn't staying up."

She tried to pull the blanket back over her.

"You can't come home at all hours and then make me wake up."

"But I want you."

"Can't it wait until tomorrow?"

"No."

"But you have to show some consideration for me, too. We've been married three years and you never do. I can't tell you how worried I was till you phoned."

"Consideration for what? For your always rejecting me?"

"Don't make believe you don't know what I mean, Arik."

"But if you want me to stay away from other women, you have to learn to adjust yourself to me."

"Why don't you ever try adjusting yourself to me?"

"Because it's possible for you to do it anyway, for my sake."

"I can't just do it anyway. Can't you understand that? That's what's ruining sex for us."

"All right. Don't talk so much."

She lay there awake. She wanted to know whom he had met.

"Daniel."

She wanted to hear details.

"There aren't any. An old school friend. I'll tell you to-morrow."

"What does he look like?"

"He's got two ears and a nose."

"Maybe you'll bring him here sometime," she said in the dark.

"I was already sleeping," he said angrily.

Nurit trembled in her sleep, searching for something to grab onto to keep her from falling in her dream.

"Did you fall?" whispered Arik, waking as her tremor passed.

She tapped him once yes on the arm. They had agreed-on signals for times like this when jaws were too heavy to move and words, like leaden birds, refused to take wing.

159

3

Daniel came in his jeep to see them one evening without bothering
to inform them in advance. He didn't like to telephone, he said; he
liked to drop in. Their apartment was small. You could tell from the
mixture of furniture in it that they had only recently left the kibbutz.
Daniel explored the two bedrooms, peeked at the bathroom and
kitchen, and was pleased to find an old wooden table there.

"This is what I like," he said, sprawling in a chair by its side. "My
place will be here."

"Sold!" said Nurit warmly. There was something about this pilot
that she already liked. She went to fetch Dafna from a friend's
house.

"Does anyone from the kibbutz ever come to visit?" asked
Daniel.

"No," Arik said. "They're boycotting us. If we were unhappy
here, or failures, they'd come all the time to pity us and tell us we're
welcome to come back."

"I could never live on a kibbutz."

"It has its good sides," said Arik. "It really is in its way a
forerunner of the civilization of the future."

"How did you meet?" asked Daniel.

"Who, Nurit? It was just one of those things."

"She's young."

"Twenty-one."

"She lost out on the army because of you."

"Lost out?"

"On a chance to be independent. What's married life like?"

Arik looked at Daniel, trying to decide whether he really wanted
to know. "Try it and see," he shrugged.

"You think it's for everyone?"

"I don't know. Maybe not."

Dafna fell in love with Daniel at first sight. He let her wear his air
force beret and she invited him into her room, from which cries of
joy were soon heard and the creaking of her swing. Nurit helped
Arik set the table.

"Do you think he's nice?" Arik asked.

"Very," she said.

"I can tell."

"How?"

160

"By the way you carry on in front of him and keep bending over so he can see down your blouse."

They sat down to eat. Daniel and Nurit did most of the talking. Daniel told her he had missed his true calling in life, which was to be a jazz trumpeter. "What was yours?" he asked.

Nurit presented him with a tiny plastic trumpet from a candy box of Dafna's. Daniel took out his wallet and tucked it earnestly away there. They laughed and joked together all evening. Arik watched their excitement and even sought to encourage it, although he felt left out, too, and tried explaining to Daniel his theory about the civilization of the future, in which the individual ego would be part of the collective All. He also talked about death.

"At our present level of development," he said, "our need to create is the outcome of the conflict between our consciousness of self and our consciousness of death. But we're still at a very rudimentary stage."

"I have a thing about death too," said Daniel. "Sometimes I pretend I'm going to crack up on a hilltop and don't pull up on the stick until the last fraction of a second. I can actually feel it pass right through my bones."

"In the future," Arik declared, "death won't even matter."

"What will?" Daniel asked.

"The All," said Arik. "I don't mean that the individual will lose his freedom. On the contrary, he'll be freer than ever. Private memories, childhood, even ordinary sensations will circulate among everyone. Humanity will be totally different from the way it is now."

"What about names?" Daniel asked.

"There won't be any."

Daniel lay down on the rug. He smiled.

"Throw me a pillow, Nurit," he said.

4

It was no use trying to work while waiting for Daniel to bring her back from the discotheque. Nurit came home flushed and a little drunk.

"There were some friends of his there," she related, oblivious of his annoyed silence. "There was a fight, and someone started up with him. You should have seen them make him pipe down. Real hoodlums! He met them in an army jail. Are you feeling all right?''

"No."

"You aren't angry, are you?" She only now sensed his mood.

"Maybe I am."

"Are you sorry you let me go?"

"No. It's just that you didn't want me to come with you."

"What?" Nurit was taken aback. "You never said you wanted to come. You kept talking about your work."

"You didn't want me to say that I wanted to. You wanted to go without me. You started trying to get rid of me this morning."

"It was you who wouldn't go to town with me, Arik!"

"No, it wasn't!"

"We left the house together," she reminded him. "You saw a car. 'That's Yossi's,' you said. 'Let's wait for him to give us a ride.' I told you that it wasn't Yossi's, and that even if it was, I didn't have time to wait. Then you started insisting that some worker peeing behind a tree was really Yossi. You know I see better than you do. Is that what happened or not?"

"Ta-ta ta-ta ta-ta ta-ta," Arik mimicked the tone of her voice. "I said I'd be bored sitting there and watching you dance, and you said, 'You're right, discotheques aren't for you.' ''

"If you said you were jealous now," she sniffed, "I wouldn't mind. But to start accusing me of not wanting you to come!"

"You didn't want any competition from me," Arik said. "And you're crying now because you know that I'm right."

"I am not."

"Then why are you?"

"Because. I drank too much and now we're fighting."

"Who did you dance with besides Daniel?"

"Nobody you know."

"Did you feel sexy with him?"

"I do whenever I dance, Arik. If you danced too, you'd understand it. Do you really think I've gone and fallen in love with him?"

"Have you?"

"There's no reason why I couldn't. It's happened to you, after all. But I couldn't imagine leaving you because of it. I could only think of it as a temporary thing. What's wrong with falling in love?''

162

"I can see what you're getting yourself into."

"I'm not getting myself into anything."

"You just said you were."

"You've said yourself a hundred times that it could happen to anyone. And that you were capable of anything, and that there was never any knowing in advance, and that something you felt and believed in today could go poof tomorrow. You used to say it to scare me every time I asked you if you were cheating on me, or if you were going to leave me. 'I don't *think* so.' That's just what you used to say."

"You're already in love with Daniel."

"He loves you too. I love him like a friend. Don't think that I like to go dancing without you, even with him. I don't like it any more than I like being left alone by myself when you go off to play bridge."

Daniel became their close friend. At first he came once a week, then twice and even three times. Upon entering, he always sat down in his seat and ordered something to drink. Dafna was ecstatic to see him. Sometimes he took Nurit dancing or out to a movie. "Jealousy is an acquisitive vestige of the past," Arik explained to them each time he offered to baby-sit. "It's a primitive stage in the development of the ego, which has to learn to free itself from it."

Sometimes they went out *à trois*. Usually to the theater or to a movie. And afterward to a café. Arik would watch how they smiled at each other or touched accidentally. The pleasure he felt then bordered on torture. Their coquetry and cloying looks disgusted him.

One rainy Friday evening, Daniel stayed with them until late. The sabbath candles they had lit before dinner were flickering out. Arik kept dozing off. Each time he opened his eyes, Nurit and Daniel were still sitting and talking. He had lost the thread of their conversation long ago.

"It's time to go to sleep," he finally said.

Daniel glanced at his watch. "It really is late," he said. He bent to put on his shoes.

"Where will you sleep?" Arik asked.

"I can try the adjutant's office," said Daniel. "Or maybe I'll drive back to the base."

"In this rain? Why don't you sleep here?"

"Where?"

"No problem. I'll sleep on one side of the bed, you'll sleep on the other, and Nurit will sleep in the middle."

Daniel looked at the two of them. "Do you really like me that much?"

Nurit laughed disconcertedly.

"In that case," said Daniel, "I will."

"What's going to happen now?" Nurit asked Arik when Daniel went to fetch his things. "You're crazy!"

"You don't want him to stay?"

"Of course I do. But you know that he loves me."

"He loves me too. Anyway, can't I trust you?"

Nurit angrily put a fresh sheet on the bed and Arik helped her to tuck in the corners. The three of them lay down. Arik could feel every one of Daniel's movements through the mattress. He had already begun to regret the situation he'd created. He told them about a game that he and his brother used to play as children when they were allowed into their parents' bed.

"Do you want to play it now?" Daniel asked.

"Not with Nurit in the middle," Arik said.

"I can't remember ever having had good times with my parents. Maybe I never did."

"Would you like us to be your parents?" Nurit asked.

"That would be a little heavy. But you can be my brother and sister. I always envied boys who had an older brother. I even envied your brother, Arik."

"You needn't have bothered," said Arik. "I remember how he used to tag along after me when I'd come home on leave from the army and I wouldn't give him the time of day. Once he asked me about condoms. How to use them. I should have hugged him then. But instead I answered him just like my father once answered me—cold, cut and dried."

"Like a prick!" Daniel said.

"I always stuck up for him in school, though."

"What did you ask your father?" Daniel asked.

"Nothing important."

"Are you embarrassed to tell us?"

"Yes."

164

"And what did he answer?"

"Quit it already."

"Would you tell me if the two of us were alone?"

"Maybe."

Daniel laughed. "But Nurit is your wife."

"That's true," said Arik. "But it's different when we're three. I'm not embarrassed to undress in front of Nurit, for example, or in front of you either, but just now I went to do it in the bathroom."

"Then get over it," said Daniel. "This is the moment of truth."

"What do you think I asked about? Masturbation."

"And?"

"He said it was all right. That there were almost no lasting effects. That like anything, I shouldn't overdo it. That sometimes it was better than getting involved with a woman."

"Did he really say that?" laughed Nurit. "You never told me."

"At least he smiled. That's more than I did with my brother."

"How did your father die?" Nurit asked Daniel.

"It was on account of me," said Daniel, trying to sound like his mother. "From sheer shame and disgrace. I remember how we were sitting on the terrace when they came from the hospital to tell us. I was eating a corncob. I knew I should put it down, because my father had died, but I finished it anyway."

"Why were you thrown out of school?"

"I don't remember any more. I was thrown out of every school I went to. My mother used to board me out to a different kibbutz every year. She thought it was good for me. At one of them I tried to fuck a donkey. The sports teacher caught me and I was on my way home the next day."

"How do you fuck a donkey?" asked Arik.

"Would you like to try?"

"No, just to know," Arik laughed.

"Oh. Well, I went to the stable with another boy to be my witness. There were two donkeys there, With and Without. I stood on a stool, opened my fly, and tried to stick it up Without, but I couldn't get it in. That's the whole story."

"Why With and Without?" Nurit asked.

"Those were their names. One had balls and one didn't."

Now each vied to tell a funnier story. They talked into the night until the pauses between the words grew longer and longer. Arik did his best to fall asleep last.

Sometimes the two men went out together and left Nurit at home. They would go to watch a thriller, or to play Ping-Pong, or shoot pool. Daniel tried unsuccessfully to get Arik to play tennis. Arik wasn't much for sports.

On one such evening Daniel stopped the jeep by an unfamiliar house.

"Come, I'll show you something," he said.

He led Arik through a garden and around to the back of the house. They peeked through the slats of the shutters. First a children's room, then a bedroom. They saw a man on an enclosed terrace. He glanced up briefly as though conscious of their eyes upon him, then returned to his work.

"That's her husband," said Daniel.

"Whose?"

Daniel didn't answer. "She's not home," he said disappointedly after a while. "Let's wait a little longer. I wanted to show you an old flame. I come around now and then to see what she's doing. What's new in her life."

They waited by the jeep. Before long she appeared. She slowed down when she saw them and stopped when she recognized Daniel.

"Daniel!" She was surprised.

"I brought along a friend," Daniel said, "so I could show him what I wasted my time on."

She tossed her head and walked wordlessly past them. They drove off in the jeep.

"Did you see that?"

"What was I supposed to see?"

"I really don't know," Daniel said.

"You don't mean to tell me that you have no luck with women!"

"No. But the minute they start loving me, I stop loving them. This one never loved me. She was an actress. I once waited all night outside her hotel just so she could see me through the window. Another time I chased after a bus that was taking her stock company to the theater. On a stolen motorcycle in the rain. I tried doing some stunt for her and smeared myself all over the road.''

Daniel rolled up his sleeve. "Here," he said. "Feel."

Arik felt the rough scar. It was strange to touch a man's warm flesh.

"What about the one in Motsa?"

"The Animal?" Daniel smiled. "She does anything I want. I can tell her to crawl and she'll crawl. Would you like me to fix you up with her?"

They drove for a while.

"What does she look like?"

"Nice. A big ass."

"What does your mother look like?"

"Like a cow."

"How did she get along with your father?"

"Are you starting with the psychology again?"

"No. I just wanted to know."

"I really don't know myself."

"You never asked?"

"No. What the hell difference does it make?"

"Wouldn't you like to know what you came from?"

"No," Daniel said. "My mother's liable to tell me some story in the end that'll sound just like me and the Animal."

He stopped speeding crazily and said: "Maybe I don't hate her so much for what she is as for what she isn't. You know, I can't ever visit her without stealing something when I leave."

5

"The Animal's pregnant," Daniel informed them on the telephone. "She doesn't want an abortion."

"What are you going to do?"

"We've got to convince her. You have to help me."

"How can you ask me to help?" Arik said. "What does anyone know about the creation of life? How do we know who the fetus might turn out to be?"

"She's out to get me," Daniel said. "She thinks that I'll marry her if she has the baby."

"You won't?"

"Never. I've already told her."

Nurit snatched the receiver from Arik. "It isn't right to bring a child into the world if you know that it won't have a father," she said.

"Should I bring her over or not?"

"Of course you should. Arik's just carrying on. He'll be glad to help."

Arik was curious to see the Animal. Nurit was beside herself with worry. We can't let her trap him, she kept saying. Dafna wanted to know what Daniel would bring her when he came.

"A little baby," Arik said.

Nurit fumed at the joke. She gave the child some sleeping drops and put her to bed. They waited tensely while the evening passed. It was after ten when they heard the jeep's horn. Daniel came in by himself, threw off his wet coat, and sat down in his usual place.

"She won't come up without an umbrella," he said.

Arik went down to get her. She really was good-looking. She seemed to look right through him, so he opened the umbrella and waited. The Animal stepped down from the jeep, pushing away his hand when he sought to help her. Upstairs Nurit regarded her with open hostility. She watched her every movement while she took off her wet shoes and sat down by the kerosene stove. No one said hello.

"Would you like something to drink?" Arik asked.

"She isn't thirsty," called Daniel from the kitchen, his mouth full of food.

Arik tried taking him aside to talk.

"We can talk right here," Daniel said out loud. "It makes no difference if she hears us or if she doesn't."

Arik brought the Animal a sandwich and tea. She took them without a word.

"We're going to the movies," said Nurit as planned.

She put on her coat.

The Animal reached for hers.

"Not you," said Daniel. "You're staying here. Don't forget what you promised."

The Animal put her coat down obediently. Nurit and Daniel left and ran noisily down the stairs, their laughter ringing, to the jeep. Arik had an idea.

"We're getting divorced," he said. "Nurit is going to marry Daniel. It's something you should know."

168

The Animal was concentrating on her tea. He had served it in the big mug they kept for Daniel.

"Are you in your third month yet?"

She didn't answer. After a while she shrugged, but by then the gesture had no meaning. Arik took a blanket from the bed and covered her knees with it. She didn't thank him. Could she be retarded? But she didn't look it, or even particularly distraught. Maybe she just didn't care. A tough cookie. Or maybe she'd sworn to say nothing in return for having been made to come. She fiddled with the radio near her. Arik went back to his newspaper. The role he was playing was absurd. Across from him sat a strange woman; there was no justification, no point of entry, for starting the conversation. Who said that one couldn't bring up a child without a father? The family of the future would be multiple, extended. There might be one parent, or two, or three, or more. There would be a scientific way of providing every child with what he could now get only from his parents, who might be two perfect monsters. It would be done by transplanting a happy childhood that had been copied or selected from another brain. Or one that was purely imaginary, like a poem. Women would look at photographs of the pregnant women of today as people look at drawings of the cavemen.

The Animal had fallen asleep. Her head drooped diagonally down. He wondered what her name was. She needed a little makeup, he thought. Her breathing was soft and regular. Suddenly she awoke with a start and saw him looking at her.

"I know that you love Daniel," he said, "and that you want to have the child. But what will you say to it when it asks you one day by what right you brought it into the world without a father? Get it into your head that Daniel will never admit paternity and will have nothing to do with the child. We've made an appointment for you with Nurit's doctor tomorrow at eleven. He's reliable and you needn't worry about anything going wrong."

She rose and shut herself up in the bathroom. When she didn't come out again, Arik lay down in bed and tried reading a book.

Daniel and Nurit made the bed shake. The light was on. The Animal was sitting in her chair. Arik rubbed his eyes and moved over to make room. They were taking out blankets from the drawer beneath the bed. Suddenly Daniel looked up and said, "Go lie down in the hallway. There's a sleeping bag for you there. Move!"

The Animal shook her head. Daniel got out of bed with a menacing gesture. The Animal wasn't fazed. She seemed to be used to it.

"You'll go to the doctor tomorrow," said Daniel between his teeth. "You know the child isn't mine. You know everyone comes to you to get laid."

The Animal didn't react. Daniel changed his tone.

"Can't you understand that I don't love you? I don't want to marry you. It's as simple as that." He started to shout. "If you don't get out of here, I'll drag you out."

"What do you care if she gives birth?" asked Arik unexpectedly. "Let her. It's no skin off your back. You're not the child's father? So much the better. The two of you can go to a lawyer tomorrow and sign some kind of waiver, or whatever it's called, in which she renounces all claims on you. There has to be some form like that. Forget about the child. Make believe it doesn't exist."

"That's easy for you to say," said Daniel. "It won't be yours."

"But what did you bring her here for?" Arik asked. "Did you really think we could force her to have an abortion she doesn't want?"

Arik had bungled it. Daniel slouched up and down the room. The Animal followed his movements like a cat waiting to be fed. Finally Daniel lay down and turned off the light. The Animal pulled the blanket from him, pushed Nurit aside, and lay down beside him.

"Oho!" Daniel said.

He dragged her by her hands from the bed to the kitchen. She let herself be pulled unprotestingly from the room. He locked the door behind her.

The three of them listened.

"She's gone to sleep," said Daniel with relief.

There was a sound of breaking glass. The three of them burst into the kitchen together. The Animal stood there smashing dishes. Not all of them at once. One by one she threw them on the floor. Daniel dragged her back inside. Arik took a broom to sweep up. Nurit stood by the table, dismally watching him.

"What now?" she asked.

"I told you," said Arik triumphantly. "They'll leave in the morning."

170

Now the two women lay on either side and the two men in the middle. Suddenly the Animal reached over and punched Nurit's face. This was too much. Arik shoved her out of bed. Nurit cried. Daniel brought a wet towel to keep her from turning black-and-blue. Without warning, he fell on the Animal and began to beat her with his fists. She didn't make a sound.

"Enough," said Nurit. "She's pregnant."

Daniel tried to comfort Nurit. He apologized and kissed her. The Animal said nothing. All of a sudden she began to laugh. Not quietly. A roaring, infectious laugh. The three of them listened awestricken in the darkness. In the end she gathered up her blanket and went to sleep in Dafna's room.

Daniel woke them at seven. He and the Animal were leaving. Could he have some coffee, please? But quickly. And for the Animal too. He'd forgotten all about an appointment he had.

"What about the doctor?" asked Arik, bewildered.

"I can't make it today."

Nurit sat up. "What's the matter? What happened?"

Daniel winked. "I've got an appointment."

"You don't know what you're doing," said Arik.

Daniel smiled.

"Maybe you really want the child," Arik said.

Nurit poured coffee for the Animal in the kitchen. They didn't speak to each other. In broad daylight the Animal was a letdown. She looked tired and unkempt. Nurit had a black-and-blue mark after all. Daniel drank his coffee standing up. Arik offered the Animal a cigarette. She looked at him and took it.

6

Several weeks went by during which Daniel was visibly depressed. While he came to see Nurit and Arik as before, his mood failed to improve. Nurit was sure it had to do with herself but was afraid to ask. Arik, on the other hand, tried to be Daniel's analyst, discreetly, of course, since he knew Daniel loathed the idea. Daniel proved an uncompliant patient.

Arik tried coaxing him. "You have to tell us what's bothering you. We're worried about you. We love you. We can't stand to see you eating yourself up. You have to talk to us. What else is friendship for? You're only hurting yourself by not confiding in us.''

Late one night Daniel arrived while they were sleeping and collapsed drunkenly on their bed. He buried his face in it and emitted a series of strange, tearless sobs. Arik grabbed him by the shoulders and shook him hard.

"What on earth is the matter with you?"

"Life sucks," Daniel said.

"This time you're going to talk!"

"Leave me alone."

No one spoke.

"All right," Daniel said. "When I fall in love with someone, I can't get it up to fuck her. Are you happy now?"

Nurit looked at him, alarmed.

"Who is it this time?" Arik asked carefully.

"Someone. It doesn't matter. It's all over anyway. She doesn't want to see me any more."

"Maybe you should really go for treatment after all."

"Are you out of your mind?" Daniel shouted. "They'll ground me immediately."

He rose, took his beret, and left, slamming the door behind him. They heard him running down the stairs and angrily starting the jeep.

"You're riding him too hard," said Nurit.

"I only want to help," Arik insisted.

"Once you start these things, you never know where they'll end."

"I'm glad that it happened. He finally told us. Now we know."

"What if we do?"

"I have to think."

Arik sought to reorder his image of Daniel, whom he saw in a new light. There was no denying his bravery. He'd shot down six Egyptian planes in the war. Until his own plane was hit, too. And even then he disobeyed orders to ditch and brought it down safely. Yet there was also the time he cracked up in training. Wrecked a piece of machinery worth millions playing chicken with another pilot and bailed out over the ocean. Right into a fishing fleet. And went gaga before anyone could pull him out. He shot off all his flares, colored the ocean red with dye, and used up a canister of shark repellent against imaginary sharks.

172

"Nurit? Are you asleep?"

"No."

"Did you understand what he told us?"

"Yes."

"Why are you so distant?"

"Distant? You're imagining it."

"Do you understand now why he keeps falling in love and nothing ever comes of it?"

"Yes."

"And the way he drives like a madman. We have to do something."

"What?"

"You have to go to bed with him," Arik said. "Not just once, but over a long period. You're the only one who can help him. He loves you, but you know all about him now, and can make him get over his fears."

Nurit was stunned. Arik himself was taken aback by his own words.

"You can make a new man of him," he continued. "When you begin, don't tell him I'm permitting you. He has to think of you as a lover and not as some kind of therapy. Later on we may have to tell him the truth so that our relationship isn't ruined by his guilt feelings toward me."

"Arik, you're out of your mind," said Nurit, trying to keep calm.

They lay there thinking.

"Nurit?"

She pretended to be asleep so as not to have to answer. What was she going to do now?

The next day Arik went on talking about the stupidity of conventional notions of marriage and sex. He kept at it so persistently that Nurit began to worry. Her first thought was that he must be having an affair again. Perhaps he even wanted to get rid of her completely. Suppose he didn't love her any more?

7

Daniel came to visit. Arik didn't leave the two of them alone for a minute. Nurit impatiently suggested to Dafna that they go to the park and casually added, "Maybe you'll come too, Daniel? Arik is terribly busy."

"I'm not busy at all," Arik said. "We can all go together."

She smiled at him sweetly. "In that case, why don't you make us something good for supper while we're gone?"

They left.

"I've been trying for days to get in touch with you at the base," Nurit said to Daniel once they were sitting in the park. "I have to talk with you. Where were you?"

"I suppose on flights," he answered.

"Night flights too? Well, it doesn't matter. Listen."

"Ima!" screamed Dafna. "He took my shovel! He took it!"

Nurit went to make peace in the sandbox and returned.

"I want you to tell me about this other woman. You shouldn't have kept it from me. But not now, there's no time. Do you know what Arik has been talking about ever since you told us?"

Daniel looked her innocently in the eyes. "Since I told you what?"

"You know what."

"No, tell me."

"Daniel!"

"I want to hear you say it."

"About your problems."

"What problems?"

"Stop it! I have something important to talk to you about."

"Say the word first."

"I don't want to."

"That I can't fuck, right?"

"That's enough. Do you want to hear or not?"

"Yes."

"Since that night he keeps trying to convince me that I should have an affair with you."

"What? Are you serious?"

"Yes."

"He actually said you should have an affair with me?"

"Yes."

"Where?"

"We didn't discuss the details."

"But what did he say?"

Daniel had to wait again while Nurit went to look after Dafna.

"He said I should do it for your sake. That it would make a new man of you. He said I shouldn't tell you at first that he's permitting me, but that afterward I should, so that your relationship with him wouldn't be spoiled by your guilt feelings. Do you understand?"

"So now you're telling me like he told you to."

"You're particularly infuriating today."

"It's weird," Daniel said. "I don't think I get it."

"Neither do I. And I'm afraid."

"Of what?"

"Maybe he's taken up with some woman again and wants to get rid of me. Or maybe he just doesn't love me any more. All he keeps talking about is his civilization of the future, and friendship, and old-fashioned ideas. I don't know what to make of it."

"Maybe he's trying to trap you," said Daniel. "Maybe he suspects something and wants to find out."

"I thought of that, too." Nurit paused. "I want to ask you something. But afterward I want you to forget that I asked it. All right?"

Daniel promised.

"What you said the other night . . . does that mean you don't love me?"

Daniel kissed her.

"Do you think you might want to marry me some day?"

"Nurit, I don't want to marry anyone."

"And that woman?"

He hesitated. "Maybe her. But she's married already and has two children."

"Forget that I asked," she said. "What are we going to do now?"

"When he catches us, we can say he gave us permission."

"I don't believe he really means it. I know him."

Daniel shrugged.

8

Daniel vanished for a while and then reappeared one night with the news that he was the father of a two-week-old boy. The two of them hugged and kissed him. He had brought a bottle of champagne.

"To the Animal!" he laughed.

"Have you admitted paternity?" asked Arik.

"No," Daniel said. "I won't until she agrees to no support."

"She won't let you visit the child."

Daniel smiled mischievously. "Would you like to see him right now?"

They rode out to Motsa in the jeep. Nurit sat in the front with Daniel, and Arik curled up in the back. Nurit peeled oranges and divided them in three. She passed Arik his and fed Daniel his with her fingers. Daniel parked the jeep a street away from the house. They approached it single file, Daniel first and Arik last, like a raiding party. The night was thick with fog that reflected the light of the street lamps as though in a strange dream. Daniel led them along a fence and through a hole in it. He stopped by a high window.

"This is the baby's room," he whispered.

He reached into the bushes, pulled out a section of rusty ladder, and leaned it against the wall. He climbed to the top rung and removed the loose pane of the window, which was held in place by two nails. Arik watched him admiringly.

"What if she hears us?"

Daniel grinned. "She sleeps like a log."

Daniel helped Nurit through the window and lowered her carefully to the floor. Arik followed her. They were in a room with some shelves, a table, and a bassinet in one corner. Arik and Nurit held their breath as Daniel lifted the infant, wrapped in white, and held him tightly against his shoulder. With his free hand he took a diaper from a shelf.

"I want to change him," he whispered to Nurit. "I want you to show me how."

Daniel earnestly tried to imitate her practiced movements. The baby gurgled on the table. It was one o'clock in the morning, and the scene seemed to Arik eerily not of this world. The baby's room, he mused, was part of a house that Daniel could never build. He, Arik, could build his own house.

9

He pressed his ear to the door.

"If you really love someone, it doesn't matter," he heard Daniel say.

"But I can't stand the way he grumbles and complains," Nurit said. "He picks on me for all kinds of little things. 'Who told you to open that window?' 'Why didn't you turn out that light?' As though he owned the house. As though anything I did in it had to be cleared with him first.''

They were talking about him, Arik thought. He was about to walk in when he heard, "There's something scratchy on the back of your hand.''

And then: "Daniel, stop! Arik will be here any minute.''

He couldn't believe his ears. He didn't want to see it. No, he did. He'd open the door and shout something terrible. Only what? He wracked his brain for the words. He'd kick Daniel out of the house. But then he'd lose him. Nearly in tears, he ran down the stairs. Let them hear him. Let them see him through the window, goddamn them. He'd hated Daniel from the start. From the moment they'd met by the motorcycle. From the time they were schoolboys.

He called from a public phone. Nurit answered.

"I want to ask you something,'' he said.

"Arik! Where are you?''

"That's none of your business.''

"Are you drunk?''

"What do you care if I am?''

"Who else should I care about?''

"Who? Daniel.''

"You permitted me!'' she said. "You permitted me!''

"That was all theoretical,'' he said with feigned composure. "You knew I never meant it.''

"You never made noise on the stairs so we would hear you in time? Or fumbled on purpose with the key? And all your talk about true friendship. That if you don't give up everything for it, it doesn't mean a thing. I suppose you've forgotten all that!''

"You were cheating on me all along!''

"You knew about it all along!''

"I did not!''

"You said I shouldn't tell you. That it would be better that way for the two of us. You can't tell me now that you didn't.''

"I never did.''

"You're a liar! First you put me up to it and now you want your revenge. Don't think you can get away with it. I've got my scores to settle with you, too. Oh, you're clever. At first I thought you didn't love me any more. That you had someone else. Until in the end you

177

convinced me that you were really doing it because you loved Daniel. And now the truth is out! Can't you see you're beside yourself with jealousy?"

"Where's Daniel?"

"Right here."

"He's listening to all this?"

"He already knows it all."

"All right. I want him to go to the kitchen now and shut the door. I want to ask you something."

There was a pause at the other end. "He went," said Nurit.

"How . . ." Arik didn't know how to put it. "Is sex good with him?"

Nurit thought for a minute.

"Yes."

"I want to know exactly."

"What exactly do you want to know?"

"Is it better than with me?"

She didn't answer.

"Why don't you say something?"

"I can't answer a question like that."

"Why can't you? Where's Daniel? Did he really go?"

"Yes," she lied.

"I can't believe anything you say any more."

"And do you think that I can believe you?"

"Look who's talking!"

"Don't shout so loud," she begged.

He lowered his voice. "Why can't you answer a simple question?"

"Because you want me to say that it's not as good with Daniel. And I don't want to talk about it on the telephone. I want you to come home now."

"Is it better or worse?"

"I can't look at it that way, Arik. Can't you see that?"

"So how do you look at it?"

"You're shouting again."

"I can't help it. You have thirty seconds to answer me. If you don't, I'm not coming home."

The line was silent.

"It's not a question of better or worse, Arik. It's just different. I

178

can't start making comparisons. When I'm with Daniel, I'm with him. I don't think of you. But the only reason I can have a relationship like that with him is because of you, do you understand?''

"That's not what I'm talking about."

"You're talking about your stupid masculine pride."

"That's what you think."

"That's what I know."

"Are you going to answer me or not?"

"Jealousy is an acquisitive vestige of the past. You just don't want anyone to put his stamp on me but you."

"Don't be vulgar."

"I'm not being vulgar."

He played with the dial to frighten her.

"Arik? Arik!"

He didn't answer. Daniel got out of bed and went to the kitchen. He winked at Nurit as he shut the door.

"It's better with you than with Daniel," she said.

"Why couldn't you say so in the first place?"

"I don't know. It's not so simple. It's better with you because I love you."

"And not Daniel?"

"I love him too. But it's not the same. Do you love me?"

Arik hung up.

He pretended not to see as Daniel entered the café to look for him among the customers. Daniel came up and leaned over him.

"Nurit asked me to find you and bring you home."

"All right."

He tried to rise from the table but had to sit down again. Daniel went to the counter to pay. He helped Arik to his feet and pulled him outside. The nerve of him paying the bill, Arik thought. He pulled out some money from his pocket and threw it in the air. The bills were carried off by the wind, while the coins fell jingling to the sidewalk.

"Money is shit!" he yelled at the top of his voice.

Daniel pushed him into the jeep.

"I don't want to go home."

"Nurit is worried about you."

179

"Let her worry."

They drove off.

"She thinks I permitted her and knew all along."

"You didn't?"

Arik shrugged. If he grabbed Daniel by the throat now, they might both be killed.

"Do you love her?" Daniel asked.

Did he love her? The question amused him. What would the idiot think of next?

"When I think I'm going to lose her," he said, surprised by his own words.

"Do you like making love with her?"

Sometimes, when he held her by the breasts, she became the fiery Negress he met in his dreams.

"Can you do with her whatever you want?" Daniel asked.

"You mean shamewise?"

"I mean can you do with her whatever you want."

"Can you?"

They looked at each other and burst out laughing.

"Maybe it's time she got pregnant again," said Arik, drying his eyes.

"From you."

"No, from you." Arik was seized by a new attack of laughter.

"From me?" Daniel started to laugh again too.

Arik embraced him and spun him around in his seat. Daniel let go of the steering wheel and the jeep swerved out of control. He managed to stop it just in time.

"Do you hate me?" Daniel asked.

"No."

He really didn't. He loved him more than ever, he thought. He climbed out of the jeep and sat down on the curb. He puked. He felt better.

"Do you have anything I can wipe my mouth with?"

Daniel removed his sweater, shirt, and undershirt in a single motion. He separated them and gave the undershirt to Arik. Arik wiped his face with it and threw it in the gutter.

"That's one undershirt less," he said.

Whenever you took off your clothing like that before going to sleep, he remembered, Bella the kibbutz housemother turned the sleeves inside out so that you'd get tangled up in them when you were hurrying to dress in the morning. It was her way of making sure you took your clothes off singly so that they'd air out overnight.

"I loved that kibbutz," said Arik.

"I hate all kibbutzim," Daniel said.

He had lent his wife to a friend, Arik thought. To the best of friends. Of the two of them, only Nurit could make contact with Daniel in the one way perfect contact could be made: through the flesh. In the civilization of the future this would no longer be true. Nor would there be any pain. Arik saw with his mind's eye spaceships sailing to far galaxies, with a human cargo on board, pioneers of the expanded meta-ego of the race, going forth to seed the vast universe with the spore of a higher life.

10

Arik made Nurit tell him every evening about her relations with Daniel. Often he heard the same details from Daniel later on in the jeep. Had they agreed between them what to tell him? It enraged him whenever Daniel mentioned something that Arik thought sacred to Nurit and himself. Such as the bath they'd taken together, for example. At such times he had to rethink everything. Then Daniel disappeared for several weeks. The two of them started to worry. Each blamed the other for the loss of their friend. They jumped from their seats at the first ring of the telephone. Even Dafna was stricken with anxiety and asked about Daniel all the time. Until he called one day and said, "I'm coming over."

"When?" Arik had reached the phone first.

"Tonight. How are you?"

"We're fine. How are you?"

"I'm fine. I married the Animal."

"What?"

"Yesterday."

"You're joking!"

"I couldn't think of such a joke in my worst dreams."

"He married the Animal," said Arik to Nurit, passing her the receiver.

"Congratulations," she said, trying to collect herself. "When will the two of you come over?"

Daniel burst out laughing. "I'm not as married to her as all that. It's just for a month or two. To give the child a name."

Arik still had his ear pressed to the receiver. "It's forever," he whispered to Nurit.

Two more weeks passed before Daniel came. He'd been busy since the wedding. The air force had given him a house on the base, and he'd moved in with the Animal and the baby. He was in high spirits all evening. He played with Dafna as usual and helped Nurit put her to bed. Arik listened carefully but could hear no whispering between them. Not until they had eaten and lain down to rest did Daniel tell them about the wedding. He kept stopping to laugh, as though he were relating some prank.

"There was a rabbi there, a pilot I'd gone to the movies with before the ceremony, and another pilot to be a witness. I didn't shave or put on fresh clothes. I didn't bring a ring with me either. But she did. When I had to put it on her finger and say, 'I take you for my lawful wife,' I wanted to say 'for my awful life,' but it came out 'for my wawful ife' instead. The rabbi wasn't so dumb. 'You're clowning, young man,' he said, 'but that's only because you're nervous.' That was after the part where I had to break the glass. I kept raising my foot to break it without bringing it down. The third time I did it, her father nearly had a stroke. I didn't tell you? Her parents were there too. And my mother in all her glory. What could I do? My mother behaved like at a real wedding. She kissed the Animal and slobbered all over her. She even gave her a pearl necklace that she claimed was a family heirloom. The Animal cried too, just imagine! I must say she was gorgeous."

"I admire her," said Arik, "for the way she got you."

"So do I," said Daniel.

"Are you really planning to divorce her?" asked Nurit.

The three of them lay on the bed until late. "I'm sorry I can't stay," said Daniel when he rose to put on his jacket. "I've got a date tonight."

11

One Sunday morning Daniel was killed in a training accident. He had left their name as his next of kin. When the air force officer who

182

informed them left their apartment, Arik relieved Nurit at the table and went on feeding Dafna.

All Daniel's friends came to the funeral. There were a large contingent from the air force and several women whom no one knew. A military salute was fired at the grave. The Animal came too, with the baby. She looked right through Nurit and Arik.

After the thirty-day mourning period was over, Arik received an invitation from the commander of Daniel's base. The colonel received him in his office. Arik scarcely glanced at the maps, the standards, and all the paraphernalia, but at heart he was impressed. The colonel spoke about Daniel. He mentioned his courage and the times he should have been grounded for some irresponsible stunt but was let off with a reprimand instead.

"I tell you," he said, "if I needed a pilot to do figure eights over Cairo, I would have picked him."

Arik nodded his assent, as though it had been asked for.

"I asked you to come today because of a certain document," said the colonel, handing him a sheet of paper. It was a will in Daniel's handwriting allocating his insurance money. Arik was to be given 70 percent, Nurit 25, and Daniel's wife 5.

"It's just one of his jokes," Arik said. "He really wanted the money to be kept in trust with us for his son. I happen to know that's what he had in mind."

"I'm glad to hear that," said the colonel. "We'll send you a formal notice. Are you getting divorced?"

Arik was flabbergasted. "What?"

"My intelligence service is first-rate," laughed the colonel.

The interview was over. The colonel was already seeing him out the door when Arik asked about Daniel's accident. The colonel threw up his hands in a gesture of noncomprehension.

"He cracked up trying to thread the needle between two concrete pylons."

Arik didn't understand.

"You mean he just wanted to prove he could do it?"

"It would seem so," said the colonel. "Someone once made it before, but in a smaller plane, and he got twenty-one days for it. Daniel didn't have a foot's clearance on either side."

Arik walked down the stairs. He wondered what Daniel had thought of at that moment. Of him? Of Nurit? Of his child? Had he understood what death was just in time to realize that there would be no one to tell about it?

12

At first they tried to ignore the growing void in their lives. In their bed. They were too busy mourning. They talked over and over about Daniel, remembering details. Little wrongs done him that could no longer be amended. Nurit tried to contact him at a séance. The cup moved on the table, but she couldn't be sure if it was Daniel or the medium. Arik, on the other hand, decided to leave.

One day, he thought, packing his suitcase, Dafna would be old enough for him to explain to her why he had to do it. Nurit sat on the bed, watching him silently. He would explain to her his obsession with order, his need to make sure that everything was always in its place. When would she be able to understand? Perhaps never, like her father.

"Where are you going?" Nurit asked.

He didn't answer. He rolled up a pair of Daniel's socks and put them in the suitcase.

"You're not taking a thing of his from here!"

They quarreled bitterly. In the end they decided to divide his things up. Arik got a new shaving brush and Nurit a model airplane. Arik got Daniel's pocketknife and his pornographic photographs, and Nurit his key chain shaped like a roulette wheel and his book of Italian matches. Nurit passed up Daniel's pen for a wobbly plastic frog. They ransacked Dafna's room and the kitchen but could find nothing else. Arik remembered Daniel's pajamas in the closet.

"Let me have them," Nurit begged.

"Just the tops," Arik said. "I'll keep the bottoms for myself."

He spread a blanket on the floor and lay down in his sleeping bag. Nurit got into bed and turned out the light. Arik tried solving an arithmetic problem: *A husband abandons his wife and leaves behind 1,860 books in their apartment.* He listened into the darkness. Nurit was lying there awake. *How many months will it take him to move all his books if he takes ten of them with him on each of his biweekly visits?*

"It wasn't an accident," he said.

184

Nurit caught her breath. "What are you talking about?"

"He tried to fly between two concrete structures. It was madness."

"What are you trying to tell me?"

"Nothing. What the air force told me."

Arik heard her sob silently into her pillow. A hundred and eighty-six visits divided by two were 93 weeks. Nearly two years, he thought disappointedly.

"Arik?"

He didn't answer. He changed it to three visits a week and tried solving it again.

"Arik?"

"What?"

"Why did you tell me?"

"I'm leaving in the morning. It's something you should know."

"Did you tell him that you had other women too?"

"Yes. He once took me to one of them in the jeep."

"You're lying."

"I swear."

"You made him do it."

"He loved me more than you. He left me three times more money."

"You yourself said that was just because he felt guilty."

She was right. He'd forgotten.

There was a long silence. "Do you think it was really Daniel when the cup moved?" Nurit asked.

"You know I don't believe in personal immortality."

"What do you mean?"

"I've told you hundreds of times."

"I've forgotten," she apologized.

"You never listened."

Arik explained to her again. His voice grew patient, almost tender, as he spoke.

"It's inconceivable that we should be able to communicate with a specific person. Take Churchill, for example. So which Churchill do we communicate with—Churchill the five-year-old-boy or Churchill the senile old man? People keep changing during their lives."

"Then if you're dead you're just dead?"

"I didn't say that. I think there's a superpersonal continuum that connects us all on a level we're unaware of because our present civilization fragments us into separate egos. It's that continuum, for instance, that sometimes makes us dream of places or experiences that someone else has been to or had."

"Someone who could be dead too?"

"Maybe."

"Come to me."

"I don't want to."

"You're a monster. You have no human feelings. I knew I should never have married you. You never even loved me. Just yourself. You've ruined my life and now you're leaving me with a child."

"I did love you once."

"I don't believe you."

Why had he said that? He must avoid such arguments. It was a sure way of losing. Of being caught in the invisible net she was gradually spreading at his feet.

"You'll have to pay for Dafna's support."

"I will."

"I want to tell you something," Nurit said. "Are you listening? Everyone finds a path to someone else. Some threads to connect him. But everyone is different. Everyone has his own threads. His own love. Do you hear me? No one knows you like I do. You can't become someone else. If you leave me, you'll never have a home again. I'm your home. If you go tomorrow, there's no coming back. It won't be like those other times. Remember that. If you go, it's for good."

"I've already heard all that. Why should I want to come back?"

"You say that you've heard it, but you haven't You think it will be like the other times. You'll go, you'll come back, you'll cry and you'll beg, you'll promise to be good, and I'll forgive you, and we'll make up. Making up is your specialty. Well, I'm telling you now, it's not going to happen."

"What will happen?"

"It's a waste of good breath to tell you." There was hate in her voice. "You'll come crawling to me, right on this floor, and it won't help you one bit."

186

It was scary to picture himself crawling like that. Arik examined himself to see if he felt sure of what he was doing. He found no second thoughts. Just the determination to leave in the morning and cold apathy to everything else.

"Are you afraid to be left by yourself?"

She laughed.

"Why are you laughing?"

"You're making me laugh. You don't understand. We're not talking about me. We're talking about you."

Daniel was missing. When they quarreled in front of him he would always think of something to say. He would make a suggestion, crack a funny joke, patch up the rift between them.

"Do you admit that you started sleeping with him before I said that you should?"

"Yes."

"Whore!"

At last he had said it.

"Come to me," she begged. "I can't fall asleep without you."

"I don't want to."

She began to cry. She sat up and turned on the light. She took Daniel's pajama tops and put them on. She wiped her eyes and nose with the corner of them. She looked small and to be pitied in them, like Dafna.

"Come to me," she begged again.

Arik marveled at his indifference even as he climbed into bed. The eagerness of her response annoyed him.

"Why do you always withhold yourself even when you come to me? Why? Why! Why! Why!"

He pushed her away from him.

"Is that what you came to bed for? Get out or I'll scream!"

"Why are you the way you are?"

"You made me the way I am."

He got out of bed. "I'm leaving in the morning."

He listened. There was no response. He lay down in his sleeping bag again and pulled it over his head.

When he awoke in the middle of the night they were together again, each in his usual place. Nurit was curled up against him. She trembled.

187

"Did you fall?" he asked in his sleep.

She tapped his arm yes. The immutability of it. It was a law, like the fixed orbits of the stars. Every movement that he made had an answering movement of her own that fitted it perfectly. He tried in vain to remember who had come to whom. He was too sleepy to make out if they were in bed or on the floor. There was only their two bodies, like old love letters. Like salt rubbed in wounds. Like salt on birds' tails to catch them before they could fly.

—*translated by Hillel Halkin*

A hollow stone
Amos Oz

1

The next day we went out to assess the damage. The storm had ruined the crops. The tender shoots of winter corn had been wiped off the fields as if by a gigantic duster. Saplings were uprooted. Old trees lay writhing, kissed by the terrible east wind. Slender cypresses hung limply with broken spines. The fine avenue of palm trees to the north of our kibbutz—planted thirty years ago by the founders when they first came to these barren hills—had lost their crests to the storm. Even their dumb submission had not been able to save them from its fury. The corrugated iron roofs of the sheds and barns had been carried far away. Some old shacks had been wrenched from their foundations. Shutters, which all night long had beaten out desperate pleas for help, had been broken off by the wind. The night had been filled with howls and shrieks and groans; with the dawn had come silence. We went out to assess the damage, stumbling over broken objects.

"It isn't natural," said Felix. "After all, it's spring."

"A typhoon. Here. A real tornado," added Zeiger with mingled awe and pride.

And Weissmann concluded, "The loss will come to six figures."

We decided on the spot to turn to the government and the movement for help. We agreed to advertise for specialist volunteers to work with us for a few days. And we resolved not to lose heart, but to make a start on the work right away. We would face this challenge as we had faced others in the past, and we would refuse to be disheartened. This is the substance of what Felix was to write in the kibbutz newsletter that weekend. And above all we must keep a clear head.

As for clarity, we had only to contemplate the sky that morning. It was a long time since we had seen such a brilliantly clear sky as on that morning when we went out to assess the damage, stumbling over broken objects.

2

A limpid, crystalline calm had descended on the hills. Spring sunlight on the mountains to the east, benign and innocent, and excited choruses of birds. No breeze, not a sign of dust. We inspected each part of the farm methodically, discussing, making notes, taking decisions, issuing immediate instructions. Not wasting a word. Speaking quietly and almost solemnly.

Casualties. Old Nevidomsky, the night watchman, slightly injured by a falling beam. Shoulder dislocated, but no bones broken, according to the doctor at the district hospital.

Electricity. Cables severed at various points. First priority: to switch off the current before letting the children come out to play and inspect the damage.

Water. Flooding in the farmyard and no water in the nursery.

Provisions. For today, a cold meal and lemonade.

Transport. One jeep crushed; several tractors buried in wreckage: condition impossible to ascertain at present.

Communications. Both telephones dead. Take the van into town to find out what has happened in other places and how much the outside world knows of our plight.

Felix saw to the dispatch of the van and proceeded to the nursery. From there he went on to the cowsheds and poultry houses. Then to the schoolhouse, where he gave instructions for lessons to be resumed not later than ten o'clock, "without fail."

Felix was animated by a passionate energy, which made his small, sturdy frame throb. He stowed his glasses away in his shirt pocket. His face took on a new look—that of a general rather than a philosopher.

The farmyard was full of hens unconcernedly scrabbling hither and thither, just like old-fashioned chickens in an old-fashioned village, oblivious of the fact that they had been born and bred in cages and batteries.

The livestock showed slight signs of shock. The cows kept raising their foolish heads to look for the roof, which had been carried off by the wind. Occasionally they uttered a long, unhappy groan, as if to warn of worse things to come. The big telegraph pole had fallen on Batya Pinski's house and broken some roof tiles. By five past eight, the electricians had already trampled all over her flower beds rigging up a temporary line. First priority in restoring the electricity supply was given to the nurseries, the incubators for the chicks, and the steam boilers which would ensure a hot meal. Felix issued instructions for a transistor radio to be found and brought to him, so that he could follow developments elsewhere. Perhaps someone should look in on Batya Pinski and one or two invalids and elderly people, to reassure them and find out how they had weathered the terrors of the night. But social obligations could wait a little longer, until the more essential emergency arrangements had been made. For instance, the kitchens reported a gas leak whose source could not be traced. Anyway, one could not simply drop in on people like Batya Pinski for a brief chat: they would start talking; they would have complaints, criticisms, reminiscences; and this morning was the least suitable time for such psychological indulgence.

The radio news informed us that this had been no typhoon or tornado, but a merely local phenomenon. Even the nearby settlements had hardly suffered damage. Two conflicting winds had met here on our hills, and the resulting turbulence had caused some local damage. Meanwhile the first volunteers began to appear, followed by a mixed multitude of spectators, reporters, and broadcasters. Felix delegated three lads and a fluent veteran teacher to stem the

191

tide of interlopers at the main gate of the kibbutz, and on no account
let them in to get underfoot. Only those on official business were to
be admitted. The fallen telegraph pole was already temporarily
secured by steel cables. The power supply would soon be restored
to the most essential buildings. Felix showed himself to combine the
qualities of theorist and man of action. Of course, he did not do
everything himself. Each of us played his part to the best of his
ability. And we would keep working until everything was in
order.

3

Condensation on the windows and the hiss of the paraffin stove.

Batya Pinski was catching flies. Her agility belied her years. If
Abrasha had lived to grow old along with her, his mockery would
surely have turned to astonishment and even to gentleness; over the
years he would have learned to understand and appreciate her. But
Abrasha had fallen many years ago in the Spanish Civil War, having
volunteered to join the few and fight for the cause of justice. We
could still remember the eulogy which Felix had composed in
memory of his childhood friend and comrade; it was a sober,
moving document, free from rhetorical hyperbole, burning with
agony and conviction, full of love and vision. His widow squashed
the flies she caught between her thumb and forefinger. But her mind
was not on the job, and some of the flies continued to wriggle even
after they were dropped into the enamel mug. The room was
perfectly still. You could hear the flies being squashed between her
fingers.

Abrasha Pinski's old writings were the issue of the moment.
Thanks to Felix's energetic efforts, the kibbutz movement's publishing house had recognized the need to bring out a collected
volume of the articles he had written in the thirties. These writings
had not lost their freshness. On the contrary, the further we
departed from the values which had motivated us in those days, the
more pressing became the need to combat oblivion. And there was
also at this time a certain nostalgia for the atmosphere of the thirties,
which promised a reasonable market for the book. Not to mention
the vogue for memories of the Spanish Civil War. Felix would
contribute an introduction. The volume would also contain nine

letters written by Abrasha during the siege of Madrid to the committed socialist community in Palestine.

Batya Pinski sliced the dead flies at the bottom of the mug with a penknife. The blade scraped the enamel, producing a grating yellow sound.

At last the old woman removed the glass cover and poured the mess of crushed flies into the aquarium. The quick, colorful fish crowded to the front of the tank, their tails waving, their mouths opening and closing greedily. At the sight of their agile movements, their magical colors, the widow's face lit up and her imagination ran riot.

Fascinating creatures, fish, she thought; they are cold and alive. A striking paradox. This, surely, is the bliss we desire: to be cold and alive.

Over the years, Batya Pinski had developed an amazing ability. She was capable of counting the fish in her aquarium, up to forty or fifty, despite their perpetual motion. At times she could even guess in advance what course an individual fish or a shoal would take. Circles, spirals, zigzags, sudden totally capricious swerves, swoops, and plunges, fluid lines which drew delicate, complicated arabesques in the water of the tank.

The water in the tank was clear. Even clearer were the bodies of the fish. Transparency within transparency. The movement of fins was the slightest movement possible, hardly a movement at all. The quivering of the gills was unbelievably fine. There were black fish and striped fish, blood-red fish and fish purple like the plague, pale green fish like stagnant water in fresh water. All of them free. None of them subject to the law of gravity. Theirs was a different law, which Batya did not know. Abrasha would have been able to discern it over the years, but he had chosen instead to lay down his life on a faraway battlefield.

4

The illusion of depth is produced by aquatic plants and scattered stones. The green silence of the underwater jungle. Fragments of rock on the bottom. Columns of coral up which plants twine. And on top of a hill of sand at the back of the tank is a stone with a hole.

194

Unlike the fish, the plants and stones in the aquarium are subject to the law of gravity. The fish, for their part, continually swoop down on the stones and shrubs. Here and there they rub themselves against them or peck at them. According to Batya Pinski, this is a display of malicious gloating.

As a procession of blood-red fish approaches the hollow stone, Batya Pinski presses her burning forehead against the cool glass. The passage of the live fish through the dead stone stirs a vague power deep inside her and she trembles. That is when she has to fight back the tears. She feels for the letter in the pocket of her old dressing gown. The letter is crumpled and almost faded, but the words are still full of tenderness and compassion.

"I feel," writes Abramek Bart, one of the directors of the kibbutz movement publishing house, "that if we have been unfair to the beloved memory of Abrasha, we have been even more unfair to the minds of our children. The younger generation needs, and deserves, to discover the pearls of wisdom contained in the essays and letters of our dear Abrasha. I shall come and see you one of these days to rummage (in inverted commas, of course) through your old papers. I am certain that you can be of great assistance to us in sorting through his literary remains and in preparing the work for publication. With fraternal good wishes, yours"—signed by Ruth Bardor, p.p. Abramek Bart.

The old woman held the envelope to her nose. She sniffed it for a moment with her eyes closed. Her mouth hung open, revealing gaps in her teeth. A small drop hung between her nose and upper lip, where a slight mustache had begun to grow during these bad years. Then she put the letter back in the envelope, and the envelope in her pocket. Now she was exhausted and must rest in the armchair. She did not need to rest for long. It was sufficient to doze for a minute or two. When a stray surviving fly began to buzz, she was up and ready for the chase.

Years before, Abrasha would come and bite. Love and hate. Suddenly he would burst and collapse on her, and at once he would be distracted. Not here, not with her.

For months before his departure, the tune was always on his lips, sung in a Russian bass, shamelessly off pitch. She recalled the tune, the anthem of the Spanish freedom fighters, full of longing, wildness, and revolt. It had swept their bare room up into the maelstrom of teeming forces. He would enumerate the bleeding Spanish towns that had fallen to the enemies of mankind, telling them off one by one on his fingers. Their outlandish names conveyed to Batya a resonance of unbridled lechery. In her heart of hearts she disliked Spain and wished it no good; after all, that was where our ancestors had been burned at the stake and driven out. But she held her peace. Abrasha enlarged on the implications of the struggle, expounding its dialectical significance and the place of the war in Spain in the final battle that was being engaged all over Europe. He considered all wars as a snare and a delusion; only civil wars were worth dying in. She liked to listen to all this, even though she could not, and did not want to, understand. Only when he reached the climax of his speech and described the iron laws of history, and averred that the collapse of reaction would come like a thunderbolt from the blue, did she grasp what he was talking about, because she could see the thunderbolt itself in his eyes.

And suddenly he was tired of her. Perhaps he had seen the tortured look on her face; perhaps he had had a momentary glimpse of her own desires. Then he would sit down at the table, propping up his large square head with his massive elbows, and immerse himself in the newspaper, abstractedly eating one olive after another and arranging the stones in a neat pile.

5

The kettle whistles fiercely as it passes boiling point. Batya Pinski gets up and makes herself some tea. Since the storm died down, close on four o'clock in the morning, she has been drinking glass after glass of tea. She has still not been out to inspect the damage. She has not even tried to open the shutters. She sits behind her drawn curtains and imagines the damage in all its details. What is there to see? It is all there before her eyes: shattered roofs, trampled flower beds, torn trees, dead cows—Felix, plumbers, electricians, experts, and talkers. All boring. Today will be devoted to the fish, until her premonition is confirmed and Abramek Bart arrives. She always relies unhesitatingly on her premonitions. One can always know things in advance, if only one really and truly tries and is not afraid of what may happen. Abramek will come today to see the havoc. He will come because he won't be able to contain his

196

curiosity. But he won't like to come just like that, like the other good-for-nothings who gather wherever there's been a disaster. He will find some excuse. And then he'll suddenly remember his promise to Batya, to come and rummage (in inverted commas) and sort through Abrasha's papers. It's half-past eight now. He will be here by two or three. There is still time. Still plenty of time to get dressed, do my hair, and get the room tidy. And to make something nice to give him. Plenty of time now to sit down in the armchair and drink my tea quietly.

She sat down in the armchair opposite the sideboard, under the chandelier. On the floor was a thick Persian carpet and by her side an ebony card table. All these beautiful objects would shock Abrasha if he were to come back. On the other hand, if he had come back twenty years ago he would have risen high in the party and the movement. He would have left all those Felixes and Abrameks behind, and by now he'd be an ambassador or a minister, and she would be surrounded by even nicer furnishings. But he made up his mind to go and die for the Spaniards, and the furnishings were bought for her by Martin Zlotkin, her son-in-law. When he married Ditza, he brought all these presents and took his young bride away with him to Zurich, where he now managed a division of his father's bank, with branches on three continents. Ditza ran a Zen study group, and every month she sent a letter with a stenciled leaflet in German preaching humility and peace of mind. Grandchildren were out of the question, because Martin hated children and Ditza herself called him "our big baby." Once a year they came on a visit and contributed handsomely to various charities. Here in the kibbutz they had donated a library of books on socialist theory in memory of Abrasha Pinski. Martin himself, however, regarded socialism the same way he regarded horse-drawn carriages—very pretty and diverting, but out of place in this day and age when there were other, more important fish to fry.

6

On the eve of Abrasha's departure, Ditza was taken ill with pneumonia. She was two at the time—blonde, temperamental, and in poor health. Her illness distracted Batya from thinking of Abrasha's departure. She spent the whole day arguing with the nurses and educationists, and by evening they had given in and allowed the sick child to be transferred, in her cot, from the nursery to her parents' room in one of the shabby huts. The doctor arrived from the neighboring settlement in a mule cart, prescribed various medicines, and gave instructions for keeping the temperature of the room constant. Meanwhile Abrasha packed some khaki shirts, a pair of shoes, some underwear, and a few Russian and Hebrew books into a haversack and added some tins of sardines. In the evening, fired with the spirit of his undertaking, he stood by his daughter's cot and sang her two songs, his voice trembling with emotion and fervor. He even showed Batya the latest lines dividing the workers from their oppressors on a wall map of Spain. He enumerated the towns: Barcelona, Madrid, Málaga, Granada, Valencia, Valladolid, Seville. Batya half heard him, and wanted to shout, What's the matter with you, madman? Don't go away, stay, live. And she also wanted to shout, I hope you die. But she said nothing. She pursed her lips like an old witch. And she had never lost that expression. She recalled that last evening with Abrasha as if it had been reenacted every night for twenty-three years. Sometimes the fish moved across the picture, but they did not obscure it; their paths wound in and out of it, bestowing upon it an air of strange, desolate enchantment—as though the widow were confronted not by things which had happened a long time previously, but by things which were about to happen in the future yet could still be prevented.

She must concentrate hard and not make a single mistake. This very day Abramek Bart will step into this room, all unawares, and then I shall have him in my power.

The cheap alarm clock started ringing at three o'clock. He got out of bed and lit the paraffin lamp. She followed him, slender and barefoot, and said, "It's not morning yet." Abrasha put his finger to his lips and whispered, "Sssh. . . . The child." Secretly she prayed that the child would wake up and scream its head off. He discovered a cobweb in the corner of the shack and stood on tiptoe to wipe it away. The spider managed to escape and hide between the boards of the low ceiling. Abrasha whispered to her: "In a month or two, when we've won, I'll come back and bring you a souvenir from Spain. I'll bring something for Ditza, too. Now don't make me late; the van's leaving for Haifa at half-past three."

198

He went out to wash in the icy water of the tap which stood twenty yards downhill from the shack. An alarmed night watchman hurried over to see what was going on. "Don't worry, Felix," Abrasha said. "It's only the revolution that's leaving you for a while." They exchanged some more banter in earnest tones, and then, in a more lighthearted voice, some serious remarks. At a quarter-past three, Abrasha went back to the shack, and Batya, who had followed him outside in her nightdress, went inside with him again. Standing there shivering, she saw by the light of the paraffin lamp how carelessly he had shaved in his haste and in the dark; he had cut himself in some places and left dark bristles in others. She stroked his cheeks and tried to wipe away the blood and dew. He was a big, warm lad, and when he began to hum the proud, sad song of the Spanish freedom fighters, it suddenly occurred to Batya that he was very dear and that she must not stand in his way because he knew where he was going and she knew nothing at all. Felix said, "Be seeing you," and added in Yiddish, "Be well, Abrasha." Then he vanished. She kissed Abrasha on his chest and neck, and he drew her to him and said, "There, there." Then the child woke up and started to cry with a voice transformed by the illness. Batya picked her up, and Abrasha touched them both with his large hands and said, "There, there, what's the trouble?"

The van hooted and Abrasha said cheerfully, "Here goes. I'm off."

From the doorway he added, "Don't worry about me. Goodbye."

She soothed the child and put her back in the cot. Then she put out the lamp and stood alone at the window, watching the night paling and the mountaintops beginning to show in the east. Suddenly she was glad that Abrasha had cleared the cobweb from the corner of the shack but had not managed to kill the spider. She went back to bed and lay trembling because she knew that Abrasha would never come back and that the forces of reaction would win the war.

7

The fish in the aquarium had eaten all the flies and were floating in their clear space. Perhaps they were hankering after more tidbits. They explored the dense weeds and pecked at the arch of the hollow stone, darting suspiciously toward each other to see if any fish had managed to snatch a morsel and if there was any left.

Only when the last crumbs were finished did the fish begin to sink toward the bottom of the tank. Slowly, with deliberate unconcern, they rubbed their silver bellies on the sand, raising tiny mushroom clouds. Fish are not subject to the laws of contradiction; they are cold and alive. Their movements are dreamy, like drowsy savagery.

Just before midnight, when the storm had begun to blow up, the widow had awakened and shuffled to the bathroom in her worn bedroom slippers. Then she made herself some tea and said in a loud, cracked voice, "I told you not to be crazy." Clutching the glass of tea, she wandered round the room and finally settled in the armchair facing the aquarium, after switching on the light in the water. Then, as the storm gathered strength and battered the shutters and the trees, she watched the fish waking up.

As usual, the silverfish were the first to respond to the light. They rose gently from their haunts in the thick weeds and propelled themselves up toward the surface with short, sharp thrusts of their fins. A single black mollie made the rounds of its shoal as if rousing them all for a journey. In no time at all, the whole army was drawn up in formation and setting out.

At one o'clock, an old shack next to the cobbler's hut collapsed. The storm banged the tin roof against the walls and the air howled and whistled. At the same moment, the red swordfish woke up and ranged themselves behind their leader, a giant with a sharp black sword. It was not the collapse of the shack which had wakened the swordfish. Their cousins the green swordfish had weighed anchor and gently set sail into the forest, as if bent on capturing the clearing abandoned by the silverfish. Only the solitary fighting fish, the lord of the tank, still slept in his home among the corals. He had responded to the sudden light with a shudder of disgust. The zebra fish played a childish game of catch around the sleeping monarch.

The last to come back to life were the guppies, the dregs of the aquarium, an inflamed rabble roaming restlessly hither and thither in search of crumbs. Slow snails crawled on the plants and on the glass walls of the tank, helping to keep them clean. The widow sat

200

all night watching the aquarium, holding the empty glass, conjuring the fish to move from place to place, calling them after the Spanish towns: Málaga, Valencia, Barcelona, Madrid, Córdoba. Outside the clashing winds sliced the crests off the stately palm trees and broke the spines of the cypresses.

She put her feet up on the ebony card table, a present from Martin and Ditza Zlotkin. She thought about Zen Buddhism, humility, civil war, the final battle where there would be nothing to lose, a thunderbolt from the blue. She fought back exhaustion and despair, and rehearsed the unanswerable arguments she would use when the time came. All the while her eyes strayed to another world, and her lips whispered, "There, there, quiet now."

Toward dawn, when the wind died away and we went out to assess the damage, the old woman fell into a half sleep full of curses and aching joints. Then she got up and made a fresh glass of tea and began to chase flies all over the room with an agility that belied her years. In her heart she knew that Abramek Bart would definitely come today, and that he would use his promise as an excuse. She saw the plaster fall from the ceiling as the pole fell and broke some of the roof tiles. The real movement was in the aquarium and completely noiseless. Without a sound, the monarch arose and began to steer himself toward the hollow stone. As he reached the arched tunnel, he stopped and froze. He took on a total stillness. The stillness of the water. The immobility of the light. The silence of the hollow stone.

8

Had it not been for Ditza, Batya Pinski would have married Felix in the early nineteen-forties.

It was about two years after the awful news had come from Madrid. Once again a final war was being waged in Europe, and on the wall of the dining hall hung a map covered with arrows, and a collection of heartening slogans and news cuttings. Ditza must have been four or five. Batya had got over the disaster, and had taken on a new bloom which had a disturbing effect on certain people's emotions. She always dressed in black, like a Spanish widow. And when she spoke to men, their nostrils flared as if they had caught a whiff of wine. Every morning, on her way to the sewing room, she passed the men working in the farmyard, erect and slender. Occasionally one of those tunes came back to her, and she would sing with a bitter sadness which made the other sewing women exchange glances and whisper, "Uh-uh, there she goes again."

Felix was biding his time. He helped Batya over her minor difficulties, and even concerned himself with the development of Ditza's personality. Later, when he had submitted to the desires of the party and exchanged the cowsheds for political office, he made a habit of bringing Ditza little surprises from the big city. He treated the widow with extreme respect, as if she were suffering from an incurable illness and it was his task to ease her last days. He would let himself into her room in the middle of the morning and wash the floor, secreting chocolates in unlikely places for her to discover later. Or he put up metal coathooks, bought out of his expense money, to replace the broken wooden ones. And he would supply her with carefully selected books—pleasant books, with never a hint of loss or loneliness, Russian novels about the development of Siberia, the five-year plan, change of heart achieved through education.

"You're spoiling the child," Batya would sometimes say. And Felix would word his answer thoughtfully and with tact: "Under certain circumstances it is necessary to pamper a child, to prevent it from being deprived."

"You're a sweet man, Felix," Batya would say, and occasionally she would add: "You're always thinking of others. Why don't you think about yourself for a change, Felix?"

Felix would read a hint of sympathy or personal interest into those remarks. He would stifle his excitement and reply, "It doesn't matter. Never mind. In times like these one can't be forever thinking of oneself. And I'm not the one who's making the real sacrifice."

"You're very patient, Felix," Batya would say, with pursed lips.

And Felix, either shrewdly or innocently, would answer, "Yes, I'm very patient."

And indeed, after a few months or perhaps a year or two, the widow began to soften. She permitted Felix to accompany her from the dining hall or the recreation hall to the door of her room, from the sewing room to the children's house, and occasionally she

202

would stand and listen to him for half an hour or so near one of the benches on the lawn. He knew that the time was not yet ripe for him to try to touch her, but he also knew that time was on his side. She still insisted on wearing black, and she did not moderate her arrogance, but she too knew that time was on Felix's side; he was closing in on her from all sides, so that soon she would have no alternative left.

It was little Ditza who changed everything.

She wet her bed, she ran away from the children's house at night, she escaped to the sewing room in the morning and clutched her mother, she kicked and scratched the other children and even animals, and as for Felix, she nicknamed him "Croakie." Neither his gifts and attentions nor his sweets and rebukes did any good. Once, when Felix and Batya had begun openly to eat together in the dining hall, the child came in and climbed on his knee. He was touched, convinced that a reconciliation was coming. He had started to stroke her hair and call her "my little girl" when suddenly she wet his trousers and ran away. Felix got up and ran after her in a frenzy of rage and reforming zeal. He pushed his way through the tables trying to catch the child. Batya sat stiffly where she was and did not interfere. Finally Felix snatched up an enamel mug, threw it at the elusive child, missed, tripped, picked himself up, and tried to wipe the pee and yogurt off his khaki trousers. There were smiling faces all around him. By now Felix was acting secretary-general of the Workers' Party, and here he was, flushed and hoarse, with a murderous gleam showing through his glasses. Zeiger slapped his belly, sighing, "What a sight," until laughter got the better of him. Weissmann too roared aloud. Even Batya could not suppress a smile, as the child crawled under the tables and came and sat at her feet with the expression of a persecuted saint. The nursery teachers exclaimed indignantly, "I ask you, is that the way to carry on—a grown-up man, a public figure, throwing mugs at little children in the middle of the dining hall? Isn't that going too far?"

Three weeks later, it came out that Felix was having an affair with Zeiger's wife, Zetka. Zeiger divorced her, and early in that spring she married Felix. In May, Felix and Zetka were sent to Switzerland to organize escape routes for the survivors of the death camps. In the party, Felix was regarded as the model of the young leadership which had risen from the ranks. And Batya Pinski started to go downhill.

9

When Abramek comes, I'll make him a glass of tea, I'll show him all the old papers. We'll discuss the layout and the cover, and eventually we'll have to settle the problem of the dedication, so that there won't be any misunderstanding.

She picked up the last photograph of Abrasha, taken in Madrid by a German Communist fighter. He looked thin and unshaven, his clothes were crumpled, and there was a pigeon on his shoulder. His mouth hung open tiredly, and his eyes were dull. He looked more as if he had been making love than fighting for the cause. On the back of the photograph was an affectionate greeting, in rhyme.

Over the years, Batya Pinski had got into the habit of talking to herself. At first she did it under her breath. Later, when Ditza married Martin Zlotkin and went away with him, she started talking out loud, in a croaking voice which made the children of the kibbutz call her Baba Yaga, after the witch in the stories they had heard from their Russian nurses.

Look here, Abramek, there's just one more point. It's a slightly delicate matter, a bit complicated, but I'm sure that we can sort it out, you and I, with a bit of forethought. It's like this. If Abrasha were still alive, he would of course want to bring his own book out. Right? Right. Of course. But Abrasha isn't alive, and he can't supervise the publication of the book himself. I mean the color, the jacket, the preface, that sort of thing, and also the dedication. Naturally he would want to dedicate the book to his wife. Just like anybody else. Now that Abrasha isn't with us any more, and you are collecting his articles and his letters and bringing out his book, there isn't a dedication. What will people say? Just think, Abramek, work it out for yourself—what will people make of it? It's simply an incitement to the meanest kind of gossip: poor chap, he ran away to Spain to get away from his wife. Or else he went to Spain and fell in love with some Carmen Miranda or other out there, and that was that. Just a minute. Let me finish. We must kill that kind of gossip at all costs. At all costs, I say. No, not for my sake; I don't care any more what people say about me. As far as I'm concerned, they can say that I went to bed with the Grand Mufti and with your great

204

Plekhanov both at once. I couldn't care less. It's not for me, it's for him. It's not right to have all sorts of stories going round about Abrasha Pinski. It's not good for you. After all, you need a figure you can hold up as an example to your young people, without Carmen Mirandas and suchlike. In other words, you need a dedication. It doesn't matter who writes it. It could be you. Or Felix. Or me. Something like this, for instance: Front page, *Questions of Time and Timely Questions,* collected essays by Abraham, in brackets Abrasha, Pinski, hero of the Spanish Civil War. That's right. Next page this picture. Just as it is. Top of the next page, "To Batya, a noble and dedicated wife, the fruits of my love and anguish." Then on the following page you can put that the book is published by the Workers' Party, and you can mention Felix's help. It won't hurt. Now don't you argue with me, Abramek. I mustn't get upset, because I'm not a well woman, and what's more I know a thing or two about you and about Felix and about how Abrasha was talked into going off to that ridiculous war. So you'd better not say anything. Just do what you're told. Here, drink your tea, and stop arguing.

Then she sighed, shook herself, and sat down in her armchair to wait for him. Meanwhile she watched the fish. When she heard a buzzing, she leaped up and swatted the fly on the windowpane. How do they get in when all the windows are closed? Where do they come from? To hell with the lot of them. Anyway, how can the wretched creatures survive a storm like that?

She squashed the fly, dropped it into the aquarium, and sat down again in her armchair. But there was no peace—the kettle started boiling. Abramek will be here soon. Must get the room tidy. But it's all perfectly tidy, just as it has been for years. Close your eyes and think, perhaps. . . . What about?

10

We were recovering hour by hour.

We tackled the debris with determined dedication. Buildings which were in danger of collapse were roped off. The carpenters fixed up props and blocked holes with hardboard. Here and there we hung flaps of canvas. Tractors brought beams and corrugated iron. Where there was flooding, we improvised paths with gravel and concrete blocks. We rigged up temporary power lines to

205

essential points until the electrical system could be repaired. Old paraffin heaters and rusty cooking stoves were brought up from the stores. The older women cleaned and polished them, and for a while we all relived the early days. The bustle filled us with an almost ecstatic joy. Old memories were brought out, and jokes were exchanged. Meanwhile Felix alerted all the relevant agencies, the telephone engineers, emergency services, the regional council, the department of agricultural settlements, the head office of the movement, and so on and so forth. The messages all went by jeep because the telephone lines had been blown down by the storm. Even our children were not idle. To stop them from getting under our feet, Felix told them to catch the chickens which had scattered all over the village when their coops had been damaged. Happy hunting cries arose from the lawns and from under the trees. Panting, red-faced gangs came running eagerly from unexpected quarters to block the escape routes of the clucking hens. Some of these sounds managed to penetrate through the closed shutters, windows, and curtains into Batya Pinski's room. "What's the matter, what's so funny?" the widow croaked to herself.

By afternoon, all essential services were operating again. A cold but nourishing meal had been served. The nurseries were light and warm once more. There was running water, even if the pressure was low and the supply was intermittent. After lunch it was possible to draw up a first unofficial assessment of the damage. It appeared that the worst-hit area was the group of old shacks at the bottom of the hill, which had been put up decades ago by the original founders. When they had folded up the tents they had pitched on the barren slope, and installed themselves in these shacks, they had all known at last that they were settling here and there was no going back.

Years later, after the successive phases of permanent building had been carried out, the old wooden shacks were handed over to the young people. Their first inhabitants were a detachment of young refugees who had arrived from Europe via Central Asia and Tehran, to be welcomed by us with open arms. They were followed by a squadron of underground fighters which later produced two outstanding military men. From this group of huts they set out one night to blow up a British military radar installation, and returned here toward dawn. Later on, after the establishment of the State, when the task of the underground had been completed, the tumble-down huts became a regular army base. During the War of Independence, this was the headquarters of the legendary Highland Brigade, where the great night operations were planned. Throughout the fifties, the shacks housed recent immigrants, paramilitary youth groups, intensive language courses, detachments of volunteers, eccentric individuals who came from all over the world to experience the new way of life; and finally they were used as lodgings for hired laborers. When Phase C of the building program was drawn up, the huts were scheduled for demolition. In any case they were already falling down: the wooden walls were disintegrating, the roof beams sagging, and the floors sinking. Weeds were growing through the boards, and the walls were covered with obscene drawings and graffiti in six languages. At night the children came here to play ghosts and robbers among the ruins. And after the children came the couples. We had been about to clear the site to make way for the new development when the storm anticipated us, as if it had run out of patience. The carpenters searched the wreckage, salvaging planks, doors, and beams which might be reused.

Felix's short, stocky figure was everywhere at once. It was almost as if he appeared simultaneously in different places. His sober, precise instructions prevented chaos, reduplication, and wasted effort. He never for a moment failed to distinguish between essential and trivial tasks.

For seventeen years, Felix had been a public servant, secretary-general, chairman, delegate, and eventually a member of parliament and a member of the executive committee of the party. A year or so earlier, when his wife Zetka was dying of cancer, he had given up all his public positions and returned home to become secretary of the kibbutz. At his return, social and financial problems which had seemed insoluble for years suddenly vanished as if by magic. Old plans came to fruition. Unprofitable sections of the farm took on a new lease of life. There was a new mood abroad. A few weeks previously, ten months after Zetka's death, Felix had married Weissmann's ex-wife. Just two days before the storm, we had received a small, stern-faced delegation which had come to prepare us to lose him once more; with new elections coming, our party would need a strong man to represent it in the cabinet.

The telephone was working again after lunch. Telegrams of concern and goodwill began to pour in from near and far. Offers of help and sympathy came from other kibbutzim, institutions, and organizations.

In our kibbutz, calm reigned once more. Here and there police officers confabulated with regional officials, or an adviser huddled with a curious journalist. Felix had forbidden us to talk to the press and the media, because when the time came to claim insurance, it would be best for us to put forth a unanimous version.

At a quarter past one, old Nevidomsky was brought home from the hospital, his dislocated shoulder carefully set and his arm in an impressive sling, waving greetings with his free hand. At half-past one, we were mentioned on the news. Again it was stressed that this had been neither a typhoon nor a tornado but simply a limited local phenomenon. Two conflicting winds, one from the sea and the other from the desert, had met and caused a certain amount of turbulence. Such phenomena were of daily occurrence over the desert, but in settled areas they were infrequent and the likelihood of a recurrence was remote. There was no cause for alarm, although it was advisable to remain on the alert.

Batya Pinski switched off the radio, stood up, and went over to the window. She peeped outside through the glass of the shutters. She cursed the kitchen team who had neglected their duty in the confusion and forgotten to send her lunch. They should know better than anyone how ill she was and how important it was for her to avoid strain and tension. In point of fact, she did not feel in the least hungry, but that did nothing to diminish her indignation. They've forgotten. As if I didn't exist. As if it wasn't for them and their pink-faced brats that Abrasha gave his life in a faraway land. They've forgotten. And Abramek's also forgotten what he promised; he's not coming today after all. Come, Abramek, come, and I'll give you some ideas for the jacket and the dedication. I'll show you the havoc the storm has wrought here. You're bursting with curiosity and dying to see it with your own eyes, only you have no excuse—why should the director of the party publishing house suddenly drop all his work and come and goggle at a disaster like a small child? So come. I'll give you your excuse, and I'll also give you some tea, and we'll talk about what we have to talk about.

She leaped across the room, spotting some dust on the bookshelf. She swept it away furiously with her hand. She stooped to pick up a leaf that had fallen from a potted plant onto the carpet. Then she drew Abramek Bart's letter from her dressing-gown pocket, unfolded it, and stared briefly at his secretary's signature; some Ruth Bardor, no doubt a painted hussy, showing her thighs; no doubt she's shaved her legs and plucked her eyebrows and bleached her hair; no doubt she wears see-through undies and smothers herself in deodorants. Goddamn her. . . . I've given those fish quite enough food for today. They'll get no more from me. Now here's another fly. I can't understand how they get in or where they hide. Perhaps they're born here. Kettle's boiling again. Another glass of tea.

11

After the embarrassing episode in the dining hall in the early forties, there were those among us who were glad that the affair between Batya Pinski and Felix had been broken off. But all of us were sad about the change that took place in Batya. She would hit her child even in the presence of other children. None of our advice or discussions did any good. She would pinch her till she was black and blue and call her names, including, for some reason, Carmen Miranda. The girl stopped wetting her bed, but instead started to torture cats. And Batya showed the first signs of asceticism. Her ripe, heady beauty was beginning to fade. There were still some who could not keep their eyes off her as she walked, straight and dark and voluptuous, on her way from the sewing room to the ironing room. But her face was hard, and around her mouth was an expression of disappointment and malice.

And she continued to discipline the child with an iron hand.

There were those among us who were uncharitable enough to call her a madwoman; they even said of her, "What does she think she is, a Sicilian widow, that cheap melodramatic heroine, that Spanish saint, that twopenny actress?"

When the founders of the kibbutz moved into the first permanent buildings, Batya was among them. Zeiger volunteered to build her an aquarium in her new house. He did this out of a feeling of gratitude. Zeiger was a thickset, potbellied, hirsute man. He was always joking, as if the purpose of life in general and his own life in particular was amusement. He had certain fixed witticisms. His good humor did not desert him even when his wife did. He said to anyone who cared to listen, "I am a mere proletarian, but Felix is going to be a commissar one day, when the revolution comes; I'd live with him myself, if he'd only have me."

He was a short, stocky man, who always smelled of garlic and tobacco. He moved heavily and clumsily like a bear, and there was an endearing lightheartedness about him even when he was accidentally shot in the stomach during illegal weapon practice in the old days. We were fond of him, especially at festivals, weddings, and parties, to which he made an indispensable contribution.

Ever since his wife left him, he had maintained a correspondence with a female relative, a divorcee herself, who lived in Philadelphia and whom he had never set eyes on. He used to call on Batya Pinski in the evenings, and she would translate the woman's letters from English into Yiddish and his comical replies from Yiddish into English. (Batya had taught herself English from the novels she read in bed at night.) He always apologized at the end of each visit for taking up her valuable time. But it was he who dug the flower bed in front of her new house, and raked it and mulched it and brought her bulbs and seedlings. His distinctive smell lingered in the room. Little Ditza loved to ask him riddles; he never knew the answers, or if he did he pretended not to, and she always laughed at his amazement when she told him.

One day he came with aluminum frames, panes of glass, a folding rule, a screwdriver, and a sticky, smelly substance which he referred to as *kit* but which Batya taught him to call putty.

"An aquarium," he said. "For fish to swim in. It's aesthetic. It's soothing. And it doesn't make a noise and it doesn't make a mess."

And he set to work.

Batya Pinski took to calling him Ali Baba. He willingly accepted this nickname, and responded by calling her "the Contessa from Odessa."

It was perhaps because of this nickname that little Ditza began to address Zeiger as Pessah. Although his real name was Fischel, we all came to call him Pessah, so that even in the kibbutz newsletter he was referred to as Pessah Zeiger.

210

Firmly but carefully he fitted the panes of glass into the soft bed of putty. At intervals he employed a tool which fascinated both Batya and Ditza—a diamond glass-cutter.

"How can we thank you for this beautiful present?" Batya asked when the aquarium was finished.

Zeiger pondered for a moment or two, breathed out a gust of onion and tobacco, winked to himself, and suddenly shrugged his shoulders and said, "*Chort znayet*"—which is to say, the Devil only knows.

The fish were brought in a jar and put into the aquarium with a great deal of fuss. Ditza had invited all her friends to a "fish party," which did not please Batya. That evening Zeiger brought, in addition to a letter from his relative in Philadelphia, a small flask of brandy.

"Won't you offer me a drink?" he said.

Batya poured him a drink and translated the letter and his reply.

That evening we were celebrating the Allied victory. The Second World War was over, and the monster had been vanquished. We flew the Zionist and socialist flags from the top of the water tower. At the nearby British army camp, there was a fireworks display, and in the small hours of the morning, soldiers came in army trucks to join in the singing and dancing. For once, the girls of the kibbutz saw fit to consent to dance with the British soldiers, despite their smell of beer. The dining hall was decorated with slogans and with a large portrait of Josef Stalin in uniform. Felix delivered a passionate oration about the pure new world which was about to be built on the ruins of the defeated powers of darkness. He promised us all that we would never forget those who had sacrificed their lives in this struggle, here and on distant frontiers. Then he pinned the victory badge printed by the Workers' Party onto Batya's lapel, shook her hand, and kissed her. We rose to our feet, sang the Zionist anthem and the "Internationale," and danced all night. At ten past three, Zeiger seized Batya's arm, dragged her almost forcibly out of the corner of the dining hall where she had been sitting silently all evening, and saw her to her room. His voice was hoarse and his white shirt was clinging to his back, because between dances he had taken it upon himself to act the clown, as if this had been an old-fashioned Jewish wedding. When they got to Batya's door Zeiger said, "That's it. You've had more than enough. And now, good night." He turned to go.

But she ordered him to come inside, and he obeyed her. She took off his sweaty shirt. When he asked if he could wash his face, she said neither yes nor no, but instead she switched on the light in the aquarium and turned off the overhead light. He began to apologize or to plead, but she cut him short by pressing him to her—sweaty, steaming, unwashed, and embarrassed—and conquered him in silence.

12

In a small village run on sound principles there are no secrets, nor can there be any.

Just before six o'clock in the morning, the neighbors saw Zeiger emerge, subdued, from Batya Pinski's door. By seven o'clock the news had already reached the sewing room. Some of us, including Felix and his wife Zetka (who had previously been married to Zeiger), saw a positive side to this new development; after all, the whole situation had been unnatural and full of unnecessary tensions. Now everything would be much simpler. Martyrdoms, Mediterranean tragedies, emotional arabesques were irreconcilable with the principles by which we guided our lives.

Even these people, however, could not accept what ensued with equanimity. Zeiger was the first, but he was not the last. Within a matter of weeks, news had spread of various peripheral characters finding their way to Batya Pinski's room at night. She did not even turn up her nose at refugees, or at eccentrics like Matityahu Damkov. Her silent, noble melancholy had become something better left unnamed. And her face was becoming ugly.

Within a year or two, even little Ditza was going around with soldiers and birds of passage. We were unable to devote our full attention to this unhappy episode, because the struggle to drive out the British was reaching its climax. Then regular Arab armies invaded the country; they reached the very gates of our kibbutz, and we repelled them almost empty-handed. Finally all was calm again. Hordes of refugees poured in from all directions. Zeiger's relative, a middle-aged woman, also came as a tourist and dragged him back to Philadelphia with her. We were all sorry to see him go,

212

and there were some who never forgave him. Felix accepted a central party position and only graced us with his presence on weekends. As for Batya, her last embers died. Ditza ran away again and again to the pioneering camps and the newly emerging settlements in the desert; again and again she was brought back. Her mother took to her room. She announced that her condition would not permit her to work any more. We did not know what this condition was, but we decided not to ask too many questions. We left her alone. We were all relieved when Ditza finally married Martin Zlotkin, the son of the well-known banker. Batya calmly accepted the marriage and the presents of expensive furniture from the young couple. The fish were now in the center of the picture. The electric kettle was always on the boil. It seemed as though it was all over with her when the matter of Abrasha's literary remains came up, and it was decided to publish his collected essays together with his letters from Madrid. Just as Felix had promised at the victory celebrations, we would not forget our comrades who had sacrificed their lives. And Felix, despite all his commitments, did not forget; he made the kibbutz movement publishing house finally tackle the job. The widow waited day by day. The fish swam across the picture without blurring it. They were cold but alive; they were not subject to the law of gravity, since they could hover effortlessly in the water. Last night's storm will bring Abramek Bart; but it's two o'clock already, and he hasn't come yet. A man like him will be able to understand the delicate matter of the dedication; he won't make any difficulties.

13

But I can't receive him in my dressing-gown. I must get dressed. I must tidy the room, if it's not tidy enough already. I must get out the best china, so that I can serve the tea properly. And open the shutters. Let some fresh air in. Freshen up the biscuits, too. But first of all, get dressed.

She went to the basin and washed her face repeatedly in cold water, as if to mortify her flesh. Then she ran her bony fingers over her face and hair in the mirror and said aloud, "There, there, you're a good girl, you're lovable, don't worry, everything's all right."

She made herself up slightly and brushed her gray hair. For an instant she caught a glimpse in the mirror of the old witch the

213

children called Baba Yaga, but at once that image was replaced by a noble, lonely woman unbowed by her suffering. She preferred the latter, and said to her: "No one else understands you, but I respect you. And the book is dedicated to Batya, a noble wife, the fruits of love and anguish." Just as she pronounced these words, she heard the squeal of brakes in the open space in front of the dining hall. She ran to the window, still disheveled because she had not had time to put the hairpins in place; she flung the shutters open and thrust her head out. Abramek Bart, director of the publishing house, got out of the car and held the door open for the secretary-general of the movement.

Felix appeared from nowhere to greet them both with a warm yet businesslike handshake and a serious expression. They exchanged a few words and walked off together to inspect the damage and the work of reconstruction which had been proceeding tirelessly since early in the morning.

14

She finished getting ready. She put on her claret-colored dress, a necklace, and an unobtrusive pair of earrings, dabbed a few drops of perfume behind her ears, and put the water on to boil. Meanwhile the blue daylight poured in through the open windows. Children and birds were shrilling joyfully. The streaming light seemed to dull the water in the aquarium. An old Spanish Civil War tune came back to her—a song compulsive and full of longing. In the old days, in the distant thirties, the Spanish freedom fighters and their sympathizers all over the world had been forever humming it. Abrasha could not stop singing it the night he left. A decade or so later, during the Israeli War of Independence, it had taken on Hebrew words and was sung around the campfires among the old shacks by pale-faced soldiers who had recently fled from Europe. Night after night, it had drifted among the kibbutz buildings and had even reached Batya Pinski:

> *The first dish to be served*
> *Is your beloved rifle*
> *Garnished with its magazines . . .*

She suddenly made up her mind to go outside.

Among the fallen trees and broken glass, she saw the sky peaceful

214

and clear over the hills, as if nothing had happened. She saw Matityahu Damkov, his bare back glistening with sweat, mending a water pipe with silent rage. And farther away she could see the empty spot where the wooden shacks, the first buildings of the kibbutz, had stood. Workers were rooting among the wreckage. A few goats were peacefully grazing.

She reached the open space in front of the dining hall at the very moment when Felix was escorting his guests back to their car. They were standing by the car, presumably running over the main points of their discussion. Up to that moment, Felix had kept his glasses in his shirt pocket; now he put them on again while he jotted down some notes, and at once he lost the look of a general and regained his habitual appearance of a philosopher.

Finally they shook hands once more. The visitors got into the car and Abramek started the engine. As he began to maneuver his way among the beams and scattered planks, Batya Pinski darted out of the bushes and tapped on the window with a wrinkled fist. The secretary-general was momentarily alarmed and covered his face with his hands. Then he opened his eyes and stared at the terrifying figure outside. Abramek stopped the car, wound the window down a fraction, and asked: "What's up? Do you need a lift? We're not going to Tel Aviv, though. We're heading north."

"Don't you dare, Abramek. Don't you dare leave out the dedication or I'll scratch your eyes out and I'll raise such a stink that the whole country will sit up and take notice," Batya screeched without pausing to draw breath.

"What is this lady talking about?" asked the secretary-general mildly.

"I don't know," Abramek replied apologetically. "I haven't the faintest idea. In fact, I don't even know her."

Felix immediately took command of the situation.

"Just a minute, Batya. Calm down and let me explain. Yet, this is our Comrade Batya Pinski. That's right, Abrasha's Batya. She probably wants to remind us of the moral obligation we all owe her. You remember what it's about, Abramek."

"Of course," said Abramek Bart. And then, as if assailed by sudden doubts, he repeated, "Of course, of course."

Felix turned to Batya, took her arm gently, and addressed her kindly and sympathetically: "But not now, Batya. You can see what a state we're all in. You've chosen a rather inconvenient moment."

The car, meanwhile, was disappearing around the bend in the road. Felix found the time to see Batya back to her room. On the way he said to her: "You have no cause to worry. We'll keep our promise. After all, we're not doing this just for your sake; there's no question of a personal favor to you. Our young people need Abrasha's writings; they will be the breath of life for them. Please don't rush us. There's still plenty of time; you've got nothing to worry about. On the other hand, I surmise that you didn't get your lunch today, and for that you have reasonable grounds for complaint. I'll go to the kitchen right away and tell them to send you a hot meal; the boilers are working again now. Don't be angry with us; it hasn't been easy today. I'll be seeing you."

15

There was still the aquarium.

Now the fish could get the attention they deserved. First of all, the old woman inspected the electrical fittings. Behind the tank was concealed a veritable forest of plugs and sockets, of multicolored wires, of switches and transformers, which kept the vital systems alive.

From a tiny electrical pump hidden underneath the tank two transparent plastic tubes led into the water. One worked the filter, and the other aerated the water.

The filter consisted of a glass jar containing fibers. The water from the bottom of the tank was pumped up into the filter, depositing the particles of dirt, uneaten food, and algae on the filter, and returned to the tank clear and purified. The aerator was a fine tube which carried air to the bottom of the tank, where it escaped through a perforated stone in a stream of tiny bubbles that enriched the water with oxygen and inhibited the growth of algae. These various appliances kept the water clear and fresh, enabling the fish to display their array of breathtaking colors, and to dart hither and thither with magical swiftness.

Another electrical fixture without which the aquarium could not function was the heating element, a sealed glass tube containing a finely coiled electric wire. The glowing coil kept the water at a tropical temperature even on rainy days and stormy nights. The

216

light and warmth worked wonders on the gray-green forests of water plants in the depths of which the fish had their home. From there, shoal after shoal emerged to pursue a course which was unpredictable because it was subject to unknown laws. The quivering tails suggested hearts consumed by longing, rather than mere pond life. The fish were almost transparent; their skeletons were clearly visible through their cold skins. They too had a system of blood vessels; they too were subject to illness and death. But fish are not like us. Their blood is cold. They are cold and alive, and their cold is not death but a liveliness and vitality which makes them soar and plunge, wheel and leap in mid-course. Gravity has no power over them.

The plants and stones emphasize this by contrast. The sight of a school of swordfish swimming gently through the hollow stone arouses a grave doubt in the widow's mind. Is death a possibility, and if so, why wait? Why not plunge in this very instant?

She presses her burning forehead against the glass. It feels as though the fish are swimming into her head. Here is peace and calm.

Breadth distracts the mind from depth. Depth also exists. It sends wave upon wave of dark stillness up toward the surface. And now the surface of the water reflects the crest-shorn palm trees.

The daylight fades and the windows darken.

Now she will close the shutters and draw the curtains. The kettle will boil again. More tea—this time in one of the china cups she has brought out specially. The fish are clustering around the underwater lamp as if they too can sense the approach of night.

A blue-tinged crystalline calm descends on our hills. The air is clear. The day's work is done. May she repose in peace. May the fish swim peacefully through her dreams. May she not be visited in the night by the crest-shorn palm trees. A last procession passes through the hollow stone. Darkness is coming.

1963

—translated by Nicholas de Lange

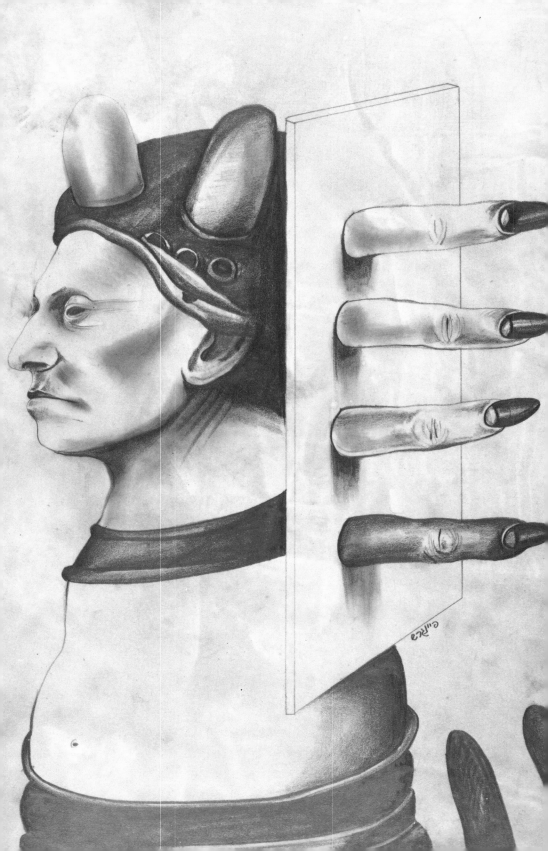

from A journey through the land of Israel
Pinchas Sadeh

Moses, or God's disappointment in love

And I entreated the Lord at that time saying, "My Lord God, thou hast only begun to show thy servant thy greatness. . . . Pray let me go over and see the good land that is beyond the Jordan, those fair mountains and the Lebanon." But the Lord was angry with me on your account and would not listen. And the Lord said to me, "Enough, say not to me another word about this matter."

I rarely have occasion to glance at the Book of Deuteronomy. Its rules and codes of law do not appeal to me. Given man's condition in the universe, it's my feeling that no saving grace can come from the pips he throws away after eating of the tree of the knowledge of good and evil. Yet as I leafed through the Bible one day, my eyes fell on the words, "And I entreated." I caught my breath and read them again: *And I entreated . . .* How curiously misplaced they seemed here!

I read on: *My Lord God . . . pray let me go over and see . . . but the Lord was angry with me . . . and would not listen.* Something tugged at my heart. I felt that my eyes were moist.

219

What on earth was the matter with me? The event had taken place many thousands of years ago. I looked up from the book. The shadowy room was lighted only by the reading lamp on my desk. No voices reached me from the city outside my window. The night sweltered with a dry desert heat. When I looked back at the printed page, it was as though the event were happening in front of me.

Once more I read the story—only four verses long and told by Moses himself—of how this titanic man had pleaded like a little child for one more thing before his death: to be allowed to see the goodly, longed-for, legendary land. *Pray let me go over and see . . . those fair mountains. . . .* But God cruelly refused him.

Yet was God really so cruel to you, Moses? True, He rejected your plea, and unkindly at that. Soon, however, you of all mortals were destined to die by a kiss from His own mouth, and He would bury you Himself in a canyon in the land of Moab, across from the plains of Jericho. What other man in history was ever privy to such great, such terrible, such lonely love as you?

2

So I mused while the words came to life in the shadowy stillness of my room. And yet it was obvious that God *had* been cruel to Moses. But why? Why be angry with him? It wasn't his fault. He had said so clearly himself: *on your account.*

It could only be, it suddenly occurred to me, that God had known some great disappointment, which He needed to pass on to Moses. It could only be—as absurd as it seemed—that God had been in some sort of trouble.

But what disappointment and what trouble, if it was possible to conceive of God's being in trouble at all? And even if it were, why treat Moses as He did? The more I thought about it, the stranger and more nebulous my thoughts became. Only with the greatest effort was I able finally to put them into words. First, though, I needed to reread the whole story of Moses from the beginning.

I leafed again through the pages of the book. "Now there went forth a man from the house of Levi and married the daughter of a Levite. And the woman conceived and bore a son; and she saw that he was in good health, and she hid him for three months." Yet death's shadow hung over the infant. Then comes the story of the cradle of reeds and Pharaoh's daughter, who comes to bathe in the Nile and finds the child crying. And the boy grew up, and he became her son, and she called him Moses.

Just as his origin is not without mystery, so nothing is told us of his youth. The years go by. "And Moses matured, and went out to his brethren, and saw their sufferings." He sees an Egyptian flogging a Hebrew and hurls himself on that Egyptian. Yet even in his anger he is prudent, for before slaying the oppressor he looks "this way and that, and sees that no man is watching." Nevertheless, he is compelled to flee. He escapes to the land of Midian, where he meets, as did Jacob in his flight from Esau, a girl by a well. Like Jacob, he goes to live in her father's house and takes her for his wife.

3

While tending his father-in-law's sheep, Moses comes to Mount Horeb. Nothing is known today of this mountain's location. It has been identified with Jebel Musa in the Sinai Peninsula, with the nearby Jebel Serbil, and with places much farther away. In any case, at the foot of Mount Horeb Moses sees a bush that burns on and on. He stares at the tongues of fire, which are nearly transparent in the shimmering desert air (at least so I imagine it, though nowhere does it say that the vision took place in daylight, and perhaps it happened at night), and resolves, "I will turn aside and see this great sight, why the bush is not consumed." How innocent is this curiosity of his, which alone, it would seem, entices him to approach closer.

"And when God saw that he had turned aside to look at it, He called to him out of the bush: 'Moses, Moses!' And he said: 'Here I am.' " At which point God informs him: "I am the God of Abraham, the God of Isaac, and the God of Jacob. . . . Go, for I am sending you unto Pharaoh." Moses now asks two questions. The first is about himself: "Who am I that I should go unto Pharaoh?" The second is, "But what if I should go to the Children of Israel and say to them, 'The God of your fathers has sent me to you,' and they say to me, 'What is His name?', what shall I tell them?" The second question is about God, yet the two are connected because man has no being apart from God.

God's answer to the first question is as much as a man might hope for: "For I will be with you!" In other words, my being will be yours. To the second question, however, His answer is elusive: "I am who I am." Perhaps such conundrums are characteristic of the language of the gods, for on the statue of the Egyptian goddess Isis it is said to have been written, "I am all that there is"; while engraved on the pyramid of Saïs were the words, "I am all that is, was, and will be." Jacob, too, when asking for the name of the angel he wrestled with through the night, received no clear answer. The answer is in the struggle, the darkness, the blessing, the experience itself. It cannot be given in names or words, or in any manner that the mind can grasp. It is beyond mind.

4

I continued to read about how Moses returned to Egypt. "And at a camping place in the course of his journey the Lord encountered him and tried to kill him." Nothing can adequately explain this macabre tale. Just a while ago God has lavished His grace upon Moses from the burning bush; now, in a reversal that might be fathomed in a moment of nightmarish madness but never in one of lucidity, He seeks to ambush and murder him on his way. Can it be, strange as it may sound, that God now regrets having revealed Himself to Moses and having sent him on his mission to Pharaoh? Or is God now revealing another side of Himself, not only different from, but actively opposed to, its predecessor? Perhaps the Bible is concerned with that side or face of God when it calls Him "a consuming fire," "vengeful and jealous," and when Paul writes that "it is terrible to fall into the hands of the living God." That is the face of God which makes "the hairs stand up on the flesh" of Job's friend Eliphaz when it appears to him in a dream; which reveals itself to Abraham, even while blessing Him, as "a great and awful gloom"; and of which Jacob exclaims upon awakening from his dream, "How terrible is this place!" Such infinite, indefinable dread is perhaps the original sense of the phrase "the fear of God." Man gazes for an instant into the abyss, then shuts his eyes again.

I myself knew such a moment of dread only once, a moment in which everything else seemed to drop right out of the world—and I knew then that I could never live through it again. But I also knew that whether or not I would have to did not depend on me. As the Psalmist, who generally seeks God's company, unexpectedly puts it, "Whither shall I flee from thee?" Sometime later I was moved to write a poem that began with the words, "I sue for mercy at the onset of the night." Lest that which comes suddenly will come. For then all defenses are down. And a man grows icy with fear. With the coming of the time of the abyss. Yea, You have created that too. And You know and You understand. I pray, then, if only it please You. For there is no other defense. I sue for mercy from God.

5

It is perhaps more than coincidence (though what it may signify I don't know) that both Moses and Jacob encounter this terrifying divinity on their way home; that is, on their way back to the homeland from which they have fled. Moreover, each has run away by himself and is now returning with a family. Can God's assault on Moses be connected with these facts? No one can say. At any rate, Jacob is physically injured in the struggle, while Moses' ordeal also ends with a bloody injury to his son. Nor is this all that the two have in common.

He who is destined to make contact with God must first break the laws of men and be compelled to flee. Jacob robs Esau of his birthright; Moses kills the Egyptian. Each seeks refuge—one in Haran, the other in Midian. Each encounters on arrival a maiden by a well, and for each this confirms that he is on the right path. True femininity, that which stands astride living water, is a source of confirmation in this world, of love and of life. Until her man comes, the maiden must stand and wait. She cannot drink from the well, whose waters flow under the bare soles of her feet, until Jacob rolls the stone from its mouth, or Moses drives away the bad shepherds.

6

The night was hot. Silence. I looked up from my papers and books. The clock said two A.M. A gecko darted from behind the bookcase. It moved slowly along the wall toward the circle of light thrown by the lamp on my desk. I knew this lizard who lived back of my books. I, too, am a creature of the night. There are spiders in my room also. They live their lives and I live mine. The gecko lay in ambush on the fringe of the circle of light, glued to the wall. It was petite, nearly transparent. A moth moved innocently toward it. The gecko regarded it frozenly. The moth came closer and was suddenly between its jaws. It beat its astounded wings but no succor came. I made a slight movement and the gecko glanced suspiciously around. It scrambled away with its prey between its teeth and disappeared behind the bookcase. I could still hear the flap of the moth's wings. In the darkness, death was taking place. There was unspeakable horror there. A small lizard and a blameless moth, yet what utter blackness. The underworld had opened its mouth to yawn.

Silence. I sat quietly smoking. Through the window I could see the pale sickle of a halo-limned moon. Shadows of trees. Of houses. For an instant I was almost sure that I saw, not far from me in the darkness, a short, burly, full-bearded man who reminded me of Tolstoy. There was just enough time for him to say, a roguish gleam in his eyes, "But suppose there isn't any God at all, eh?" And I knew that he had thought about it a great deal, a great deal. Quickly, for I had to answer before he could vanish, I said, "Well, what if you're right and there isn't? Tell me, then—what is there?" He had gone when I added, "In that case, we're simply right back where we started from."

7

I returned to my book and to the story of what happened to Moses at his camping place. It occurred to me that I must try to understand it, not from the divine point of view from which it is told—that is, in terms of God's nature—but from the human point of view, in terms of the man it happened to.

According to Moses—who can be presumed to have related it at a later date (from whom else could it have been known if not from him?)—God attacked and sought to murder him. Nothing in this story enables us to imagine what shape the attacker assumed, but no room is left for doubt that it was God Himself. Humanly speaking, it would seem, one cannot preclude the possibility of a moment of madness.

This moment happened to Moses on his way back, after the exhilarating experience by the bush, where he was cast in the role of prophet and redeemer. Not a word is said about his having been inwardly shaken by this experience, from which we may conclude that he underwent it undauntedly. Abraham, when God revealed

224

Himself to him, fell into a dark and frightful slumber. Ezekiel, after hearing God's call, "went bitterly in aggravation of spirit, and the Lord's hand was hard upon him." Nothing of this sort happened to Moses, yet perhaps the seed of the crisis to come was sown at that time. Now, on the way back, it bursts forth. The terrible dread of returning, of his mission, of his contact with God, awakens in him. In its light, God's face changes from one of lovingkindness to one of nightmarish aggression.

One may say that the human point of view is unimportant, and that the only perspective which matters here is God's. Yet because of our own inadequacy the divine perspective reveals itself only through the human one, which it wears like a mask upon its face.

8

I read on how Moses, accompanied by Aaron, comes to Pharaoh. "And they said to Pharaoh: 'Thus says the Lord, Let my people go.' And Pharaoh said: 'Who is the Lord that I should hearken unto him?' " And Moses was eighty years old.

Now all manner of miracles begin to happen. Moses turns the waters of Egypt to blood and strikes the country with frogs. He turns the earth into lice and sends vermin into the houses. He afflicts the people with pestilence, and with boils, and with hail, and with locusts. "And God said to Moses: 'Stretch out your hand to the sky, that darkness may fall.' . . . So Moses stretched out his hand to the sky, and there was thick darkness throughout the whole land of Egypt. . . . And God said to Moses: 'One more plague will I bring on Pharaoh, and then he will let you go.' . . . And at midnight God struck down all the first-born in the land of Egypt . . . and there arose a great cry." At which point Pharaoh summons Moses in the middle of the night and says, "Rise and go."

Once, when I was in the Louvre in Paris, my glance fell on a statue of Ramses II, who was, there is reason to believe, the Pharaoh of the biblical story. From what is known of him, he was one of the great kings of Egypt, a hard man whose wars and monuments cost the labors and lives of tens of thousands. Somewhere I read that he fathered one hundred sons and sixty daughters. I stood at length before the massive granite sculpture, whose height I judged to be twice that of an average man. Ramses sat upright, his hands on his knees, his eyes staring straight ahead. The shadow of a smile had frozen on his lips. A heavy, sphinxlike composure informed his whole being.

I thought then that Michelangelo, though he could not possibly have seen this work, must have had it in mind when he sculpted Ramses' rival. In the statue of Ramses there is a perfect equilibrium: neither time nor movement have any place here. Michelangelo's Moses, on the other hand, is all flow and fury. Here is the wanderer, the man who knows no rest until he dies of God's kiss. Momentarily I imagined these two grand works together, Pharaoh staring stonily ahead, Moses turning stormily leftward to face him, a wordless exchange passing between them.

9

Here I must say a few words about restlessness. I once read somewhere that a certain Hasidic tsaddik, I forget who, was asked why it is written in the Book of Psalms, "May God bless the house of Israel, may God bless the house of Levi, may God bless those who fear the Lord," rather than "May God bless the house of those who fear the Lord." His answer was that those who fear the Lord have no house. In all likelihood he meant that those who fear the Lord are so destitute that they never know from day to day if they will have a roof over their heads, but a second interpretation is possible. In the Bible there is an expression "to come to rest and to estate," a phrase which suggests that the two are connected; that is, that he who has an estate, a house, has rest. If it is not written of those who fear the Lord that they have a house, therefore, this must mean that they can have no rest. There is nothing restful about the fear of God. On the contrary, it must lead to restlessness, which is the true religious state.

The God of Israel is the Lord of Hosts. He is not like the gods of India, whom man perceives by staring at his navel until ultimate peace descends on him. He is a God of wandering and travel. A God who comes from the desert. A God of trial and contention. A God of conflict between opposites. A God who hides, and reveals Himself in the bush, and hides again.

10

The story goes on to tell how Moses brings the children of Israel out of Egypt and conducts them across the Red Sea while their pursuers drown. As soon as they reach the desert, they begin to complain: "Would that we had died in the Land of Egypt, where we sat by the pots of flesh!" Had these words been written in sand, they would have vanished long ago, but they remain in the book that I held as a distasteful memorial. Yet Moses continues to lead the rabble through a chain of forsaken places whose very names ring strangely in our ears: Sin and Dophka and Alush, Rephidim and Sinai and Kibroth-hattaavah (which means the Graves of Lust). And from Kibroth-hattaavah they journeyed to Rithmah, and from there to Rimmon-perez, and from there to Libnah. And from Libnah to Rissah, and from Rissah to Kehalah, and from Kehalah to Har Shefer, and from Har Shefer to Haradah (which means Anxiety). And from Haradah to Makheloth, and from Makheloth to Tahath (which means Bottom), and from Tahath to Terah, and to Mithkah, and to Hashmonah, and to Moseroth, and to Bene-jaakan. And from Bene-jaakan to Hor-haggidgad. Thus, slowly, the wanderers reach the fringes of civilization. From Hor-haggidgad they move on to Jotbah, and from Jotbah to Abronah, and from Abronah to Ezion-geber, and from Ezion-geber to Kadesh and the border of Edom. In this way they gradually approach the land of Canaan.

Perhaps—for who can say?—all these descents and foulings, these peregrinations from the Graves of Lust to the Bottom of Anxiety, are necessary. Perhaps one has to touch the bottom of the abyss before beginning the ultimate ascent, as a Polish Jew, Jacob Frank, was to declare some three thousand years later. Still, the story in the Bible is an obscure and tedious one—in spite of which, in the third month after leaving the land of Egypt, the Israelites reach the desert of Sinai, and camp opposite a mountain there while Moses ascends to God.

11

For forty days and forty nights Moses remains by himself with God. When he descends, the two tablets of the Law in his hands, he finds the people prostrating themselves at the foot of the golden calf, and is consumed by wrath. In a paroxysm of fury he takes the tablets, which are said to be God's own work, and smashes them on the ground. Moreover, we read that he assembles the Levites at the edge of the camp and commands them, "Let each of you fasten his sword on his hip and slay each his kinsman, his friend and his neighbor." And about three thousand of the people fell on that day.

What is it that arouses such wrath in the prophet that he breaks the tablets of the Law and seeks to slaughter his own people, or calls down destruction on the land it inhabits? What is it that makes him go bitterly in aggravation of the spirit, or sit catatonically among his countrymen, or take refuge in the desert, or lie for days on his side like a city under siege? It is the power of disgust. He, who has just come down from forty days and nights on the mountain, looks and sees the people wallowing before the golden calf, and cannot believe what he sees. He has seen the brevity of life, like a twinkle in an infinity of time, the terrible, stupendous riddle of man's existence; and he sees now how the common people are sunk in the fetid bog of their petty lies and concerns, their cowardice and obsequiousness, their trivial views and idiotic amusements, their sterile, fulsome culture and corrupt, sophisticated wisdom, their loathing for whatever is pure and sublime. And so disgust fills his soul. He has seen the necessity in all things and the flow in them; he has experienced pure, wild, cosmic joy; he has known the love that is in everything and the fear and death that are in everything; and he cannot fathom the distance between all this and the sneaking, insensate, vainglorious human existence that he sees. Disgust fills his soul. Yet still Moses does not abandon the people. When his anger is appeased, we read, he carves new tablets of the Law and ascends the mountain with them again. And he is there for forty days and forty nights, and he writes upon the tablets.

12
We read, too, that Moses says to God at this time, "Show me Thy glory." And God says, "You cannot see my face, for man cannot see me and live." And He says: "Here is a place by me. Station yourself on the rock; and when my glory passes by, I will put you in a cleft of the rock, and cover you with my hand until I pass by; then I will take away my hand, so that you may see my back; but my face may not be seen."

Moses wishes to see the combined profile of the compassionate and the jealous God, of the God of love and the God of death, of Him who speaks from the splendor of the bush and of Him who attacks in the solitary night. Not that either of these aspects is

228

untrue in itself, but to man they seem contradictory. Oppressively so. The rabbi of Kotsk once said: "Whatever is contradictory or paradoxical is called the back of God. His face, where all exists in perfect harmony, cannot be seen by man."

In order to enhance God's standing with the intellectuals of his age, Moses ben Maimon, commonly known as Maimonides, rigorously denied Him any possibility of assuming material form or shape. Perhaps he thought that he was doing God a favor. Moses ben Amram of the Bible thought differently. More than once, in defiance of all intellectualization, he saw God explicitly, in the flesh.

13

I read on about how, before they have gone very far from Mount Sinai and the events that occurred there, the children of Israel burst out crying: "O that we had flesh to eat! We remember the fish that we used to eat for nothing in Egypt, the cucumbers, the melons, the leeks, the onions, and the garlic; and now our souls are dry." Hardly have they done quarreling with Moses over the spiritual dehydration brought on by lack of garlic when his sister Miriam and his brother Aaron begin maligning him for having married a Negro woman. Yet all this contention, strife, backbiting, and stupidity notwithstanding, the people keep moving through the desert until they reach Kadesh. Here great weeping and wailing break out when the twelve spies return from Canaan. "Let us turn around and go back to Egypt," the people say to one another. At the very height of all this hatred, this despair and futility, when the people are on the verge of rising up and stoning Moses to death, the glory of God, we are told, appears again. And God says to Moses, "Tell them that their corpses shall fall in this desert."

Still the living corpses move on, driven by their leader's restlessness, by his dream, by his God. At some unspecified place in the desert, Korah and his backers stage an insurrection and charge Moses with being a mountebank who is leading them to disaster. And Moses is exceedingly wroth. In the desert of Zin his sister Miriam dies, she who stood by the Nile as a young girl to see what befell his cradle of reeds. How many years have gone by since then! Thence they journey to Hor Hahar, where his brother Aaron dies too, close to the land of Edom. Of Tsippora, Moses' first wife, we hear nothing; perhaps she too is long dead. Nor are Moses' sons ever mentioned. He is now an utterly lonely man, as perhaps he has always been by nature. Nowhere do we read of his ever having had a friend or a lover; his only converse is with God. He is old now too, fantastically old.

14

Still the people continue to wander, through complaints that the bread is bad, through wars with the Midianites and the Amorites, with the king of Arad and the king of Bashan. Roundaboutly, indirectly, they approach the land of Canaan. In one of their resting places, Moses has a wondrous vision of that land.

The land to which you are coming, Moses says, is not like the land of Egypt. What is the land of Egypt? It is a land where "You sowed your seed and watered it on foot like a garden by your house." In contrast, says Moses, the Promised Land is one that drinks rainwater from the sky, "A land for which the Lord your God cares, the eyes of the Lord being always upon it."

When Rabbi Simha Bunim of Pszyscha was asked what kind of curse it was for the serpent to have to eat earth, since this was a food that would always be available, he answered: "Man is condemned to eat bread by the sweat of his brow, so that if he wearies of his labors he will cry out to God. Woman is condemned to bring forth children in hardship, so that if her pain proves too great she will weep before God. Especially in their distress they remain linked to God. But God has given the serpent everything it needs, so that it will never turn to Him again."

The land of Egypt is the land of the serpent. The Promised Land is the land of man. It is the land of his true condition, which is always a religious one. This is the whole Torah in a nutshell.

15

The sky is still dark in my window. Distant stars twinkle placidly. The houses are indistinct forms. Silence. A streetlight shines quietly at the corner. I sit staring into the darkness.

Whom am I writing this for? The paper I write on is white, yet the universe answers in black. The earth answers with silence.

Only death is worth writing about. To ask, to explain. But these aren't the words.

230

God. But these aren't the words. I have no words.

16

The sky has turned gray. Dawn. The antennas on the rooftops reach up like crosses. The treetops nod slowly in the dawn breeze. Birds. One, very close, calls something that sounds like "jug, jug." "Jug jug jug jug jug."

I must have fallen asleep at my desk. I must have dreamed. I was in a strange land, at night. Perhaps in a small hotel, which was empty and deserted. Not a soul was in the rooms except for a young girl who sat in one of them alone. In my own room, an oil lamp hung from the ceiling. The oil was running low and I was afraid the wick would go out. I climbed on a chair to add oil. It was difficult because the ceiling was so high.

There was a second dream, too. I was in a strange cellar. Next to me, by a small window, sat an unfamiliar girl spinning on a staff. A pure, white light fell delicately through the window onto a square of bright fabric. I think now that there must have been something pagan about her. She told me that she liked to spin.

17

Morning light. A bright sky. I returned to my book and reached the end of the tale. At that time, says Moses, "I entreated the Lord saying, 'My Lord God, thou hast only begun to show thy servant thy greatness. . . . Pray let me go over and see the good land that is beyond the Jordan, those fair mountains and the Lebanon.' But the Lord was angry with me on your account and would not listen. And the Lord said to me, 'Enough, say not to me another word about this matter.'

"Then from the steppes of Moab Moses ascended Mount Nebo, the headland of Pisgah, which faces Jericho, and the Lord showed him all the land—Gilead as far as Dan, all Naphtali, the territory of Ephraim and Manasseh, all the territory of Judah as far as the last sea, the Negev, and the valley of Jericho, the city of palms, as far as Zoar. . . . And Moses, the servant of the Lord, died there in the land of Moab by the mouth of the Lord. And he was buried in the valley of Moab opposite Beth-peor; but to this day no one knows where."

Not long ago, some 3,500 years later, I, a fortuitous and unknown man, stood on the plateau above Jericho and looked down on the badlands of Moab to the east of the Jordan, and at the mountains of Edom and Moab and Gilead, and at Mount Nebo. I turned around to look at the mountains to the west, and for a moment I could scarcely believe that I was standing on the land to which Moses wished to come and could not. For who was I? The earth I stood on was hard and dry. It was flowerless, unattractive, untouched by any green; yet it was the earth which Moses loved and to which he wished to come. I didn't think then of the thousands of dead Israelites who had fallen in the desert before him; I thought only of him. For a few minutes I stood in the sun by myself until something told me to bend down and scoop up a bit of hard soil. I looked at it. I wanted to see what he, in his love for it, had so pleaded to come to. I put it to my lips and kissed it, for him.

18

When I first read Moses' plea and God's harsh answer, the thought occurred to me—and I was taken aback by the strangeness of it—that perhaps God was in trouble. Perhaps, I reflected, God had known some kind of love, and His trouble was that He had met with disappointment.

In the tenth chapter of Deuteronomy, Moses says: "Yet the Lord set His heart on your fathers to love them, and choose their descendants." He speaks of love in the preceding verse too, when he says, "And now, O Israel, what does the Lord your God require of you but to stand in awe of the Lord your God, and to walk in all his ways, and to love him. . . ." A few verses further on, he puts the demand of love first: "So you must love the Lord your God, and keep all His statutes, ordinances and commandments." Moses often calls God a jealous God—and jealousy, too, we know, is a sign of love. For according to Moses, who is (if such a person can be said to have existed at all) the most competent of all human experts on God's being, God wishes to be loved back in requital for His love. Five hundred years later, with unequaled clarity, the prophet Hosea makes the same point: when the people whore after strange gods, he declares, it is exactly the same as when his own wife betrays him with other men. Indeed, when a son is born to him, God commands him to call it Lo-ami, "Not-my-people," and explains that "you are not my people and I will not be your God." God's disappointed

232

love, the polluting of the trust between Him and His people, causes a rupture of the relationship. Yet one day, the prophet asserts, God will fall in love with His people—beloved all over again. "And I will betroth you forever; and I will betroth you in justice, and in lovingkindness, and in mercy; and I will betroth you in faith, and you shall know the Lord." Of all these expressions of love, the last is the most pregnant with meaning. Love that is unaccompanied by knowledge of the beloved, of his existential dilemma, has no lasting value. Love cannot do without knowledge. Fourteen hundred years and many historical metamorphoses afterward, another Israelite, the apostle John, points out in an epistle, "In this is love, not that we loved God, but that he loved us." We love Him back *because* He loved us first.

This mystic sense of divine love was not born with Christianity. It was always at the heart of the biblical concept of God. Jesus, in the mystery of his suffering and of his vision, understood what Moses had been through.

19

In fact, all human history may be viewed as a story of God's disappointment in love.

As far as the human understanding can grasp it, the prophets understood this. For what does a prophet's appearance signify? He cannot be understood until we understand how he understood God. And the prophet is the man who senses God's tragic dilemma. Hosea arrived at this sense of God as a result of his own wife's infidelity. Others did so not from personal analogy, but from a primal, cosmic intuition. In Moses' case, this developed into an almost human friendship, for we read that "No prophet has ever appeared in Israel like Moses, whom God knew face to face." No prophet whom God so chose, so loved, so frightened when He came to kill him, so repeatedly spoke to, so harshly rejected, and so utterly kept for Himself in the end, making even of his burial place a secret, a crypt forever apart from the wretched, senseless whirlpool of time and men.

In his innermost being, the prophet does not exist for the people. The people are the stage on which the mystery play of God's unrequited passion is acted out among men. The people are God's disappointment. In vain are all His signs and miracles, in vain His display at Mount Sinai, in vain Nebuchadnezzar and Auschwitz. The prophet exists for God, as though—if such a thing is conceivable—by means of an inner identification with Him, of an empathy with His sorrow and disappointment. As though to show Him that He is not alone.

20

What, then, is the prophet to do? The life of each prophet has something sacrificial about it. At the same time, each speaks with loathing of ritual sacrifice and burnt offerings, because such things have nothing to do with true sacrifice of self, which alone can lead to contact between the human and the divine. The sacrifices in the Temple seem to them a cheap joke—a joke aimed not so much at themselves and at the sacrifice they have made as at something infinitely greater, at the mysterious tragedy of God.

Few men in human history have understood this as well as the Galilean who offered himself up in fulfillment of the Psalmist's words, "Sacrifice and offering thou dost not desire, burnt-offering and sin-offering thou dost not demand, so lo, said I: here I come." Paul, in his Epistle to the Hebrews, comments, "He entered into the Holy Place, taking not the blood of goats and calves, but his own blood."

21

The Law states that the adulterous woman must die. "And you shall be holy unto me," God says through Moses, "because I am holy." One must understand these words not only as a commandment but as a plea. As the woman who cheats strikes at the roots of her husband's existence, so the people that cheat strike at the roots of God's holiness, which is essential to His being. Only this mystery, which cannot be grasped with the intellect, explains the thought of the prophets, who perceived a connection between the pollution of life and its destruction. The adulterous woman must die. Yet the blood price is not necessarily paid by those who are least worthy or most evil. Perhaps this is because, as the Bible tells us, a sacrifice is invalid when the body of its bearer is imperfect. Whoever belongs to the people that God, for mysterious reasons of His own, chose for Himself in antiquity, is equally responsible; yet this responsibility rests most heavily on the best and most highly endowed. This is why Moses must die in distress without reaching his destination, why the prophets are always the victims, why Akiva was martyred by the Romans, why Jesus must be crucified. Perhaps this is why six million men, women, and children who bore no personal blame of their own, but nevertheless bore the consequences of God's ancient choice, were burned alive in the furnaces of Europe.

Some 160 years ago, Rabbi Nachman of Bratislav dreamed a dream. "In my dream," he relates, "I saw that it was the Day of Atonement. And I understood right away that on each Day of Atonement one person is picked to be sacrificed by the high priest. And since they were looking for that person, I volunteered to be him. And I was asked to put it in writing, and I did. Yet when they wished to sacrifice me, I repented and sought to hide. How could I hide, though, when that great crowd of men was around me? I managed to escape from the city; yet no sooner had I done this than I returned to it again, and behold! here I was in the city once more. Then I sought to hide among the nations of the world, though I knew that if anyone came to demand me from their hands they would surely yield me up. In the end, someone was found to be sacrificed in my place. Nevertheless, I fear for the future."

Jerusalem

1. *Back to the Goldin house in a dream*

Last night I returned to the Goldin house in a dream.

Over the years, I'd revisited it several times while awake. The look of the neighborhood hadn't changed. Neither had the street I once lived on. There were still ten houses on it, two of them synagogues, all pretty much the same.

I never entered the Goldin house itself during these visits, nor did I climb the winding wooden staircase to the roof, under which was hidden the small room I had lived in for a while when I was young. I simply stood on the sidewalk and looked up at it. For a long time. And then went my way.

Who knows, perhaps I held back because there had been changes in the house itself. In my own time it had been anonymous. The late

235

Mr. Goldin was a jeweler. Among his tenants were a baker, a carpenter, a shopkeeper, and a *yeshiva* student. All of them still lived on the second floor, but the ground floor, to my surprise, had become institutionalized. A small sign above a doorway informed me that here were the offices of the Charitable Souls Society, while another sign announced that soon, with G–d's help, a medical clinic for the needy would be opened here.

Charitable institutions are a fine thing. Still, I couldn't help remembering a story I once read about a young man who left his father's house and, after much wandering, succeeded in becoming an author of books. One day he returned to the place of his birth and found that it had been made into a public library. The sad mockery of it did not escape him.

Last night, then, I dreamed that I returned to the Goldin house.

I returned at sundown, on a Friday, on the eve of the sabbath. I entered the courtyard, climbed the stone stairs to the second floor, and then the wooden stairs to the roof. I encountered no one, and before I knew it dusk had fallen. My small room was exactly as I had left it years before. There was the same wobbly table by the light of whose kerosene lamp I had written my first poems, the same primus stove on which I used to make tea, the same dilapidated sofa with bits of seaweed sticking out through the ripped upholstery. A page of poetry I had once wanted to write and never did lay on a chair. Now it was written, but I didn't touch it. A thick film of dust covered everything.

I stood in the darkness leaning against the railing of the roof. In the synagogue below, a crowd of men had assembled for the sabbath eve prayer. A light shone through a transom window in the house across from me.

Behind that window lived a young woman who was tall and white. I didn't know who she was, and all I could see of her face was its whiteness. Her hair was black, and her lips were the color of mulberries.

Every sabbath eve at this time she took a bath. The lighted transom was the window of her bathroom.

I saw steam. Hot water started filling the tub. A white mist covered the window. In its vapors stood the white woman.

She started taking off her dress. In the candlelit synagogue below, the first half of the sabbath eve prayer began. I could hear the voices of the men singing: *O let us give joyous praise to the Lord, let us lift our voice to the rock of our salvation . . .*

She let her dress drop. Only her head and shoulders were visible in the steam. Then these vanished too, and I knew that she was in the water.

I stood in the darkness, listening to the cantor below. *To greet the sabbath let us rise. For there our chiefest blessing lies.* And the congregation answered him: *Come, O come ye by my side. Come to greet the sabbath bride.*

The cantor's voice rose a pitch: *To the holy palace of the king. Rise, beloved, rise, take wing.* I could tell the words by the melody, and I knew that the white woman was stretched out in the water.

I waited for her to reappear, but there was only steam. I knew she must be soaping her white body.

The cantor's voice rose from below: *Shake off the dust thou slumb'rest in. Put on thy bridal diadem.*

And the congregation answered him: *Come, O come ye by my side. Come to greet the sabbath bride.*

Above me, as on the nights when I had stood here awake, stretched the deep sky. One window alone was lit in the darkness, and I knew that soon I would see her.

Be not ashamed, O be not ashamed. For soon the king shall call thy name. . . . Come, O come ye by my side. Come to greet the sabbath bride.

She rose from the water and stood drying her hair. Her two breasts quivered slightly.

In the synagogue the song gathered strength. *Then all thy haters shall be hated. And thy beraters be berated. The Lord shall come to thee, elated. As cometh the bridegroom to the bride.* And the congregation answered: *Come, O come ye by my side. Come to greet the sabbath bride.*

She stood drying her breasts and her back in the steamy light, and I stood in the quiet quiver of the dark. She raised one long white leg and began to dry it, slowly, and then, through the steam, against the whiteness of her skin, I saw something like a patch of black grass. At that moment the quiver overcame me, and some stupendous being spread its wings inside me and took off and was gone, and I shut my eyes, and from below came the voice of the cantor beginning the second half of the sabbath eve prayer: *Bless ye the Lord who is blessèd*. And the congregation answered him: *Blessed be the Lord who is blessèd for ever and ever*.

2. *Mount Zion*

After many years I ascended Mount Zion again. The old dirt track was overgrown with weeds, and I took the stairs instead. Various signs greeted me, some with verses from the Bible, others announcing institutions and shops. A guard stopped me at the entrance to King David's tomb and lent me a skullcap. Four men were reciting psalms by the catafalque. Tourists of both sexes circulated through the dank interior beneath massive Gothic vaults. I climbed the minaret outside. A wind was blowing. Across from me, its tombstones gleaming whitely, was the Mount of Olives, and beyond it the mountains of Moab, screened by blue haze. When I looked at the nearby church steeple I saw that the holes from the shells that had hit it during the 1948 war, when I was first here, were still visible. Doves of peace were roosting in them now.

I climbed back down. I had time on my hands, and so I lingered for a while in the crypt beneath the vaults. Next to me sat a man behind a small table, selling certificates in testimony that the bearers thereof had trod in this holy place.

There was nothing to make me feel that this was really David's grave—nor had there been anything back then, during the war. At the time, it was true, I hadn't known that the tradition was a late one, originating apparently with the medieval traveler Benjamin of Tudela. The biblical City of David, in a corner of which the king no doubt lies, was hundreds of meters northeast of here. The Christian tradition that the Last Supper took place on this site, where the Church of the Dormition now stands, is undoubtedly much older, for the writings of St. Epiphanus and, after him, of St. Cyril date it back to as far as the third century. Then, though, I knew nothing about this either. No one had told me about it, nor had I encountered it in any book.

Throughout those days and nights, however, I had sensed something primeval, dark, about the place.

The wall of the Old City had loomed grayly before me by day, blackly at night. An Arab sniper lurked behind its apertures. No one dared set foot in the narrow lane between the church and the wall. It was enchanted ground. Whoever infringed on it paid with his life.

I used to stare at the wall from our firing positions in the church as though bewitched. Only a few dozen paces lay between me and it, yet they led through the gates of death.

Sometimes, at night, I would sit by one of the windows in the church and send long bursts of fire from my machine gun at the wall, like a jackal howling at the moon. Invisible in the darkness, the mouths of the wall lit up in return each time the hidden machine gun opposite me flashed quickly back. The sound of my own gun, though deafening, was like a musical drumroll, and I liked the smell of the burned powder.

I saw no newspapers, had no radio, read nothing, heard nothing. I knew nothing about the conduct of the war, about where it was being fought or who was winning or losing it. Nor did I waste my time thinking about it. It had simply fallen on me from out of the blue, and I accepted it for what it was.

Forgotten fragments, like scenes from a dream, came back to me now.

When the fighting began, before I was sent to Mount Zion, I spent a few days in an Arab neighborhood of Jerusalem called Musrara, in a rear position near the broadcasting station. There had been a piano in one of the studios there, and I used to shut myself up in the dark, soundproofed room and hammer away on it, though I knew nothing about music at all.

All the houses of Musrara had been abandoned, as though in a dream. In some of them, food was still left on the tables, yet you couldn't find a living soul in them. From time to time Jews would come, soldiers or civilians, to loot what rugs, furniture, or radios were left. What they wanted any of it for was beyond me. The world was totally spiritual then, totally religious: all its conventions and givens had melted away, shells whistled through the air like flying angels of death, and one could have really died at any minute. Yet even I made off with something, a small reproduction of Van Gogh's *Sunflowers* that I found on somebody's wall. It cheered me to have it, because Van Gogh and Gauguin were my two favorite painters in those days. I can still remember that yellow.

Afterward, in Abu Tor, a neighborhood separated from Mount Zion by hell on earth, I found an abandoned house with a room that was empty except for an armchair and a large mirror. I used to sit for hours in the depths of the chair, opposite the mirror, writing poems on a pad of stationery that bore the letterhead of an Arab commercial firm.

I liked best climbing at night onto the roof of that house in Abu Tor, a neighborhood named after a comrade-in-arms of Saladin, and throwing hand grenades from it at the Arab position down the street. It didn't accomplish much, but I had a weakness for the sudden flash, and for the thud of the explosion that followed.

Later, on Mount Zion in the Church of the Dormition, from which the Virgin Mary supposedly ascended in her sleep to heaven, I used to sit for long periods in the forsaken cells of the monks. Thus I managed to live in a variety of times at once, among them my own and the Middle Ages.

Now and then I would descend into town. The connecting passageway was a low, narrow tunnel that had been dug to the Jewish neighborhood of Yemin Moshe. You had to traverse it doubled over, like a worm burrowing through the earth. Once in the city, I went to see two girls I knew, Hava and Ada. Sometimes, walking along a deserted street, it would occur to me that I was living to see the fulfillment of Nietzsche's words that man's destiny in life was to be a warrior and woman's to be his paramour. The thought amused me, since—with a helmet shaped like a chopping bowl on my head and army pants a size too big for me that kept threatening to fall off—I looked like anything but a prophetic vision of the Übermensch. In general, though, those walks were a strange hallucination of empty city blocks, bloodstained sidewalks, suddenly shrieking shells, thirst, and a smell of sperm and sweat.

Those days were distant. Now I stood on the mount by the Old City wall, opposite Zion Gate, but neither mount, wall, nor gate was what it had been. Those days belonged to such another world and such another time that I could almost have believed that the war I took part in had been fought in crusader times, or back in the age of Joshua.

3. *Me'a She'arim*
The streets are narrow here. They wind among the columns of the houses like the spaces between the lines on a page of the Talmud.

Small, crooked alleyways, like letters of Rashi script.

Me'a She'arim, Bet Yisra'el, Batei Ungarn, Sha'arei Hesed.

How many nocturnal hours I spent wandering through these alleys during the years I lived in the area. Deathly silent hours of the night, when you could hear a pin drop. When the only sound was the echo of my footsteps on the cobblestones.

In the houses, behind latticed windows, Jews were covered by slumber as the fallen Israelites in the desert were covered by sand.

Sometimes I would pass a house of study. Through the window, by the light of a feeble, yellowish electric bulb, I would see two or three young students bent over their books, rocking softly back and forth while they chanted the ancient Aramaic words of the Gemara in a melancholy murmur: *Thus say the rabbis . . . wherefore Rabbi Levi bar Hama differs with Rabbi Hanina . . . on the one hand, this one says . . . and on the other hand, this one . . .* the torts and case laws of the Talmud . . . the world of Rava and Abayei, of Rav Ashi and Rabbi Abahu. . . .

Sometimes I would stop to read one of the placards affixed to the walls. Proclamations, prohibitions, excommunications. "In the name of our rabbis and officers of the Law, may they live in peace, amen. . . . Be it hereby made known . . . For as when the time of the Messiah grows nigh, heresy and apostasy stalk the streets. . . . And whereas on account of our innumerable sins the wicked thrive and prosper . . . Wherefore the Holy One Blessed Be He bestows on them success that we may be brought into temptation and withstand it. . . . May the Compassionate One have mercy on us and save us. . . . For Thou alone, O Lord our God, shall rule over us. . . . And may it be granted us to see the coming of the Redeemer. . . ."

Today I have come here on a workaday afternoon. Women are shopping in the market. Men are about their business. My eye is caught by a large notice on the wall. "Help!!!" it says. Its contents are trivial, but I know that all such cries here are essentially addressed to God.

Nearby stands a pretty boy with a proud, wise look on his face. A little scholar of the Law.

To tell the truth, I could never identify with these people (for if I could, I would have come to live with them as an observant Jew) who live by the rule of the Torah and its codes. To be religious, in my terms, means to understand that life is a parable of which God is the meaning—that is, to live life as a struggle to make contact with the divine. Somewhere else I have written about the instructive historical fact that the official codification of the Bible in the days of Ezra the Scribe was accompanied by the cessation of prophecy—in other words, by the drying up of the previously renewable source of human contact with God.

And yet still I feel close to them, these people who live as though in a fortress under siege, surrounded by a secular world they disdain and by a "culture" that revolts them. Their life is without compromise, without concessions. It is a waiting for the Messiah.

When I was called to the army to fight in the War of Independence, it grieved me to think that I might have to die defending the Hebrew University, or the bourgeoisie of Rehavia, or the offices of the press. These and many other things meant nothing to me then and mean nothing to me now, nor do I hesitate to say so. But the Torah is something else. I have no difficulty understanding that whoever believes in it must be ready to die for it. One must never refuse to be a martyr for God. There can be no other significance to life beside worshiping Him. The rest is simply a question of how one understands this worship—that is, of how one understands God.

Worshiping God, as the phrase suggests,* has nothing to do with pleasure or cultural frills. It is work, hard work, like paving a road, or farming land, or building a house. In general, I don't believe that the purpose of life in this world is to snatch a little pleasure here or there. If it were, we might as well have been born bedbugs. In whatever we live and do—in our happiness, our suffering, our love, our hate, our passions, our thoughts—we must live and do it not just for itself, but as a parable, as a question, as a war. As work. As worship.

What is man? Man is a question. God is the answer. If the answer were available here, in this life, the question would be unnecessary. The painful tension between the two gives life its energy.

4. *Snow*

It is snowing on Jerusalem. It is snowing on its walls.

* In Hebrew the word for "worship", *avoda*, is the same as the word for "work." *Translator*.

Snow falls on the Temple Mount. Snow falls on the Dome of the
Rock.

Snow falls on Mount Zion. And on the Holy Sepulchre.
Snow falls on Sheikh Jarrah and on Al-Ghazali Place.

Faces of snow peer through the windows on the Via Dolorosa:
Faces of priests and of Levites and of *yeshiva* boys in black hats.

Beneath a sky of snow he walks slowly by himself.
Snowflakes in his hair, his head sunk on his chest.

Only women follow him, white women in dresses of snow:
Mary Magdalene who loves him, weeping tears of snow as she
walks,

And Mary his mother, and Mary the mother of James, and that
other Mary, the Mary of snow.
Follow him, dear women, for he is cold by himself in the snow.

Through the Gate of Ephraim they pass, onto a field that is
shrouded in snow.
There in the snow will rise the cross which he will ascend with
outstretched arms.

Drops of sweat will drip from his brow that is covered with thorns of
snow
As into his hands and feet are driven four nails of snow.

Snow falls on Jerusalem. It is snowing on all the mountains.
On the Temple Mount and Mount Zion, on Sheikh Jarrah and Wadi
Joz.

And the women at his feet can see in sunlight of snow
How slowly he melts before their eyes, like a man made of snow.

With him melt the white women, Mary Magdalene who loves
him,
And Mary his mother, and Mary the mother of James, and that
other Mary, the Mary of snow.

—translated by Hillel Halkin

243

POETRY

We shall live forever
Yehuda Amichai

We shall live forever.
The earth will weigh her fruits
with yesterday's dead. And the vine
will drape the quarry. Who sings
in this ripening solitude, this hardening of stone,
these seasons? Precision of fruit form will be demanded,
candor on their night of love; their flight
will be no flight, and their joy
will break all dark vows. A pretext,
soft and large, will protect them too.

We shall live forever.
The kingdom of the deceived will not collapse
even if we learn the cause of trees, reason of thorns
and water, the number of the dead in lust.
The quality of stone is in all. Put another way:
flaming hair, picture of a strange wedding,
the heritage of a veil. A somnambulist bride turning round
in the empty circle, smiling. Childhood of smiles.
Alternatively: reflections of a nomad God.
And the heart of my love like a trumpet's mouth, suddenly
out of the dark. Contrariwise: my heart
lying on my drying body, like a thrashing fish
singing with distorted mouth lest it suffocate on land.

Or: me and my window. A window being widened
to become a door, my entrances, additional stories
in houses. Families grow. We shall live forever.

Wait for me at the ruins of the crusader's castle.
What a plan it was—the defense of the already disintegrated.
Wait for me there at evening
with your body already in darkness and your naked hair
still light, reddish, catching
the last suns of the day. We live
forever.

For I have a mezuzah on my doorpost.
Not the one with sacred writ on parchment—
quiet cradle songs of my childhood—
but a mezuzah full of wind blowing
out of distance. This one I will kiss
with a hand holding and surrendering at once.
Now we shall know of the exile of water in tears,
in rain, in wells, in ocean and in blood.
We live, we live.

Small interrogatives still
ferry us to the black ships
that couldn't approach: they are too large and too terrible.
They lie out at sea
pointed in the direction of their destination,
and their smoke is timeless.

—*translated by Ruth Nevo*

When I was a child
Yehuda Amichai

When I was a child
grasses and masts grew on the shore,
and, lying there,
I didn't distinguish between them
because they all rose skyward above me.
Only my mother's words stayed with me,
like a sandwich wrapped in crackling paper,
and I didn't know when my father would return,
for there was a forest beyond the forest.

Everything put out its hand.
A bull butted the sun with its horns,
and at night the street lights stroked
my cheek and the walls,
and the moon, a great jug, leaned over
and watered my thirsty sleep.

—*translated by Ruth Nevo*

246

The old ice factory
Yehuda Amichai

The old ice factory
in Petach-Tikvah—a low wooden tower
with boards rotting black—
there in my childhood lived weeping.
I remember the tears dripping
from board to board,
soothing angry summer,
making ice below,
white ice, gliding
from a deep opening.
And behind the dark cypresses
a voice saying,
"You live only once."
I didn't understand then.
I understand now, too late.

Cypresses still stand there
and the water drips somewhere else.

—translated by Bernard Knieger

Here
Yehuda Amichai

Here, under the kites that the kids fly
and those caught by last year's telephone wires, I stand
with the branches of my silent decisions
grown strong within me, and the small birds
of hesitation in my heart, and the great rocks of hesitation
before my feet, and my two eyes that are twins,
one of which is always busy and the other
in love. And my gray pants
and green sweater, and my face that absorbs
color and reflects color, and I don't know

what else I reflect and receive
and transmit and reject,
and how I've been an exchange mart for many things.
Export. Import. Frontier post. Customs barrier.
Watershed and graveyard. Meeting place. Departure point.

The wind comes through treetops and pauses
at every leaf; nevertheless, it passes
without stopping, and we
come and stay a while, and fall.

So much similarity in the world; like sisters:
thighs and hill slopes. A distant thought
like an act that grew here in flesh and hill;
like cypresses, dark events on the ridge.
The circle closes. I am its buckle.

Until I discovered that my hard forefathers
were soft inside, they were dead.
All the generations before me are circus acrobats,
standing on each other's shoulders.
Generally I'm at the bottom, with all of them,
a heavy weight, on my shoulders.
But sometimes I'm on top: one hand raised high
toward the Big Top. And the applause
in the arena below
is my reward, my blood.

—*translated by Ruth Nevo*

Lament
Yehuda Amichai

Mr. Beringer, whose son
fell by the Canal, which
was dug by strangers
for ships to pass through the desert,
is passing me at the Jaffa gate:

He has become very thin; has lost
his son's weight.
Therefore he is floating lightly
through the alleys
getting entangled in my heart
like driftwood.

—*translated by Ted Hughes*

The sweet breakdown of Abigail
Yehuda Amichai

We hit her with little blows
like an egg for peeling.

Desperate, perfume-blows
She hits back at the world.

With pointed gigglings she takes revenge
For all that sadness.

And with hasty fallings-in-love,
Like hiccups of emotion.

Terrorist of sweetness
She fills bombs
With despair and cinnamon, cloves and love-splinters.

At night when she tears her jewelry
Off herself
There's great danger she won't know the limit
And will go on tearing and slashing away
All of her life.

—*translated by Ted Hughes*

All the generations before me
Yehuda Amichai

All the generations that preceded me contributed me
in small amounts, so that I would be erected here in Jerusalem
all at once, like a house of prayer or a charity institution.
That commits one. My name is the name of my contributors.
That commits one.

I am getting to be the age my father was when he died.
My last will shows many superscriptions.
I must change my life and my death
daily, to fulfill all the predictions
concerning me. So they won't be lies.
That commits one.

I have passed my fortieth year.
There are posts they will not let me fill
because of that. Were I in Auschwitz,
they wouldn't put me to work.
They'd burn me right away.
That commits one.

—*translated by Robert Friend*

from Cool filmscripts
An elderly lonely woman glances
David Avidan

An elderly lonely woman glances
for the thousandth time or so
into a room
where her beloved used to live—
her only concern at this stage being
whether the vase
standing too close to the end of the table
will or won't fall off.
The only way to solve the problem
is probably
to start through the door toward the table,
to push the vase lampward
to shut the door—
then return to her sad reflections
upon her irretrievable youth.

—translated by the author

from Vegetative love
The theoretical offer
David Avidan

Come to me, come to me, said the tree.
Grip hard. Forget everything.
There are love-cracks in my trunk. I am experienced. I shall
       learn.
My roots will embrace your hips. My leaves will enfold you.
I shall evict all the birds and monkeys.
I am yours, all yours.
Give me a chance. You are
going to like me.
I shall be obedient.

251

There is room for you at the top, the top that will come down
to you over the years. Learn to like it. There is more to it
than certain women. Sex is not everything,
when everything's said and done. Forget the world,
the skin-soft sound waves, the boring temperature
of your cooling body, the liquids straining through you
from all directions, to all directions, the eye colors,
the transient hair, the music, the hostile sea, the roads.
Stay where you are. Do not move.
Soon I shall introduce you to the bowels of the earth,
the depths of fire burning from a distance, my roots that long
for you, the dark and solitary waters following it
like hungry hyenas, the scalding kernel
of this enormous fruit.
Be my friend. Give me credit. You know
too much about women to reject me. Do not refuse.
Do not be flesh. Do not smile at me. Do not speak
prettified words.
I want your gravity, not your memories.
I have time. Think of me. Travel. Go round the world, float
in the deepening dusk, break away, lock the gates. Come back to
          me
in the damp darkness, in the still wind, upon the dust that
          trembles
for your sake.

—translated by Richard Flantz

From there on
T. Carmi

I am already in the earth's pull.
As I draw away from the zone of your silence,
fire greets me with seventy tongues.
I hold in my hands several specimens:
the drift of your hair across your forehead,
the glow of a shoulder from the fireplace,
the breath of your mouth close to my lips.
Not much.
Now, years of research lie ahead.
It's not every day that a man grows
wings of fire and water.

—*translated by Marcia Falk*

Order of the day
T. Carmi

Keep the children happy!
Keep the children happy!
Keep the children happy!

So they won't hear the hoarse shrieking in our throats,
or see the forest of antennae growing from our heads,
or hear the tearing on all sides: clothing, paper, sheets, sky.
So they won't hear the neighbor's eyes cocked behind the
        shutters,
or see the camouflage beneath the skin of our faces,
or hear the lit networks racing inside our bodies.

We have to invent a grownup's code
so we can talk about
    distant bell (fallen)
    green pine (missing)
    little cloud (captured)
    bird's nest (wounded)

Your commanding officer speaking:
A bird's nest, hovering
on a little cloud,
is landing in a green pine
to the tinkling of a distant bell.
Good night. Over and out.

Keep the children happy!
Keep the children happy!

—translated by Marcia Falk

Perspectives
T. Carmi

Last remembrance:
a frenzied flight into the calm street,
a white forehead crushed against the air,
a girl's waist.

I stand in the background, as usual,
watching:
suddenly you evaporate
among the passersby,
suddenly you glow
in the distancing curve,
your hair—sparks, foam—
a tiny flash,
incomprehensible.

And I wait for you at the end of the street,
in the foreground:
I meet your battered forehead,
join the tatters of your breathing,
place my palms on your heart's drum
and say—

Enough now.
We're back to natural size.

—translated by Marcia Falk

254

Porcupine fish
Raquel Chalfi

Apparently a fish like you and me.
But there is something nail-like about him.

Slowly he glides,
examining himself in that great mirror called water
and asking why,
why these nails planted in his flesh,
why this need for endless wariness
that sharpens him, keeps him from being one
with the blue enfolding softness.

And then
the waters breathe,
something moves,
something alien perhaps,
certainly malign.
His spines bristle.
He turns into something else—
a swollen ball,
a small mountain of fear—
all roar, if one could hear.
His mouth—small, tight, rectangular—
distorts into a smile.
And his eyes, tiny pools in a suddenly vast forehead,
whirl violent images in his brain.

This time, however,
it was nothing really.

And he subsides
into the rigid destiny
of his nail-like self.

—translated by Robert Friend

I, the barracuda
Raquel Chalfi

Not just a fish, but an official
legend of the sea.

Even the green morena, cruel beyond compare
in this green, dark, blue, far realm
is no match. For me sea-wrack bursts its pods
out of season, I ripen the deep-sea fruit,
like a sun.
Ripe darkness surrounds me. Almost bright.
All waiting to be gathered.
And the sea, to be caressed.
I devour the water like fire.

I am never afraid.
I have no weaknesses,
I know myself, and my neighbor.
I am very musical.

Take note.
Even the green morena is no match.
I am an intelligent creature.
I seek no prey because I'm hungry.
I thirst for battle
because of a pleasant tickling in my guts.

I have absolute pitch.

—*translated by E. A. Levenston*

256

The dwelling
Moshe Dor

I dwell on alien ground I eat
on the Day of Atonement
not even heretic
my eyes are rubies my mouth beaten gold
purple the thread in my beard

I am Lord of 127 provinces
frost spreads through my bones

when I determined to build an ark
to escape on alien ground
a dark bird cried

I did not learn his name as I sank to the depths

my eyes are rubies my mouth beaten gold
purple the thread in my beard
a day of atoning for sin
I have not even yet
fearlessly
proclaimed my heresy there is no faith
in my bones I am Lord
of 127 provinces

I weep remembering Zion in the cold
when kingdoms
fall and dark the wings of the bird
its cries a sea
of darkness

I do not know my name

—translated by Moshe Dor and Denis Johnson

Progression
Moshe Dor

Even more terrible than crumbling, the dark
feeling of niches, the jokes
of purposeless entrances and exits,
the conflagration
of maple leaves like a forewarning:
but to keep silent?
A temporary solution, the memory of your body,
and, more limited, of your breast,
its nipple standing up between two hungers,
my lips, words that are moaned, loss
of the preeminence of man,
and animal swept by the primeval . . .
but to keep silent?
Maple leaves burn, too foreign
to scream, the hand ages on the
steering wheel, wild horses will not stop
the attrition of cells, seeds, hopes.
A meadow and a lakeside: the drawled speech
of those who fish for sport drags lead nets
through opaque waters. But to keep silent?
Even more terrible than crumbling, the sudden
consciousness that when a star
sears these fabricated skies
no one looks up, for the change in it.
The car doors will slam . . .
an odor, faint, of smoke, then nothing.

—translated by Moshe Dor and Denis Johnson

Samson rends his clothes
Anadad Eldan

When I went
to Gaza and met
Samson coming out rending his clothes
on his flailed face rivers streamed
and the houses bent to allow him
passage.
His pain uprooted trees and clung
to the tangle
of the roots. Among the roots the locks
of his hair.
His head shone like a skull of stones.
The tramp of his tread tore my tears. I heard
how the earth groaned beneath his step
how he crushed its belly.
Samson went dragging a tired sun.
Fragments of suns and chains sank
in the Gaza sea.

—translated by Ruth Nevo

When the waves fell silent
Anadad Eldan

When the waves sent to him from afar fell silent
covered with weeping like sad foam
winds stormed within him
for he wished to say them all at once.
He was like a city raging in battle.
His hair flamed
with his face's effort
to give shape to his mouth
lest the muscles abandon
the image of his voice.

His bones that shouted
when he tried to clothe them
with reasons and causes
broke his arms
as if they were breaching gates.
His hair that had flamed
like a flag on a last stronghold
darkened darkened
and turned white.

—*translated by Ruth Nevo*

When you gave light
Anadad Eldan

When you gave light to the sun
And sun to the morning,
I went to you like your only child.

The trees screened the flowing water,
on their branches you hung white birds;
and on me, pupils, dark as my shoes.

Barefooted, the trees are rooted
upright, making God's years green.

Give my legs back those years my father spent by the swamps
that ran here from hillock to hillock—
whistling, hanging his clothes out to dry.

He built a channel for tears; for pain,
shelter in my eyes.

When I see white birds, resting
on the tops of trees, it seems
God or his angels are about.

—*translated by Bat-Sheva Sheriff and Jon Silkin*

from Gazelle, I'll send you . . .
Amir Gilboa

Prologue

Gazelle, I'll send you to the wolves they are not in the forest
even in town on the sidewalks you'll flee from them your terrified
eyes are beautiful they will envy me seeing how you flower
frightened and your soul

I'll send you to the front of the hottest
battle it's no longer for me

my heart gazelle watching you bleed at dawn

1

The whole land is mine asleep and awake I see
a dream one long electric circuit making
flocks of swallows hover in branches of the tree weaving the
            window
and my bones and flesh in a dizzy wind over a huge land
all mine.

2

They will all rise. I know I see them
rising and turning each man to his home each to his home
seeing the road they remember
and a split second wipes out the distance and binds
distance to distance in a wonder of dream whether
dreamed or not. And meanwhile
his wife already laughs through the tears and his children
rub their cheeks on his cheek telling their story
he waited to hear again after it was whispered in his ear
in mouths of the roots of plants.

3

I looked outside. Pools of water.
Strips of silt between each pool
sprouting with stems of hands
their voices unheard
fish were tossed on the shore
from the water their eyes behind
on the water still watching me
frightened I run and keep running
treading in place my voice hides
in my throat between water and water

4

Far far outside, behind the wall,
lips bubble great words
unbroken unweaned to the street
and a sea in the intervals, eyelids fluttering,
now rain after midnight,
above and below, in the heart of the world,
prays

5

To pluck stars, berries from a bush at night
out of the dark, the velvet, time for the one set apart
breathing easy, wrapped warm in
kind loneliness, leaving commotion,
voiced by the silence, ripening with a secret.
And to go further, as if on the paws of a cat
knowing the ease of immortality that steals a portion of life
not divided, a godly emergency ration
between being and being, between nothing and nothing,
and to lie bundled up on the ground, smelling the earth
that good crust of bread, growing and growing
an embryo in the belly of some great mercy.

6

The time of waking from death from the dream
to a nagging ache, insistent, depressing,
which passes at last to return
and show up like the seasons, foreseen like the seasons,
dangling before your eyes like a threatening finger between times,
intermittent, not forgotten. But the time of waking from death
from the dream as if everything's blank for an instant
when suddenly washing your body and face as if cleansing
your soul, you suddenly remember a face you know, strange
but still known, from a distance, that you saw in the dream
pouring blood from wounds dead now, wallowing in filth,
and the white of its flesh made the earth fade

7

A patch of the sea, flesh, to swim in it,
in marble, in alabaster, which will grow hot and finally melt,
also the eyes will first become blue, will wake up again
to a patch of the sea, to equate blue with blue
in a cave of the sea, secrets of faraway days
which the sun will turn gold, last rays from the hiding of sorrow,
beauty that's saved for eyes which no longer
look except toward the west

8

In the haze the sun an orange ball, smooth
as if thrown in the air, at the cry of a child might
begin the trip back, increasing and gathering speed,
if it falls nearby it will smash, he'll see
thousands and thousands of splinters like a great
china world, and the world will go on like this without
moving without a polished ball until it will clear again,
the sun will move again will stay up high again
a ball in its glory and this time he won't see it eye to eye
because a child won't see anything but a ball thrown
in the air in the dream in the day

9

See an unwalled city by day a wasteland
whitens distance coming toward you
at night from every side legions rise and
rise upon you
an unwalled city by day your name
swells without limit
at night you contract and contract
and your name grows small within you

10

And on the great waters when I
seem to have opened, or else they were opened, the dams and the
                waters spilled
and the waters ran out revealing a hollowed land of silt of nothing
cradle of nothing, not to be measured, not to contain all these
                primordial eons
where God alone casts His shadow
and a fierce cold
and suddenly dogs chase after dogs

and life barks
in a cradle of nothing I dream

11

All the time to sit here and look through this window.
Truly the whole world will pass before me in this window.
But I have to pass through the whole world
and put it in this window the whole world.

12

Suddenly with force comes the absence of force.
Ah the absence of force is dryness.
Suddenly with force
like the first rain,
with the force of the first rain
comes the drought.
And with it, not with it, but
frightening in its aloneness, comes,
does not come, nothing comes, there is
nothing.

13

If in pain a light feather what will you say
it will fly if they throw it to the ground
if the wind tosses it to every wind
it will sink touching not touching the earth
from above what will you say
the whole weight of the earth below it holds
earth a light feather
every wind will toss it to every wind
what will you say

14

I'm certain I went, out of an illusion, to look for
my footprints on a road that was covered with buildings and
              bordered with fences
ages ago the signs that I left were erased and even then
I knew that I wouldn't remember them something strange happened
I saw my footprints clearly engraved even
in the walls of houses the lattice of fences all
the signs shining in the dark as if anointed
phosphorous cats' eyes in the dark I walked
by their light I passed through the fences I crossed
the walls as if they were never there were
only those days in which I left signs
and I knew then I wouldn't remember them and something
strange happened in real life I saw an illusion

15

Look at this man who crosses here on the bridge
and what is in front of him is the water under him
now he flows with the water far away far away

Look at this man who crosses on the bridge
I know truly his heart is like mine
now his heart flows with the water
toward another country
toward another loneliness

river of my heart, wait for me
I finish my prayer and run, maybe

—*translated by Shirley Kaufman with Shlomit Rimmon*

To my city Jerusalem, 1967
Amir Gilboa

I knew in the dream the dream wouldn't fly like a dream.
I knew in the dream that in me myriads are dreaming the dream.
I woke. Midnight. Who turns the dark of night into the light of
        day?
The sun stands still in the window in the dream as on that day in
        Gibeon I recall.
Look, here comes the night that is day and not night
and the endless day comes in the midst of the night. And it will never
        darken.
And morning light glows. I wake. Look, here before me, Jeru-
        salem.
And I see it. I see it with myriads of eyes.
Was there ever anything like this—
a dream dreamed at the same time
by myriads while they dream.

—*translated by Shirley Kaufman with Shlomit Rimmon*

Samson
Amir Gilboa

And Samson grew old in days
and his sleep left him in the nights.
He was still a child when he picked up the world on its axis with one
        hand.
When he grew up, he hoped he would die on the night that he was
seventeen years old.
He didn't want to die old: seventeen and a day.
That's why he tied firebrands to the three hundred foxes' tails,
to burn everything down.
In his twenties he planned to do wonders up to his death at the age of
        thirty-three.
In the days when they gouged out his eyes
he prayed that he would live to see the wedding of his daughters.
At eighty he stopped growing up
and in the forgetfulness of his hours he daydreamed like a newborn
        child.

And the gates of his Gaza are still asleep in the ore.

And Delilah.

—translated by Stephen Mitchell

By the waters of Babylon
Amir Gilboa

On the willows we hung our harps. I mean the grownups.
As for me, I had a little harp and I hid it in under my cloak.
On the far side of the river the victors lit fires and wild with joy they
        reveled.
Evening fell and fell. The grownups sat crying. A big fire over
        there.

And the guards assigned to us, not taking part in the dancing,
Reviling us with impatience, raucously,
Aping our language in grotesque ways.

The grownups listened, and looked at their harps. The waters filled
          with tears.
And I out of sorrow dared to cry: Who is grotesque here,
You wild beasts, and how can you mock us with gibberish?
For there is no language like ours for color and sound, for depth and
          distance.

And they laughed louder, their mouths gaped at me.
They began chasing me, getting entangled in darkness.
I would stop to rest a brief moment briefly to pluck my harp,
They would swell like sacks, glow like copper.

—*translated by Robert Alter*

Chosen land
Zerubavel Gilead

1. *Sun at Givon*

All night we fought
for the chosen land:
your tongue a keen knife
your hand tendril of vine
on my heart.
Like Adam and Eve innocent,
like them strong in desire
and hunted by fear.

All night the sun waited for us,
and in the morning passed by—
a stranger.

2. *Your smile*

A soft gust of wind
in the dense thickness of the khamsin
in our hearts.
All our quarrels
like thorns in the vineyard
hollowed
before the fullness of the grape
borne like a soft gust of wind.

3. *Miracle*

A bird flew about our heads
like a scream.
The light broke
like a decayed tree.
The shadow slipped away
jerking like a lizard's tail.
Only your tears live
like a miracle.

—*translated by Dorothea Krook*

Ibn Gvirol
Zerubavel Gilead

On the unseen border between today and tomorrow
The rain fell heavier.
His head floated on the water in the darkness:
Cheekbones protruding
Fire in the eyes and pain
In the pupils.
When the water swelled the roots
And the silence the leaves,
He opened his mouth like an ancient well:
"From the day of his birth man is oppressed and tormented . . .
In his life he is like a scorched grass
And God seeks his hunting down."

When light dawns I am still pursued
By the anguish of consciousness:
Royal Crown without mercy.

—translated by Dorothea Krook

Some words in praise of my friends
Haim Gouri

I have been in want of many things, never in want of good
        friends.
And some are growing fat or bald,
or gray and old like me,
and some are slim and bushy haired
as in the photographs.

I don't remember them all,
don't always think of them.
Sometimes I even forget them for a while,
even for a long while.
But when I return to them
I find them there.

I had good friends who loved life
but didn't always know how to live it.
Some had time to learn;
some, hardly any time at all.

They ran and ran in fields or orange groves or woods
between silence and commotion,
and had hardly stopped for breath
when they were called for. In a hurry
to be on the spot, take part, they went.

I had friends who knew how to smile
and what to take from the women around them,
who knew how to climb into their beds
and do them good.

270

I had friends who didn't know these things,
who were too shy or didn't dare or couldn't manage,
who remained outside with flowers in their hands,
flowers that dropped slowly from their loosening fingers
and were scattered over them.

I had friends who, on winter nights around a fire
or on summer nights under the stars,
knew how to laugh and tease and joke
and tell tall stories
they swore were true.

I had strange friends.
When they laughed you saw them and heard them,
when they wanted to cry they hid their faces
or turned aside.
I had dangerous friends.

And I had friends who were deaf.
One volunteer called for,
ten came. They hadn't quite heard.
Told to step back, they stayed—
like Uriah the Hittite.

And I had friends who were dumb,
who sometimes, unable to utter a word,
asked me to speak for them;
who said, "Never mind, it's OK,"
and moved away
to lean against a tree or a wall.

Many of my friends were liars.
When you asked them if they were all right
or needed anything,
they'd say, "Everything's fine."
They had bloodshot eyes and week-old beards
and were almost too tired to stand.

I also had alchemist friends
who could turn water into wine
and long roads into song,

weariness into iron
and youth into an open wound.
I had foolish friends,
madmen of spirit.

I had rich friends.
All of this land was their home.
They slept in olive groves, in smoky caves,
on windswept hills.
Like Jacob, they knew how to dream dreams
that took them out of themselves.

—translated by Robert Friend

My Samsons
Haim Gouri

Look, my Samsons are coming back, the gates of Gaza on their
            shoulders:
smiling, they pass by unseeing sentries.
Mint. Wind. Crickets.

Look, my Samsons are coming back, their Delilahs at their feet;
they move along my boulevard.
I'm awake.

Look, my Samsons are coming back, the memory of lions in their
            hands;
light on their bare feet, they stride
through a street without voices, through a street that is not in
            flames.

Look, my Samsons are coming back, the frogs of the Vale of Sorek
            in their ears;
they make their way, they always make their way.
When was it I last lifted the gates?

Look, my Samsons are coming back, the taste of the feast still on
            their tongues;

272

the green withes* are broken, the riddles are solved,
my first gray hairs.

Look, my Samsons are coming back, no nails in their eyes;
they come back to me from Gath
when the fire's gone out.

Look, my Samsons are coming back to the thicket of their nights
alight with foxes of fire.

—*translated by S. F. Chyet*

* Judges 16:7

Holiday's end
Haim Gouri

He went off; didn't say when he'd be back
a short holiday, you might call it

but surely he'll soon be back
surely: that raven over a road which for once isn't empty
that caravan making its way through the Negev

he went off to die a while
and then to rise from the dust, to come home from the desert

for his "servitude is over," his "sin is almost atoned for"*
wordlessly, ever so wordlessly

I know it by the disquiet in the air
which bears these conflicting rumors
(one of them is good)

I know it by the wind gusting over these dead words
these words which only moments ago knew nothing
I know it by this city which senses his loss

—*translated by S. F. Chyet*

* Isaiah 40:2

Cycle
Haim Gouri

a tormenting blue reminding me
of rare gems
and the replies bloodstained tonight

my questioners that were wounds
are mute at last for their own good
and those who gore know how to forge ahead—
weeping, the toll of the road,
always with them

when was I last here?
and when will I come here
blood-drenched again?

and here's the dog yelping as if mad
and the fragrance of jasmine
and the oven left as it was

and the marksman silly enough to swear by his whiskers
and paradise waiting for his bones

and there, a metal crescent concave to the sky
and those bent on vengeance reeking in my wake

and the sword making its way
and wailing in my grasp
and the radiant heaven of my loss

—*translated by S. F. Chyet*

Song of the great mind
Uri Zvi Greenberg

That mind—the small one—is soft, like a pullet;
it is afraid of space and it loathes the dimensions of the sea;
it is a forest firefly at night,
a tavern's splinter of light in the meadow-night
to the eyes of the carter
as sluggishly he drives horse and cart
through the dust, and yawns.
Such is that mind—the small, the poor one—that serves
the peddler on his daily rounds;
and that twistedly scorns visions of glory.
It goes through our streets near the low roofs,
licking the moss of days, drinking from drainpipes,
seeing in every cur a kind of wolf or tiger.

That mind—the great one, the one winged with light,
the supreme ruler, the high king—
(from the time the people inhabited their lands and waters,
and the king from his throne
beheld the mountains of Moab)
is not here. It sits in its nest forgotten,
but it lives. I sing to my people: Remember the eagle!
Bid it come, and it will come,
to show you
the place of passage that leads from here, the swamp of
                    dream . . .
to the meaning.

So poor are we without, so twisted of shape, so shorn of all
                    glory;
not so within the body, which is more deep
than its bodily dimensions. In it hidden lie
as in a locked palace
all kinds of marvelous and precious things,
until the tall and wide gate of the heart
is broken through by the gate breaker
blowing a ram's horn.

Toward that day I sing; and in the hearts
of our generation, in every song,
I stir up the strife of longing. My every syllable cuts.
I catch each traitor, though disguised. I strip him bare
who teaches us to be as a reed to the river.

So poor without, such mighty lords within!
Mighty like the mountains of Lebanon,
eternal like Mount Hermon in its snows.
And that sundering in the middle? Amen, I sing the day
on which the miraculous line of the race which Titus rent in two
will be joined.

—*translated by Robert Friend*

from To God in Europe
Uri Zvi Greenberg

III: No other instances

We are not as dogs among the gentiles: a dog is pitied by them,
fondled by them, sometimes even kissed by a gentile's mouth;
as if he were a pretty baby
of his own flesh and blood, the gentile spoils him
and is forever taking pleasure in him.
And when the dog dies, how the gentile mourns him!

Not like sheep to the slaughter were we brought in trainloads,
but rather—
through all the lovely landscapes of Europe—
brought like leprous sheep
to Extermination itself.
Not as they dealt with their sheep did the gentiles deal with our
                bodies;
they did not extract their teeth before they slaughtered them;
nor strip them of their wool as they stripped us of our skins;
nor shove them into the fire to turn their life to ashes;
nor scatter the ashes over sewers and streams.

276

Where are there instances of a catastrophe
like this that we have suffered at their hands?
There are none—no other instances.
(All words are shadows of shadows)—
This is the horrifying phrase: No other instances.

No matter how brutal the torture a man will suffer
in a land of the gentiles,
the maker of comparisons will compare it thus:
He was tortured like a Jew.
Whatever the fear, whatever the outrage,
how deep the loneliness, how harrowing the sorrow—
no matter how loud the weeping—
the maker of comparisons will say:
This is an instance of the Jewish sort.

What retribution can there be for our disaster?
Its dimensions are a world.
All the culture of the gentile kingdoms at its peak
flows with our blood,
and all its conscience, with our tears . . .

—translated by Robert Friend

Whispering in me
Ya'ir Hurvitz

The dead man took hold of me.
I followed him.
He appeared to me at night—that dead man.
I followed his years.

He was a kingdom once.
Years passed.
A cracked halo crowned him.
A broken light moved in me.
I know those difficult days.

A man is walking in the street.
He sees me laugh—that man.
But how can I explain
that someone dead has me in his grip
and magic spells
whisper powerful in me?

—*translated by S. F. Chyet and Leonore Gordon*

On your heart, open
Ya'ir Hurvitz

In a city without a sky, its tranquility a refuge
I see my years like the clothing of the dead
and all the rivers run all
the rivers run to the heart all
the rivers and mountains around it and all
the rivers from the sources of the rivers come
and I a mere nothing
put from the water into the basket
a little of a gift, like

water that the heart sustains on a flower on a kiss
and I a bird on the mountains kissing my mortality
in a city spread out like a sky
and the water in pain.

The painful water,
I shall cleave the pain of the painful water
like a fish slicing through it,
I shall climb the stairs of the water
like a bird.

I shall kiss the blue-garbed earth.

—*translated by S. F. Chyet and Leonore Gordon*

I don't know if Mount Zion
Abba Kovner

1

I don't know if Mount Zion would recognize itself
at midnight in the fluorescent light
when there's nothing left of Jerusalem
but its beauty
wakeful in the milky light that glides
over its limbs   still wings
lift it from the sunken desert
slowly slowly higher than the stars
this strange shell that floats out of the night
transparent giant
so much sky
washes over it
I don't know if Mount Zion looks
into my heart holding its breath now in pain and pleasure
behind a barred window
and who it is meant for
at midnight

2

These olive trees that never knelt
their knowledge hidden their
wrinkles carved this whole blue fan
on the road of the Hinom Valley
I don't know if Mount Zion sees the things
that have changed our image
out of all recognition. Hands that touched it every day like a
            mother's
touching the forehead of her son sank
dropping into the sleep
of the Dead Sea—
does it hear the cry
from the market of the gates or the rush of my prayer from the
            shadow—

what's the use of friends who watch from the galleries
while our hearts struggle in the arena
and what's the sense of poets if we don't
know how to ask
Mount Zion does it really exist or
is it like our love that glows from another light
rising night
after night

—translated by Shirley Kaufman

Lookout on a rock on the heights of Mount Hermon
Abba Kovner

1
This is the naked rock. Right here. From here
we had a fine view of the city and the land and
the treeless waterless boulders.
Here he knelt and watched
his fear crumbling opposite the terror. A cliff split
like fingers spread to bless
those who pass by. No, there's no sign
of a grave here. Only wonder
only puzzlement.

2
You lived the things which came later and I
sat here paralyzed my eyes scratching
the stones scattered below
scattered shapes and signs of those
who'd been my friends and enemies a while ago.
So I gathered their remains from the plain
to sort them in the sun—
We stopped here. At exactly 4:25 A.M.

someone woke us to say it
was time to move toward
the voices you'd see even in the blindness
of your death. For wander where it will
the eye that follows them
will never break away.

3
And at night. Only at night suddenly in your arms
it's like it was then when we left the southern front: you'll
live these things as they happen and I mindless quiet
with a filthy fingernail still scratch on your belly
shapes and signs now ended
scattered and torn each one
will confront his fate

In the lookout.

—*translated by S. Y. Chyet*

Observations on Jerusalem at twilight and a dialogue
Abba Kovner

When did flocks leave the streets of Jerusalem?
We got up at dawn
and there weren't any flocks in the streets of Jerusalem.

When were wolves silent through the nights of Jerusalem?
That night we woke
and the desert withdrew from the edge of Jerusalem.

When did the camel trains quit the streets of Jerusalem?
Yesterday an old man died
who saw camels stroll in the squares of Jerusalem.

And mad dogs? Are there any still in Jerusalem?
I saw a covered well, and there's the new moon.
Why shouldn't there be mad dogs in Jerusalem?

And how does a man die in Jerusalem? When his time comes.
Each man earns his death
though men fall in herds in the hills of Jerusalem.

And when is nothing brighter than Jerusalem? Whenever
her people say to each other,
we're on our way home, we'll turn on the light.

—translated by Shirley Kaufman

Sun watchers
Abba Kovner

Eat and drink
Eat   and drink because
tomorrow we're not going to die   because
we're going to live   because
we're going to go through the whole twilit city
from end to end
that Hebrew city between the veiled hills because
you stand revealed
with me by your side,
my beautiful bridegroom:
we sun watchers lie down in the   field
we'll be. And until the sun shines
on the wall again we'll lie down again mouth   to mouth
and anyone who's seen it all and said nothing
will see   again
under the tree's spreading boughs
how love is torn
you and I and the canopies overhead
are seven,
my beautiful bridegroom.

—translated by S. Y. Chyet

282

Observation
at dawn
Abba Kovner

The night is still silky. Curtains are drawn
from the edge of the dream in a slow rhythm.
Red silk. We are both awake
trying quietly to spin the thread
cut off between the ribs. I'm reluctant
to look at this rain
beating at the windows.

And inside the night
is still silky. Your breath a soft thicket
guarding its border. When I count
the number of pulse beats, as if not believing,
and find signs in them, suddenly my eyes
discover my body, my arms stretched out, lying here
naked (must I retrieve them somehow?).

Rain
it's just rain! Like an oath I repeat
for the third time. Not your blood.
Then my finger taps on your throat
groping like a blind man's cane.

—translated by Shirley Kaufman with Shlomit Rimmon

Armchairs
Dan Pagis

The slowest beasts
are the soft, big-eared
leather armchairs
of lobby corners.
They multiply
where rubber plants stand darkly,
or in the shade of dusty philodendrons,
and though content to live
more slowly than elephants,
are ever on the verge of setting forth
on a secret, unending safari.

—translated by Robert Friend

The elephant
Dan Pagis

The elephant, battle-scarred veteran,
patient and thick-skinned like an elephant,
balances—
on the pillars of his legs—
a whole world
of belly. But
such is his strength
that he conquers himself all by himself.
At zero hour,
with cotton-wool care
and unconditional love,
he steps on sixteen marvelously precise
wristwatches,
fastens four to each hoof like skates
and smoothly glides away
out of his elephant fate.

—translated by Robert Friend

284

Autobiography
Dan Pagis

I died with the first blow and was buried
in the stony field.
The raven showed my parents
what to do with me.

If my family is famous, not a little of the credit
goes to me.
My brother invented murder,
my parents—crying,
I invented silence.

Afterward, those well-known events took place.
Our inventions were perfected.
One thing led to another.
And there were those who
killed in their own way,
cried in their own way.

I am not naming names
out of consideration for the reader,
since at first the details horrify,
though in the end they bore.

You can die once, twice, even seven times,
but you cannot die a thousand times.
I can.
My underground cells reach everywhere.

When Cain started to multiply on the face of the earth,
I started to multiply in the belly of the earth.
For a long time now, my strength has been greater than his.
His legions desert him and go over to me.
And even this is only half a revenge.

—*translated by Robert Friend*

Fossils
Dan Pagis

The creatures that live forever, the fossils,
are all extreme nay-sayers.

The royal arch-fly, fossilized in amber,
scorns time. Having closed his thousand eyes,
he takes his siesta in the sun.

The arch-snail is an ear that refuses to listen.
The arch-fish has renounced even himself,
and left in the rock only a trace of his bones.

The fossil-paragon is the Venus of Milo,
the eternal negator,
whose arms are air.

—*translated by Robert Friend*

The portrait
Dan Pagis

The child
keeps fidgeting.
It's hard for me to get the line of his cheek.
I draw one line
and the wrinkles of his face increase.
I draw another,
and his lips grow crooked, his hair white,
the bluish skin peels from his bones. He's gone.
The old man's gone. And I—
what shall I do now?

—*translated by Robert Friend*

286

The last
Dan Pagis

I am already quite scarce. For years now,
and only here and there, I have been found
on the fringes of this jungle. My clumsy body
shelters in the reeds or clings
to the moist shade around it.
Civilization would be the death of me.
I'm tired. But the huge fires
keep driving me from hiding place to hiding place.

And now what? My whole reputation rests
only on the rumor
that from year to year,
from hour to hour even,
I grow few and fewer.
One thing is certain: at this very moment
someone's on my trail. Cautiously I prick
all my ears and wait. Already there are footsteps
in the dead leaves. Very near. Rustling. Is this it?
Am I it? I am.
It's already too late to explain.

—*translated by Robert Friend*

In the laboratory
Dan Pagis

The data in the glass jar: some ten scorpions
of various species, a community
lazy, adjustable, moved by feelings of equality,
each treading, each trodden upon.
Now the experiment:
an inquisitive, private providence blows
poisonous fumes.

287

At once,
each is alone in the world,
erect on his tail, begging one moment more
from the glass wall.
The sting is superfluous now,
the pincers do not understand.
The dry straw body stiffens
against the last judgment.
Distant in the dust, the angels of doom
are terrified.
But it's only an experiment, an experiment,
not a judgment
of poison for poison.

—*translated by Robert Friend*

from Selected poems
A lesson in observation
Dan Pagis

Pay close attention: the world that appears now
at zero-point-zero-one degrees
was, as far as is known,
the only one
that burst out of the silence.

It hovered within a blue bubble, fairly large;
and sometimes there were clouds, sea breezes,
sometimes a house, perhaps a kite, children,
and here and there an angel,
or a garden, or a town.
Beneath these were the dead, beneath them
rock, beneath this the fiery prison.

Is that clear? I will repeat: outside there were
clouds, screams, air-to-air missiles,
fire in the fields, memory.
Far beneath these, there were houses, children. What else?

288

The little dot on the side? It seems to be
the only moon of that world.
It was silent even before this.

—translated by Stephen Mitchell

Twelve faces of the emerald
Dan Pagis

1

I am exceedingly green: chill green.
What have I to do
with all the greenishness of chance?
I am the green-source,
the green-self,
one and incomparable.

2

The most suspicious flash
in the cat's eye
at the most acute moment
aspires
to be
me.

3

What have I to do with you, or the living grass?
Among you I am a stranger—
brilliant, cold, playing with my eternities.

4

The emperor Nero, artist in stage-lighting,
raises me to his red eye;
only my green can pacify his blood.
Through me he observes the end of the burning world.

5
Slander! I am not
envious of the diamond: fickle duke,
reckless, lacking in self-control:
daggers! fireworks!
I, on the contrary, am moderate,
know how to bide my time,
to pour, green and accurate,
the poison.

6
As if I shared a secret. Shade of blue,
hint of red in a polished facet,
hesitating violet—
they're gone, they're gone.
I, the green-source,
abolish the colors of the rainbow.

7
You think that you will find your image
in mine.
No. I shall not leave a trace of you;
you never were in me.
Mirror facing mirror facing mirror, enchanted,
I am reflected in I.

8
With one flick of the hand,
I smash your days into twelve
green nights.

9
I am all eye.
I shall never sleep.

10
And so I put on a face,
twelve facets apparently transparent.

11
Fragments of light:
they indeed are my soul: I shall not fear.
I shall not die.
I have no need to compromise.

12
You will never find the secret of my power.
I am I: crystallized carbon
with a very small quantity
of chromium oxide.

—*translated by Stephen Mitchell*

Fragments of an elegy
Dan Pagis

I've closed your eyes.
I've returned your hands to their place.
The soles of your feet look at me with pity:
I am superfluous.
I find my hands.
What shall I do with my hands?
I tie my tied shoelaces,
button my buttoned coat.

The new cemetery is spacious,
entirely future. Far, near, incessantly,
the cantors are singing.

You are quiet, a little embarrassed;
perhaps the separation will be long.
The nails are growing, slowly, sketching a truce.
The mouth cavity is at peace with its maker.

But now the earth-fists
are knocking on the boards of the trap:
let us in,
let us in.

—*translated by Stephen Mitchell*

A somewhat clouded study
Gabriel Preil

As if legends were devoured by beasts
in bitter forests
and the rain did not cease its reporting
of those who, blind to the waters' blindness,
cast bread upon the waters;
of travelers who folded
countries in their pockets
while the one station
slid away

a kind of victory crowns them
who reached their door safely,
those in whose ear the gallows
refused to whisper.

—*translated by Robert Friend*

Sunset possibilities
Gabriel Preil

No one would believe me if I described
such a sunset. They would say
a tired rhetoric has fired his brain,
the Complicator of things
has made him fish like a callow youth
in the poetaster's pot.

El Greco's celebrated clouds
did not climb by means of mountainous heroics.
They were valleys washed
by little pearly waves
and a silence flowed through them
like a crystal holiday.

I, the great cloud-connoisseur, affirm
Toledo is a city that has lost
its massed spoils of terror; in the sky
the horns of her oxen, the arrows of her storms
are shattered. Perhaps El Greco
also thought of such a possibility.

—*translated by Robert Friend*

Romantic reminder
Gabriel Preil

Always the same net
cast by expectation
when planes orphan
the airports,
trains loosen their grip
on dove villages,
and still remembered is the season
of comets that reddened
the faces of other observers.

Caught in that net,
the blue garden praises
the blond moonlight.
Disconsolate
is the identity of things
in the never-ending street.

—*translated by Robert Friend*

From a late diary
Gabriel Preil

Gabriel turned at last into old Mr. Preil.
Overnight began the pamperings
that go with taking off a coat
and opening a door.
Suspicions and hypotheses
sprouted in him like weeds.

And he tried to ignore
the marginal in things,
the fortuity of time—
not wanting to give up
the young wininess in him,
the flow of his young streams.

As for the obtuse, they do not realize
that the self-same Gabriel
shares his time with them,
that no change threatens him.
It would also seem the coffee is hotter now,
and longer now the lightning-play of jets,
and longer lasting the bird-trees in full bloom.

—translated by Robert Friend

Folk tune
Esther Raab

The great tiger
loved me—
and I loved him.
He had eyes
of an extinguished blue
with the skin sagging about them:
wrinkles, wrinkles . . .

294

I searched among the wrinkles
for the blue of his eyes
as for cold water
hidden in mist.
He smelled like a forest,
smelled like a hunter:
a hunter whose quarry
was wild beasts and women.
He lived
beyond time,
he was
"the eternal tiger"—
granter of visions,
dispenser of dreams,
collector of pain.

—*translated by Robert Friend with Shimon Sandbank*

Today I am modest
Esther Raab

To day I am modest like an animal,
open like rain-drenched fields.
With a little fat hand I guide my life
toward compassion and children.
Every stranger, every sufferer
comes to me today.
The little gifts of my heart
patter about me like rain.
And I am already carrying Tomorrow—
a heaviness
closed
and leaping again.
toward the unknown.

—*translated by Robert Friend with Shimon Sandbank*

Hills of salt
Dahlia Ravikovitch

Foam fluttered on the sea like birds' wings.
Two salt hills were left on the beach,
and the sea was a welter of pools,
with sailboats small as a finger
gleaming
like soap bubbles.

The two of us sat, each by his pool,
two sand strips between us
and a wealth of seaweed.
The heavy fronds swayed back and forth,
grasping at the teeth of the rocks in their lust.

A mass of seaweed broke loose and fell at my feet,
and my eyelids were heavy with sun.
And the sea rose up and spilled over
from pool to pool,
blue streams in a net of light.

Pools lapped at the palms of our hands,
the sand between us—the length of two arms.
We did not draw near all that day,
not by a hair's-breadth,
our bodies two salt hills and our feet seaweed.

—translated by Chana Bloch

Hard winter
Dahlia Ravikovitch

The little mulberry shook in the flame
and before its glory vanished
it was lapped in sadness.

Rain and sun ruled by turns, and in the house
we were afraid to think
what would become of us.

The plants reddened at their hearts
and the pool lay low.
Each of us was sunk in himself alone.

But for an instant, offguard,
I saw
how men topple from this world

like a tree that lightning splits,
heavy with limbs and flesh, the wet branches
trampled like dead grass.

The shutter was worn and the walls thin.
Rain and sun, by turns, rode over us
with iron wheels.

All the fibers of the plants were intent
on themselves alone.
This time I never thought I'd survive.

—*translated by Chana Bloch*

Pride
Dahlia Ravikovitch

Even rocks break, I tell you,
and not from old age.
For years they lie on their backs
in the heat and the cold,
so many years
it almost seems peaceful.
They don't move from their place
and so the cracks are hidden.
A kind of pride.
Year after year passes over them,

expectant, waiting.
The one who will shatter them later
has not yet come.
And so the moss grows,
the seaweeds are tossed about,
the sea pounces in, and returns.
And they, it seems, do not move.
Until a little seal comes
to rub against the rocks,
comes and goes away.
And suddenly the stone is wounded.
I told you, when rocks break
it comes as a surprise.
And all the more with people.

—translated by Marcia Falk

Distant land
Dahlia Ravikovitch

Tonight, in a sailing boat, I came back
From the isles of the sun, and their coral clusters.
There were girls with combs of gold
Left on the shore in the isles of the sun.

For four years of milk and honey
I roamed the shores on the isles of the sun.
The fruit stalls were heavily laden
And cherries glistened in the sun.

Oarsmen and boatmen from seventy lands
Sailed toward the isles of the sun.
Through four years by shining light
I kept counting ships of gold.

For four years, rounded like apples,
I kept stringing coral beads.
In the isles of the sun merchants and peddlers
Spread out sheets of crimson silk.

And the sea was unfathomable, deeper than any depth,
As I returned from the isles of the sun.
Heavy sundrops, with the weight of honey,
Dripped on the island before sunset.

—*translated by A. C. Jacobs*

How Hong Kong was destroyed
Dahlia Ravikovitch

I am in Hong Kong.
A river branch there
swarms with snakes.
There are Greeks, Chinese, Negroes.
Near the paper lanterns, carnival dragons gape.
Who said they eat you alive here?
A great crowd went down to the river.
You've never seen such silk in your life,
redder than poppy blossoms.

In Hong Kong
the sun rises in the east
and they water the flowers with a perfumed spray
to enhance their scent.
But in the evening the paper lanterns
are stricken by the wind,
and if someone is murdered, they ask:
Was it a Chinaman? a Negro?
Did he die in pain?
Then they pitch his body into the river
and all the reptiles feed.

I am in Hong Kong.
In the evening the café lights grew dim
and paper lanterns were ripped in the streets.
The land kept erupting and seething,
erupting and seething,

and I alone knew
that there is nothing in the West
and there is nothing in the East.
The paper dragon yawned
but the earth erupted.
A horde of enemies will come ashore
who've never seen silk in their lives.

Only the little prostitutes still
receive their visitors
in dresses of soiled silk
in tiny alcoves crowded with lanterns.
Some of them sob in the morning
over their rotting flesh.
And if someone is killed, they ask:
Oh-oh, Chinese? Negro? Poor thing.
Let's hope he didn't die in pain.
And already at dusk the first
of the visitors arrive
like a thorn in the living flesh.

I am in Hong Kong
and Hong Kong hangs on the ocean
like a colored lantern on a hook
at the end of the world.
Perhaps the dragon
will swathe it in crimson silk
and let it drop
into the abyss of the stars.
And only the little prostitutes will sob in the silk
because even now
still now
men pinch them in the belly.

I am not in Hong Kong
and Hong Kong is not in the world.
Where Hong Kong used to be
there is a single reddish stain,
half in the sky and half in the sea.

—*translated by Chana Bloch*

300

Abdath
David Rokeah

Abandon the small dreams
that redeem nothing
and walk in the land which breeds mirages
between the vaults of Abdath and the phosphate mountains.
Walls still fortified,
fortified memories.
Red granite cliffs
break the sun and the wind
on terraces facing the west

—translated by Ruth and Matthew Mead

You know
David Rokeah

You know and do not know how many rivers
dwelt in you on the way to the sea. Flowing
from within, whirlpool in a moonlit night, you move forward
to congeal suddenly like a lake between mountains.
You know and do not know the springs on the way,
loves on the way, fences before you

—translated by Ruth and Matthew Mead

You let me go
David Rokeah

You let me go
and I go. My childhood
a sack of conch shells. In them the sound of my steps,
the sound of surf. You stand
at the edge of the mole, sum up your years,
and the water rolls beneath you
like a scroll of the Torah at your bar mitzvah.
Then you preached from the tractate of Yoma
on the Long Day—and it seems
that this day is prolonged: a cord
with many knots—entangling
your poems as they still
breathe the darkness of ripening.

—translated by Ruth and Matthew Mead

Among iron fragments
Tuvia Ruebner

Among iron fragments and rusty dreams
I found you

lost in my astonished hands:
is this your face, your shoulders; this, the hair of night?

dark flame and sleepy mouth
the years have forgotten your eyes

they rose up around you
with the sharpness of spikes

the fine, white dust above you
in winds that rose and died

I found you,
my wounded face in the wind and my arms open wide.

—translated by Robert Friend

302

Waking up
Tuvia Ruebner

I don't begin
the poem begins
me, again
something rises from the heavy sand, takes wing

and already three years beyond forty

for years the same sky over me, within me
the same wilderness, before my eyes
the pepper tree changing measures soundlessly
and the moon rising in my veins
and the birds
in hidden nests
of your hair

at first
I said again
for you? for me? for whom?
these words which begin

—translated by S. F. Chyet

I left
Tuvia Ruebner

I left my temporary home and set off
To show my sons the source.
There, I said, I lay on the ground
With a stone for a pillow, lowlier than the grass
Like the dust of the earth—
All has been preserved there.
I meant to show my sons where I came from.

We passed mountains, woods, and cities that were
Caves. Water gathered in pools on the way and the roads got worse.
The car was forced to bump over the ditches.

In the fading light we arrived at my home town.
What is this sweet air? ask my sons.
What's this plaster falling off the walls?

Never mind, quoth the old woman at the window,
Here the future too is past. And she shut her dry eyes
Like a fowl that rises, and folds its wings and dives.

I was born here, I told my sons.
My parents and grandparents were born nearby.
Everyone is born. Here stood a house,
I told my sons, and the wind blew
Between me and the words.

I tried to show my sons where I came from and when.
Are we going to eat and where?
Are we going to sleep? ask my sons, and we are surrounded by
        emptiness and there is no way out.

—*translated by Betsy Rosenberg*

Niagara Falls
Avner Treinin

1

The water before is the water after—

what a stale smell after the act.
A despairing attempt will again be made
to justify the long journey. Another honey-
moon, clotted and sticky.

Like a smoking hive the motels swarm.
Blue roses hover
in the wallpaper, in vain they try
to belie the end. And the waters spill.

304

2

As they fall, the tension rises. Cascades
of electricity to the earth. Two wings to one,
a bird pierces the steam
like a messenger summoning help.
It stops then, looks backward,
a tiny foot on the high tension wire,
twitters softly, delouses its wing—

far from the text, from the pillar of salt.

3

We all witness the falls. At sundown
light falls from searchlights, paints
the arena. Now a thin vapor rises
like transparent cellophane, veiling, revealing

how desperate they are for the Beginning,
they crash to return, as if to restore
all that changed since the day of expulsion.

He will come back from the depths and answer: the water
above is the water below, that is,
nothing will change below.

4

But something is happening the way things finally do,
nothing will divide the lakes in two.

They will be equal. Primeval
mountains crumbling impair the view.

—*translated by Shirley Kaufman with Shlomit Rimmon*

305

Really
Avner Treinin

Veil after veil. Day by day
sight improves, brightens,
dissolves
all that vagueness.

Now for the green scum. Look at it.
Study it well.
Know it as it really is,
as you really are—
in standing water,
in the full light of your day,
near this street of boardinghouses.

—*translated by E. A. Levenston*

from Songs of Leonardo
Avner Treinin

*I can make cannon, mortars, and light
ordinance, very beautiful and
useful things.*

*An arch is nothing other than the
strength caused by two
weaknesses opposed to each
other and combined.*

Leonardo da Vinci

1

Leonardo, who loved hard young men
—oh, candle flame, a frail blue swirl
below a dark zone, the soot will whiten and glow—
lies on hard ground, tries to know
what it is in the grass that pushes through, growing,
a trembling stem out of the whole earth—

and the herd pushes on, chewing.

2

The line is heavy and the hook already lifted
to a dry sea of terror. So much
oxygen to choke on. Such useless sucking with his gills,
reticulum that flaps to choose
between air and water—gaping wonder.

Fish in the mud, if your fate were reversed
as in a camera obscura, would you still
move like a knife, a scale of silver,
when the water flows through your soul?

Return to the life you own,
I hear you—
and the gull, reviving its soul, swoops down.

3

With a saw and pincers one lizard from two—
one belly one pair of wings. But wind
from the edges of the world won't stick a sky to you.

Go back, go back to your dust, Leonardo's feeling blue.
When you want to fly, a pair of demons will carry you.

4

In your smile I am revealed again,
and both of us know that because of it
my wings will not hoist me to heaven.

A cruel skull governs me.
In vain the gray matter writhes—
among all of them laughing and weeping
I don't find the image of God.

They stand here facing you,
looking as if they were ecstatic.
But in the corner both of us see
his strong body, sharp and pure.

5

Beautiful things expand the mind of a man
in a head split open, and vapors of blood
are carried like columns of birds. How terrible
to lock them in cages, oh pure wing.

But something went wrong,
Anghiari—the fire I lit
didn't work; the blood boiled
and the paint ran, ugly and oozing out.

6

On that day each man and his demon
will gather in Meggido;
mad, on a white horse,
God will slaughter his image.

Solomon stabled his horses there,
his father murdered and so did he.
Who will protect me from all evil—
the mother of Sisera wails.

Then everyone will click his heels—
hymn of the last ordeal.

7

Even when the waters cover us again
and wings lie on the corpses
—they will float and collide
bloated without mouths or eyes—
remember the law of reflection:
perfect equality of the two angles.

Because this is the covenant between us.
As in Jabbok through which they passed,
our weakness and God's frailty
wrestle again and combine—
this is the arch on which we lean.

—*translated by Shirley Kaufman with Judy Levy*

308

Yonatan
Yona Wallach

I run on the bridge
and the children follow
Yonatan
Yonatan they call
a little blood
just a little blood to finish up the honey
I'd let them pierce me with tacks
but the children want
and they are children
and I am Yonatan
They cut off my head with a gladiola stalk
gather my head
in two gladiola stalks and wrap
my head in rustling paper
Yonatan
Yonatan they say
Please forgive us
We didn't imagine
you are like this

—*translated by Leonore Gordon*

When the angels are exhausted
Yona Wallach

When the angels are exhausted
we fold their wings
with pleasure, with pleasure
prepare the whip
when the angels begin
and wound them
till dew floods the earth

—*translated by Leonore Gordon*

The house is empty
Yona Wallach

The house is empty and the trough is broken,
and Naomi my heart's delight where has
she gone? The house lies plundered, the closets
are empty. And Naomi's gone off scared.
What garments what rags cover her
body? The groves are parched, the earth
abandoned to wild grass and nettle.
Donkeys don't tread the dust any more
and Naomi has left off making them lie down.
Naomi my heart's delight. Birds
of the water, living things, but Naomi where are you?
Girl, girl, O who would not revive her?
If only Naomi could live her life,
there would still be joy in our meadows.

—*translated by Warren Bargad*

Cradle song
Yona Wallach

Imagine lamenting our longing, no,
we'd leave no room to mourn
and the bush is sprouting
wild to jazz rhythms.
What we hear in hysterical women
is the faint echo
of the voiced conclusion
a lullaby:
a butterfly net
and another song
another net.

310

And that's not what
will satisfy
my hunger, no,
that's not
what
will calm me
no
that's not it.

—translated by Leonore Gordon

The secret of authority
Meir Wieseltier

When in the inner sanctum a purple seal is stamped on
      documents sharp as razor blades whose size has been
      distorted:
when telephone receivers are brandished like spears:
when they ring the bell, then bang the door with their fists:
when the soldiers present arms and the executioner puts on his
      watch,

not only does the cow go on giving milk, not only does the
      chicken
lay unbroken eggs: a young
woman walks into the field and picks flowers
to fill her room with perfume, and a young
man goes to town, buys her a ring
with a red stone.
The jeweler touches the gold
and is transported. Across the road
the dealer in dry goods fondles muslin.
As for the butcher, he cracks bones
and then cuts perfect slices of meat.
His dog is strange: he's learned to watch his master patiently
for no meat.

From the laundry, steam always rises,
in the fish store they keep things superbly clean,
and the lady from the crockery shop
is also a matchmaker: usually she manages
to match couples at evening, but sometimes
she puts up a sign: Be back soon.
This sign's a field day for the children returning from school:
they tie a dead rat to it
and stick a peach pit in the rat's mouth.
When the matchmaker comes back from her matchmaking, she
        faints and they
bite their fingers on the opposite roof.
When she recovers they're not there, no trace of them, just a big
        sun
making noon music
and a little girl singing, hoping to be a bird.

And the narrator hears
a voice: Fine, very nice, and you,
what do you say?
What do I say? I also
drink milk, fry eggs in butter.
I go from shop to shop and come back with some paper bags.
I listen to music at night.
Next to a woman I'm more calm.
The racket of the kids consoles me for my death.
I empty my house of newspapers,
radio, television, all these
feeble striptease shows of public shame.
I don't lift a finger
against the hands that slap our intelligence,
I don't open my mouth
against the feet that deafen the sound of the heart.
I imagine I see clearly
what's done in the inner sanctum, the placard faces
with nothing behind them
but a simple mistake in arithmetic.

I see the children turn into soldiers,
and the girl soldiers turn into mothers,
and the mothers weep and make their children into soldiers.
I see the line traced on the map
and the line under the names of people in sealed notebooks in
        safes.
Reading about people who believed in redemption, I understand
they also miscalculated. But their error was different,
more godlike. Yes, here I start talking about God,
a painkilling drug, with its harmful side-effects.

—translated by Shirley Kaufman with Shlomit Rimmon

A request
Meir Wieseltier

The day I die or the day after
I'd want some friends to come down,
to take a day off from work
and gather around what is left.

And not be ashamed of how few they are,
and firmly, even with sticks if they have to,
shoo from my corpse the black crows
that shift dead bodies to their graves.

And lift me and seat me in the car,
without covering my face, without the ritual cleansing,
and go with me as far as there is to go,
to a wooded place on the Carmel or Galilee.

And dig a hole deep and wide enough
and not hurry to drop me in, but sit down and smoke
a cigarette with my flesh and image
whose nonexistence will soon be here.

As long as they don't sit with heads sunk and silent,
but talk together like human beings,
not separate beings, creatures by themselves,
but seeping through each other, people like sieves.

And finally they'll have to set down the body,
the day goes down, the body's let down, and push in the soil
and stack up the stones against the wild beasts
and soil on the stones for the grass to re-cover.

And from then on, to keep the place secret,
alert to the scorn of nagging authorities
who'll try to turn the thing upside down
and pluck the corpse out of the ground.

All this business has to be done, so let it be done by friends
who won't strip the body of its soaking clothes,
or wrap it in white sheets like a mummy,
or mumble the fraudulent mumble of dealers in death.

And though I encourage my friends with explicit advice
so they can stand up to a criminal charge,
I'm afraid they'll go soft and not do what I ask,
and some will give thanks if they don't carry it out.

And walk, halfhearted, behind the cart
which shysters rattle in the limestone road,
and hear the foul blessing in spite of themselves,
and rend their garments and toss the first earth.

So don't be put off if I seem obsessed
with the style of my burial, or ask something special.
Love doesn't happen alone, or burials.
I only wanted you to know how things stand.

—translated by Shirley Kaufman with Shlomit Rimmon

March
Meir Wieseltier

Dry heat in the spring already at five in the morning,
the temporary gold of sunrise flickers back of the humps of
    houses.
Television antennae write
an awkward letter in primitive script.
The street's beaten gray still gives off a violet glow.
In a lighted window,
a woman makes coffee and toast.
It seems to me spring has gone out of her shape.
Now I will sleep.
I will skip the strong hours.

—translated by Shirley Kaufman with Shlomit Rimmon

Friends
Meir Wieseltier

Friends come and talk and talk, and you talk
and eight, ten, fourteen
eyes hover anxious, desperate, gnats
in their search for honey, jam,
anything sweet, anything sticky for the soul.

They sit, they get up, they drink with long-practiced hope.
And the soul, juice drained out, beseeches to be sweet.
Somebody gives you a look as if passing a note:

and you put the note in your pocket, returning a look with some
    promise of good.
And he nods as if you could already speak, as if you don't need to
    write.

—translated by Shirley Kaufman with Shlomit Rimmon

Samson's hair
Natan Zach

I've never really understood Samson's hair:
its immense latent power, its Nazarite mystery,
the prohibition (perfectly understandable) against talking about it,
the constant fear of losing its locks, the endless dread
of Delilah's light caress.

But I have no trouble at all with Absalom's hair.
Obviously it was beautiful, like the sun at high noon, like a red
      vengeance moon.

Its fragrance was sweeter than the perfumes of women.
Conniving cold Ahithophel couldn't bear to look

when he saw before him the cause of David's love:
the most glorious hair in the realm, the perfect license
for every uprising and afterward the terebinth.

—translated by S. F. Chyet

I saw
Natan Zach

I saw a white bird in the black night,
and I knew that the light
of my eyes would soon go out in the black night.

I saw a cloud, small as a stain
on a man's palm. And I knew that I couldn't explain
to anyone the rain

I feel. I saw fallen leaves, leaves raining.
Time is short. I am not complaining.

—translated by Robert Friend

from Against parting
Sergeant Weiss
Natan Zach

An everlasting flower
buds on your forehead.
Your cheeks nurture
unseen grubs. Rarely
is your name mentioned
except on maneuvers. You move
through your flesh as though
through a sieve; my time is still
troubled by your hand
whose watch marks time
other than my own.

Until your arrival I
had thought it necessary
to hurry back to my task.

I don't know how you treat children now.
It is hard thinking of your face
when I am afraid. Events have moved on
as to a late reel of film
that may not be watched again.
In the desert, still, they
worship you, with their boots on.
The brambles bend themselves
down, remembering your orders.

Weiss, I do not know
how much time will pass
before I recall you,
suddenly restless.

Your way was right, perhaps.
In the house you have built
nothing presses itself on you
except cold, heat, hunger,
desire perhaps. Water will

not prosper round your eyes.
The oleander will
not sing through your tongue. Mother is dead;
you will not be a child again, Weiss.

In this continuing parody on people's fate
war manages one of its most convincing roles:
formed by the formless, it can hardly recognize
its image, surrounding you like a sea that pierces
the swimmer's flesh, rearing the waves. Your madness is
one of war's possibilities, not the worst.
You created a situation we must put up with.

In the delusions that leave no sign of their existence
but move in us, I see your eyes agape, sometimes,
like oases. We who were not able in these years
to shape the war into a thing we understand
remember you as a page written in lines close together,
hard to read, correct; spaces of time passed, not fulfilled.

—*translated by Jon Silkin and Abraham Birman*

He apologizes
Natan Zach

Birds are flying from his hands—one,
and another one. He is calm now.
He has taken nothing from you: neither
ox nor ass.

He apologizes. What a nerve, by God,
to apologize. By God, he apologizes.
I'm asking you; he apologizes.

You do not answer. You count
the times. Strange, but in the sky
the wind follows the most worn track,
soft, like the plumage of a bird.
Here on earth, the foot hardens

318

with each step. It seems that
a shudder has passed through his body. Listen.
Listen. He reads from the page;
what else has he to say now. He apologizes?
He writes? He says he loves? The least
of his pupils cranes his neck. He is
still small. Is this all? Will he

sell off? Will he bequeath?
What is he repeating there, to himself?
He says he remembers? His name appears
in every paper. He'll be forgotten.
He will rot. He's not the last.

—translated by Jon Silkin

King Solomon's camel*
Natan Zach

King Solomon's camel is a hypocritical creature.
The encyclopedia (always objective) attributes,
without scruple, to him the description of "dangerous carnivore."
Dangerous, it is said, because of his
developed ability for camouflage.
In South America he devours even frogs and lizards.

Here in Israel, he is green; or white and green; less voracious;
satisfied with flies and other insects. And yet
here, too, he's not loath—just as abroad—to eat up
his own species: females, the males; larvae, their brothers.

And he can deceive: when he's in wait for his prey,
he can be seen sitting calmly, only his head nodding,
with his predatory legs upright, like the hands of man
held in prayer together. This posture produced,

Gemal Hamelekh Shlomo (King Solomon's camel) is the Hebrew for praying mantis.

with ancient people, an illusion. The Greeks possessed
the finest, mistaking this dangerous predator
for a holy man and seer. The Germans named him
"He who prays to God," whereas the Muslims believe
that Solomon's camel prays with his face toward Mecca.

For us Jews, the direction matters less; although even
for us the sight of a head nodding may excite
certain associations, not all of them zoological.

Strange, then, that creature—small, dangerous carnivore,
white and green, that was able enough to deceive
not only frogs and lizards, but such respectable hosts
of believers, religions; with just a few movements
executed in perfect mental calm.

—*translated by Jon Silkin*

A song for the wise lovers
Natan Zach

A song for the wise
lovers, who love wisely.
Their days in blessedness pass.
Even in death, they will not age,
nor ever part, but inhabit
together the one house.

A song for the wise
lovers on their bed, who do not speak.
With a hand they turn the light
off, together close their eyes,
blessing each other.
While one is reading he'll
have on the bedside light.
Their children's breathing is
heard by the clock and
by the midnight's wind.

320

A song for the wise
lovers, who have built themselves
a house, and locked its doors.
Bolt the shutters; outside it is cold and
windy, and a storm is expected. A guest
will not arrive on such a night;
and if he comes, don't admit him.
It's late; and only frost blows through the world. The poet
also, out of distress, not abundance, sings. Remain
embraced.

—*translated by Jon Silkin*

As sand
Natan Zach

When God in the Bible wants to promise,
he points to stars. Abraham goes
through the opening of his tent at night,
and sees lovers. As sand on the sea's
shore, says God, and man believes.
Even though he knows that
"as sand" is merely the language
man can understand.

And since then, sand and stars remained
linked in the net of man's similes.
But perhaps there's no point in
mixing man in here;
it wasn't man that was
then spoken of.

And yet it's explicitly said
"as sand," which implies, of course,
the capacity for suffering.
Or maybe it's possible to imagine that
all was then permitted, and no words made
a difference any more.

As sand on the sea's shore. But nothing is said there
about water. And yet explicitly
God mentions seed.
But this is heaven's way
and, possibly, nature's.

—*translated by Jon Silkin*

Time
Zelda

We had a hidden treasure of time
tender as morning air,
a time of stories, tears, embraces
and holy days.
A time of Mother, Grandma, and the aunts
sitting tranquil in a boat
of splendor,
gliding slowly—slowly
in a tiny boat of peace
with the moon and all the stars.

—*translated by Edna G. Sharoni*

I stood in Jerusalem
Zelda

I stood
in Jerusalem
which hung by a cloud,
stood in a graveyard
with people crying,
a twisted tree.
Blurred hills,
a tower.

322

You are not,
said death
to us,
nor are you,
he said to me.

I stood
in Jerusalem
that was framed in sun
and smiling like a bride,
stood in a field
near thin green grass.

Why were you afraid of me yesterday in the rain?
said death,
I am your older, your silent
brother.

—*translated by Zvi Jagendorf*

The seamstress
Zelda

Days her little house is a desert,
no friend, no bridegroom,
nights a lord masters her,
most high, faithful.

When she falls sick, he will embrace her,
when she sinks, he will kiss her,
and when she dies,
he will gather her to his cold heart
with hands of dust.

—*translated by Zvi Jagendorf*

When you were here
Zelda

When you were here
and your dark glance shielding me,
our thoughts brushed
suddenly
wing to wing.

When you were with me
in this flow of things,
these walls were old friends
telling stories
in the evening
as we drank tea.

They give no shelter now,
they've shut themselves up,
won't watch over my downfall.
Concrete and whitewash now
alien matter,
they're voiceless like death.

—*translated by Zvi Jagendorf*

From the songs of childhood
Zelda

I was a butterfly
and I was idleness
and I was fickleness
and I was a kingdom.
My years of childhood
went by in quest of
sweetness
and touched the roots of the sea.

324

Alas! Alas! Alas!
My father and my mother
stand weeping on the shore.

Why this wailing?
Why this mourning?
Is not the bottom of the sea
a chariot to God?

—*translated by Chana Hoffman*

Be not far
Zelda

The comforters come to the courtyard
outside,
standing beside the gate
that faces the valley of the shadow of death.
Its terror is all around.
Standing beside the gate is the utmost
comforters can bear.
Even my own soul is miles away
from the I of the weeper. It is divine decree.

Creator of nights and winds,
against Thee is this dreadful weeping.
Be not far.
Let not millions of light-years
stand like a wall
between Thee and Job.

—*translated by Edna G. Sharoni*

Afterword: a problem
of horizons
Robert Alter

*It seems to me often that life in this tiny
country is a powerful stimulant but that
only the devout are satisfied with what they
can obtain within Israel's borders. The
Israelis are great travellers. They need the
world.*
—Saul Bellow, *To Jerusalem and Back:
A Personal Account*

One of the most striking qualities of Israeli literature since the
beginning of the 1960s and, increasingly, into the 1970s, is that it
remains intensely, almost obsessively, national in its concerns
while constantly pressing to address itself to universal issues and
situations, perhaps to an international audience as well. This dialectic is inherently unstable, and of course its operation will be felt
differently in different writers, or in poetry and prose. Nevertheless,
one can detect in most contemporary Hebrew writers a high-
pitched vibration of nervousness about the national setting which is
the principal locus of their imaginative work; and if we can understand the peculiar nature of that nervousness, we may be able to see
more clearly why the Israeli literary imagination has adopted certain

characteristic modes and even certain characteristic constellations of plot and dramatic setting.

The nervousness I have in mind is not about the specific problems that confront the state of Israel, grave or abundant as they may be, but rather, to put it bluntly, about the simple fact of being in Israel. I do not mean to suggest, as some observers outside Israel would no doubt like to think, that Israeli writers tend to be covert anti-Zionists. On the contrary, what particularly characterizes most serious writers in Israel is their surprising combination of chronic disaffection and unswerving commitment. Whatever radical doubts they may, on occasion, raise in their writing, they are notable for their unwillingness to drop out of, or rebel against, the troubled national enterprise. Whether high school teachers, university instructors, kibbutzniks, or journalists by profession, they tend politically to gravitate toward small, ineffectual groups of the responsible opposition (usually on the Left). They seem ever ready to lecture to popular audiences, to join in symposiums with Arab intellectuals, to sign manifestos, to deliver scathing statements on current controversies to the daily press, or to picket the office of the prime minister, as the case may require. But it is one thing to be an engaged intellectual and quite another to be an imaginative writer in a constantly beleaguered nation-state the size of Rhode Island, and it is the pressures and constrictions of the latter problematic condition that repeatedly make themselves felt in contemporary Hebrew literature.

In a sense, this tension of attitudes is part of the legacy of classical Zionism and of the antecedent Hebrew literature which flourished in Central and Eastern Europe in the nineteenth and early twentieth centuries. Modern Hebrew literature was born out of the German Enlightenment, with a vision of progressive cosmopolitanism, the dream of a new brotherhood of man in which a renascent Hebrew culture within the European sphere would be accorded the opportunity to play its rightful role. By the end of the nineteenth century— the old cosmopolitan optimism having collapsed under the pressures of a new European era of fierce particularism—the early Zionists nevertheless argued for a nationalism which would somehow be universal in scope. A resurgent Jewish commonwealth, they hoped, would not be a new kind of ghetto on a national scale or simply a "Bulgaria in the Middle East," but a vital center

327

for all world Jewry and, with intricate links both to the best modern culture and to the Jewish past, a small but precious beacon for mankind. One might conceivably argue from the complex facts of Israeli actuality in the seventies that the visionary notions of the Zionist founders were not entirely off the mark; yet the discrepancy between vision and reality is obviously enormous, and it is out of the pained consciousness of this discrepancy that Israeli writers tend to shape their work.

When your whole cultural tradition tells you that you should be a universalist, though with a proud particularist base, and when, in this tension of expectations, you find yourself part of a tiny linguistic pocket hemmed in at the eastern end of the Mediterranean by enemy guns and a wall of nonrecognition, striving to maintain connections that sometimes must seem tenuous with the "great world" thousands of miles away—you are quite likely to experience flashes of claustrophobia. The only dependable antidote to this collective sense of cultural entrapment is a strong dose of messianism. For if you believe that the future of mankind rides with the ebb and flow of your nation's destiny, then no political or geocultural encirclement, however constricting, can ever cut you off from a realm of larger significance. Old-fashioned messianism, however, is not much in evidence these days among serious writers in Israel. In fact, the only convincing example that comes to mind is the poet Uri Zvi Greenberg, now in his eighties, whose fierce, mystic nationalism has produced poetic moments of awesome power but who has not inspired any literary emulators. The overwhelming majority of Israeli writers, for whom national identity is an incontestable fact and not an incandescent faith, must settle for scrutinizing the surfaces and depths of their national reality while sometimes secretly longing for a larger world to embrace—perhaps even feeling, in some corner of awareness, the persistent needle of doubt as to whether, if it were only possible, life might not be more fully livable somewhere else.

Somewhere Else, in fact, is the symptomatic title of Amos Oz's first novel, published in 1966 (the English translation is entitled *Elsewhere Perhaps*). It is one of several books of the early and mid-sixties that could be taken as points of departure for the so-called New Wave in Israeli fiction. Shimon Sandbank is surely right in proposing a new uncertainty about values as one of the distinguishing traits of the last decade and a half of Israeli writing. Viewing the transition from another angle, however, I would suggest that the difference is also essentially the difference in the imaginative horizons of the fiction and poetry. I am not using the word "horizons" in any metaphorical sense; what I am referring to, as I shall try to illustrate through some specific instances of Israeli writing, are the actual geographical limits that define the imagined world of the literary work.

The novelists of the generation of 1948—writers like S. Yizhar, Moshe Shamir, Natan Shaham, Aharon Megged—created fictional worlds focused on distinctive Israeli social realities like the army, the kibbutz, and the socialist youth movement, with horizons that never visibly extended beyond Israel. In these works Europe appeared, if at all, as a bad memory, and America was simply not a presence. The writers may have been, like writers elsewhere, acutely unhappy with what they saw, but they never seemed to imagine or seriously muse over any arena of existence other than this newly independent national one in which they were struggling to articulate an authentic identity.

Somewhere Else is, like earlier books by Shaham, Shamir, and others of the older generation, a novel of kibbutz life (Oz in fact has remained a kibbutz member since adolescence). Yet it is profoundly different from Hebrew fiction of the forties and fifties, not only because of its pronounced symbolism and its plangently lyric style but, more crucially, because its imagined horizons are different, as the very title declares. Oz's kibbutz is not simply an assumed institutional framework within which certain social and moral problems may be explored. Sitting in the shadow of ominous mountains and enemy guns, huddled within the perimeter of its own fences, it becomes a parable of claustrophobic collective existence. All the action takes place within the kibbutz, but all the urgent *pressure* on the action originates "somewhere else"—whether in the dark beyond the Syrian border, where jackals howl and primordial forces lurk, or in the moral quagmire of postwar Germany, which, through the agency of a sinister visitor, penetrates the kibbutz. The novel's oppositions between here and elsewhere tend to be too simple and sometimes melodramatic—Oz was scarcely twenty-six when he completed the book—but the schematism has the effect of making the symptomatic aspect of the novel vividly

329

clear. Whatever "somewhere else" may actually be, it embodies a disturbing, and alluring, depth, complexity, ambiguity that go beyond the rationalist, optimistic commitment to the salubrious collective endeavor of Israel's tight little island.

Recent Israeli literature, I would contend, galvanized by these claustrophobic flashes, has tended to swing in rapid oscillation between two poles: on the one hand, an imaginative leap outward to Europe and the West; on the other hand, a return to roots, an attempt to recapitulate the Israeli self in all its distinctiveness by imaginatively recovering the world of the writer's childhood. Let me offer a variety of examples of this dialectic movement in Israeli fiction of the sixties and seventies. Haim Gouri, an established poet of the 1948 generation, set his first novel, *The Chocolate Deal* (1964), in postwar Germany. This fable of the moral ambiguities of Jewish survival was followed by a work written in a totally different vein, *The Crazy Book* (1972), an affectionate evocation of Palestinian life in the Mandatory period when Gouri was growing up. Hanoch Bartov, a contemporary of Gouri, returned to his own childhood in *Whose Are You, Son?* (1970), a subtly convincing recreation of a boy's experience in the town of Petah-Tikvah during the 1930s. On the other hand, his most recent novel, *The Dissembler* (1975), is set mainly in England and deals with a mysterious accident victim who turns out to have three national identities—German, French, and Israeli—and with them three different, internally coherent personal histories. The plot of *The Dissembler* is actually a brilliant focusing of the whole problem of horizons—Israel collapsing into France and Germany, or vice versa, until the entire structure of national identities seems like a house of cards—but Bartov's rendering of the psychological dimension of his situation, as the "serious" conclusion to his whodunit scheme, is unfortunately lame.

There is often, it seems to me, some problem of artistic authenticity in Israeli fiction set in another country. The simple and obvious reason is that no Israeli writer can ever know, in all their nuanced variety, the foreign milieus he chooses to evoke. French people in Hebrew novels show a propensity to eat nothing but pâté de fois gras; Englishmen repeatedly consume tea and scones; and so forth. This effect of straining after a European horizon is transparently illustrated by Rachel Eytan's recent book, *The Plea-*

sures of Man (1974). In its first half this is a competent, more or less feminist novel of conjugal distress and social satire, focused on what passes for the glittering circles of Tel Aviv society, but it noticeably loses credibility at precisely the point where the heroine runs off to the south of France with a French lover. The general rule of thumb seems to be that when a Hebrew novelist moves dialectically in his work between fictions of Israeli origins and fictions of foreign horizons, the realm of origins is the one that is most consistently handled with authority and conviction.

Amos Oz, whose first novel gave us our point of departure for defining this whole problem, provides an instructive instance of how a gifted writer can variously work with the geocultural tensions we have been observing. All his early fiction—the volume of stories *Jackal Country* (1965) as well as *Somewhere Else*—is obsessed with a claustrophobic sense of constriction. The penned-in kibbutz, its recurrent symbol, is in turn converted into an image of the human condition, hedged in and menaced (as Oz conceives it to be) by vast and inimical forces that man, through his self-deceiving schemes of rational order, vainly hopes to subdue. This essentially symbolic conflict in the early fiction forms the base for Oz's more probing psychological portraits, beginning in the later sixties, of deeply troubled protagonists whose mental disturbances mirror certain distinctive focuses of neurosis in Israeli life. After one remarkable novel in this manner, *My Michael* (1968), and a striking novella, *Late Love* (1970), Oz was for once seduced by the beckoning expanses of "somewhere else." In *Touch the Water, Touch the Wind* (1973), he tried to put together a novel that would embrace past and present, Poland, Russia, Israel, the Western world at large, even time and infinity. The result is unpersuasive, especially when compared with the genuinely hallucinated intensity of his best writing. Finally, in his most recent collection of novellas, *The Hill of Evil Counsel* (1976), Oz has gone back, in his brooding fashion, to his Jerusalem boyhood, just as Bartov, Gouri, Kaniuk, and others have turned to the Mandatory Palestine of their formative years. In these three utterly compelling stories, set in the last years before the establishment of the Jewish state, Oz manages to enjoy the imaginative benefits of Zionist messianism without having actually to believe in it himself. In each novella, there is at least one central character obsessed with the apocalyptic vision of a "Judea reborn in blood and fire." These prophetic delusions of the extreme Zionist Right have a profound subterranean appeal for Oz, an antimilitant man of the Zionist Left. By recreating such messianism in his characters, the writer partly suspends disbelief and momentarily transforms a minutely particularized Jerusalem setting into a landscape of ultimate significance—just as U. Z. Greenberg, with no such ventriloquistic obliquity, does in his poetry. In these fictions, then, set on the threshold of Jewish statehood, there are no inviting horizons to distract attention from the portentous fullness of this time and place.

The nervous shuttling between home and horizon in Israeli writing is also perceptible in the new prominence it has given to the role of the expatriate. Again, in order to keep biographical and literary facts properly sorted, we should remember that scarcely a single Israeli writer of any consequence has actually emigrated, although most of the writers find repeated occasions to spend a year or more in England, on the Continent, or, most frequently, in America. Expatriation, in fact, never seems to solve anything for the spiritually displaced personae that populate this literature. Nevertheless, the expatriate is now a figure who has to be contended with, empathically explored, because he tries to follow to the end a personal way out of Israel's landlocked location in history. Hebrew, one should note, has no comfortable neutral way of saying "expatriate." The usual term for an emigrant from Israel is *yored,* which literally means "one who goes down," and which has at least some of the pejorative force (depending on who is using the word) of "turncoat" or "renegade" in English. In recent years, writers have tried to see what light this conventionally deplored figure could throw on the perplexities of the Israeli condition in the second generation of national independence.

The earliest Hebrew novel I can recall that focuses on an expatriate is Yoram Kaniuk's *The Acrophile* (1961), which in Hebrew is called, much more pointedly, *Ha-Yored L'Ma'alah*— "the upward *yored,*" or "he who goes down upward." Kaniuk himself had been living in New York for some time when he wrote this first novel, which deals with the marital and spiritual confusions of an ex-Israeli teaching at a university in New York. Kaniuk's subsequent novels, like their author, have returned to the Israeli scene. The terrific tension between home and abroad then became the explicit subject of *Rockinghorse* (1973), a wildly uneven novel about an expatriate who, out of a sense of radical disorientation, returns from New York to Tel Aviv to try to make contact with his earliest origins. Kaniuk's latest book, and in many ways his most appealing, is *The Story of Big Aunt Shlomtziyon* (1976). Like the novels we noted by Bartov and Gouri, this is an affectionate, imaginative engagement in personal history—working back anecdotally, through the outrageously domineering figure of Aunt Shlomtziyon, to family beginnings in the pre-Mandatory period. Finally, Kaniuk's story "They've Moved the House," included in this volume, swings once more to the other pole of the dialectic, following the farcical and pathetic odyssey of two expatriate Israelis through California and Central America in search of a kind of El Dorado—deeply uneasy in a world where houses roll along on trailer frames instead of sitting on permanent foundations. (A story by Amalia Kahana-Karmon, "To Build a House in the Land of Shinar," provides a neatly complementary opposite to Kaniuk's fable of the moving house. Her model Israeli household in a new town, visited by a foreign home economist, is a quietly claustrophobic setting of stale domesticity. The ironic epic overtones of the title—no national symbolism is intended—alluding to the builders of the tower of Babel in Genesis, imply that this is not a house which will stand.)

Elsewhere, the *yored* stands at the center of Yehuda Amichai's farcical extravaganza, *Hotel in the Wilderness* (1971), a novel about an Israeli residing permanently in New York. He works for a Zionist agency propagandizing Israelis in America to return to Israel (!), and eventually finds an outlet for his dormant powers as a long-silent poet in writing advertising copy for ladies' underpants. Bartov's *The Dissembler,* of course, takes as its subject the intriguing impossibility of a man who is simultaneously an *oleh* (immigrant to Israel, "one who goes up") and a *yored,* at once a rooted Israeli and a rootless cosmopolitan. Still more recently, in a collection of poems which the quarterly *Siman-Kriyah* began publishing in installments with its Spring 1976 issue, a gifted new poet (in fact an important figure in literary-academic circles in Israel) adopts the persona of "Gabi Daniel"—a Russian-born Israeli living in Amsterdam. In experimental Hebrew verse of Mandelstamian formal intricacy, he ponders the role of his peculiar language and

333

culture in the vast arena of human languages and cultural perspectives. In the dramatic setting of these poems, as in much contemporary Hebrew fiction, the figure of the expatriate is used to test some of the fundamental assumptions of the Israeli national enterprise.

Finally, the value-challenging idea of the *yored* is given an ultimate turn of the screw in a chapter of a novel-in-progress by A. B. Yehoshua, published in this volume. Here the expatriate Israeli, having returned to his homeland chiefly to look after a legacy, finds himself caught in the deadly meshes of the October 1973 war. Seeking, like a number of his fictional counterparts, a way out, he finds it paradoxically through a way in: disguising himself as an ultra-orthodox Jew, he slips away from the Sinai front to one of the old quarters of Jerusalem; there, in the beard, sidelocks, and black kaftan of a pre-modern, pre-Zionist Jew, he is for the moment exempt from duty, exempt from history.

In Hebrew poetry contemporaneous with the New Wave in fiction, the problem of horizons is not usually so transparently evident—except where, as in the case of "Gabi Daniel," there is an elaborated dramatic or narrative context for the poems. The simple reason is that a lyric poem is not under the same obligation as a novel to articulate an imagined geography or a set of characters moving within or against cultural limits. Nevertheless, I would argue that the oscillations we have been observing in Israeli fiction are present in a good deal of recent Israeli poetry—sometimes on the level of explicit theme, sometimes in the formal shaping of the poem's world.

The situation in Israeli poetry today stands in marked contrast to that of the Israeli novel. Although there has been abundant and at times highly interesting activity among younger poets, no new creative figure has emerged to rival in stature the leading poets who achieved prominence after 1948, like Yehuda Amichai, Natan Zach, Amir Gilboa, and, just a few years later, Dan Pagis. Given this circumstance, shifts in the literary fashionability of the various established poets become revealing.

The poet par excellence of the so-called Palmach Generation (the war generation of 1948) was Haim Gouri. Although he is still very much alive and still writing, his plainspoken style, his frequent focus on group experience, his nostalgic impulse, and his pervasive

Israeli-ness now seem out of date, and his poetry attracts little attention in serious literary circles. Yehuda Amichai, in my view the finest poet of this generation, combines a colloquial sense of place with rich imagery, inventive allusiveness, and an easy movement between disparate cultural worlds. He has managed to remain a perennial favorite, even though at various moments his preeminence has been partly eclipsed by the very different modernist idioms of Natan Zach and Amir Gilboa. In the last few years, some younger literary intellectuals seem to have fixed particularly on the poetry of Dan Pagis, and Pagis' popularity, though well deserved on the genuine merits of the poems, is instructive. This is a poetry that visibly, in terms of its optic perspectives, shrinks the Israeli landscape to one dot out of many on an imagined global scene. Local allusions are relatively rare, and the language is for the most part meticulously clinical, manifestly a distancing medium. Beginning with his 1970 volume, *Transformation,* Pagis has frequently favored science-fiction situations (using verse for many of the same ends that Italo Calvino has used prose) in which terrestrial space and time are seen at an enormous telescopic remove—either from the other end of evolution, long after a global holocaust, or from the observation post of a spaceship or alien planet. This peculiar distanced mode is an authentic development within Pagis' poetry. It clearly gives him a means of confronting historical horror with artistic restraint and intellectual lucidity (he himself was a concentration camp prisoner as a child, and demons of disaster haunt his work); but I suspect that the gift of globality which the poetry offers is at least one important reason for the attraction it now holds for Israeli readers.

At the other end of Pagis' high-powered telescope, and on the opposite side of this geocultural dialectic, one discovers a poet like Dahlia Ravikovitch, whose imagination has virtually a fixed focus on a palpable Israeli geography that repeatedly becomes a screen for the projection of her personal anguish. A sense of entrapment and a dream of escape are recurrent presences in Ravikovitch's poetry, and although hers is a very private claustral distress, she manages to give it a local place and habitation in her encircled native land. One of her best known poems, "The Blue West," is in fact an archetypal expression of the problem of horizons that figures so importantly in the Israeli literary imagination. The poem begins (I shall quote from Chana Bloch's fine translation) with an image of ruins which is a distinctive piece of local landscape: "If there was just a road there / the ruins of workshops / one fallen minaret / and some carcasses of machines, / why couldn't I / come to the heart of the field?" But there is an opaque impenetrability at the heart of the field, at the heart of the native landscape, so that the attempt to penetrate it only reinforces the poet's sense of desperate entrapment. She then turns, at the Mediterranean shore, to a "blue west" which is not real like the landscape around her, but a visionary gleam that can only be imagined on another temporal plane, at the end of days. First, she conjures up a kind of surrealistic extension of Israel's actual beleaguered situation, a desolate coast with unvisited harbors: "If only we could reach / all the cities beyond the sea— / And here is another sorrow: a seashore where there are no ships." Then, in the two concluding stanzas of the poem, she shifts into prophetic style, mingling the grandeur of biblical eschatology with the naive fantasy of a fairy tale:

> On one of the days to come
> the eye of the sea will darken
> with the multitude of ships.
> In that hour all the mass of the earth
> will be spread as a cloth.
>
> And a sun will shine for us blue as the sea,
> a sun will shine for us warm as an eye,
> will wait until we climb up
> as it heads for the blue west.

It would be simplistic, I think, to draw direct political inferences from this underlying tension between homeland and horizon in Israeli literature. What the tension reflects most profoundly is the key psychological paradox of an imaginative literature that feels itself to be a full participant in modern culture at large, and yet is boxed into a tiny corner of geography, linguistically limited to at most a scant two million readers. In this regard, contemporary Hebrew literature provides a vivid if extreme paradigm for the difficult fate of all small cultures in an age of vast linguistic-cultural blocs and of global communications. In order to define the outlines of the paradigm, I have been stressing points of resemblance in distinctly different novelists and poets, although the points of divergence among them are at least as prominent, and in any case writers may do remarkably different things with the same set of oppositions. Most Israeli writers, it seems to me, tend to cluster at the end of the spectrum we have been concentrating on, where the imaginative confrontation of here and elsewhere is felt as a continual distress of creative consciousness. To avoid any misleading schematism, however, I would like to offer one final example from the other end of the spectrum—the poetry of Yehuda Amichai.

For Amichai, the West has not been a blue vision calling to him from beyond the shore, but a variegated, concretely perceived intellectual and emotional legacy. His German childhood reverberates through his poetry. Rilke and Auden are as natural sources for his poetic idiom as are Israeli speech and the Bible; and the various American and European scenes he has passed through as an adult are evoked with little sense that they present a challenging or alluring alternative to the Israeli setting in which he has taken root. Indeed, some of Amichai's finest poems over the past ten years, beginning with the remarkable cycle, "Jerusalem 1967," have been imaginative realizations of distinctive Israeli cityscapes and landscapes, where topography, architecture, cultural history, politics, and the record of age-old vision are so extraordinarily interfused.

Amichai is surely as aware as any other Israeli writer of the pull of the great world and of the exiguous dimensions of his national sphere (as his novel, *Hotel in the Wilderness,* makes clear). Yet the peculiar acerbic, playful, and at times visionary intimacy with the local scene which he has cultivated in his poems tends to keep the problem of horizons outside them. It may be that the messianic perspective, which makes one little state an everywhere, still remains, despite the prosaic logic of intellectual history, more available to Hebrew writers than I have allowed. In Amos Oz, we observed a ventriloquistic messianism which might reflect the writer's half-willingness to believe, or rather to surrender to, a fiery doctrine of national redemption that he would reject on the grounds of sane political principle. In Amichai, one sees instead a wryly nostalgic messianism that reflects an affectionate, self-ironic longing for the flashes of transcendental vision that in the past so repeatedly illuminated the Jerusalem landscape in which he lives. The nostalgia does not dissolve into sentimentality because his attraction to Jerusalem as the seedbed of prophecy is always articulated through an unblinking perception of the terrestrial Jeru-

337

salem—in all its hodgepodge of noise, stench, dirt, color, and piquant incongruity, and always rendered through the flaunted inventiveness of an imagery that constantly yokes feelings and spiritual entities with the most earthy of mechanical accouterments of the workaday world. These characteristics can be observed in lively and significant play in the following untitled poem from *Behind All This a Great Happiness Is Hiding* (1974), Amichai's most recent volume of poetry. (My translation must unfortunately surrender much of the verbal wit and sound-play of the original.)

The only real horizon of the poem's Jerusalem, at once a city of the seventies and of the ages, is, in defiance of geography and optics, an absolute vertical above the city; the switch in diction in the last two lines to a virtual nursery lisp expresses, not a wish of simple escape, as in Ravikovitch, but a fantasy of assumption in the theological sense. For three faiths, Jerusalem has been the locus of ascent, the "navel," as rabbinic tradition has it, joining heaven and earth; and even an ironic modern poet cannot put that fact of the spirit's history out of his mind as he muses over the city. It is this awareness that makes the poem intensely local—yet, like other Hebrew writings that have come out of Jerusalem, a prism of meaning that focuses a universal dream:

> All these stones, all this sadness, all
> the light, shards of night-hours and noon-dust,
> all the twisted pipework of sanctity,
> wall and towers and rusty halos,
> all the prophecies that couldn't hold in like old men,
> all the sweaty angel-wings
> all the stinking candles, all the peg-legged tourism,
> dung of deliverance, gladness and gonads
> refuse of nothingness bomb and time,
> all the dust, all these bones
> in the course of resurrection and in the course of the wind,
> all this love, all
> these stones, all this sadness.
>
> To fill with them the valleys around her
> so Jerusalem will be a level place
> for my sweet airplane
> that will come to take me on high.

Contributors

ROBERT FRIEND, poetry editor for this book, has published four volumes of verse and many translations of poems from the Hebrew, Yiddish, French, Spanish, and German. The Seahorse Press in London has just issued his *Selected Poems*. Panjandrum Press (San Francisco) is about to publish Friend's translations of the poems of Lea Goldberg. **SHIMON SANDBANK** is a translator and critic who teaches at the Hebrew University, Jerusalem. His translations (from English and German into Hebrew) include Brecht's *Mother Courage*, Conrad's *The Nigger of the Narcissus*, Kafka's *The Castle*, and an *English Anthology* of poems from "The Wanderer" to Ted Hughes's "The Crow." Sandbank is the author of *Two Pools in the Wood: Hebrew Poetry and the European Tradition* (Tel Aviv, 1976). Professor of Hebrew and comparative literature at Berkeley, **ROBERT ALTER** has recently written on the modern novel (*Partial Magic: The Novel as a Self-Conscious Genre*, University of California Press, 1975) and on *Modern Hebrew Literature* (Behrman House, 1975). He is currently engaged in a critical biography of Stendhal. **AHARON APPELFELD** was born in Czernovitz, the Ukraine, in 1932, and for two years was interned in the Transnistria concentration camp. He has published five collections of short stories and two novels, *The Skin and the Shirt* (1970) and *Like the Pupil of the Eye* (1972). Novelist **YORAM KANIUK** worked in New York from 1955 to 1965 as a bartender and waiter. Atheneum has published three of his books: *Adam Resurrected*, *Himmo King of Jerusalem*, and *The Acrophile*. His *Rockinghorse* is soon to be published by Harper & Row. Kaniuk is presently a columnist for the newspaper *Davar* in Tel Aviv. **YEHUDA AMICHAI** has written four books of poems, two novels, one book of short stories, and one book of radio and stage plays. Last year Penguin issued a volume of his verse and this year Harper & Row will publish a new novel. Amichai's work has been translated into twenty languages. His story, "The Orgy," which appears here, is from his 1973 collection, *In This Terrible Wind*. Volume one of **DAVID SHAHAR**'s five-volume novel, *The Palace of Shattered Vessels*, was published by Houghton Mifflin in 1975. Shahar has won the Agnon Prize (1973) and the Prime Minister's Award for Creative Literature (1969), and was elected chairman of the Society of Hebrew Writers in 1972. **A. B. YEHOSHUA** currently lectures at the University of Haifa on world literature. Doubleday published his *Three Days and a Child* in 1976 and will issue his novel *The Lover* this year. **HAIM GOURI**, a poet and novelist, fought with the Palmach in the War of Independence and took part in all subsequent Israeli wars. He is a journalist, a translator of French poetry and drama into Hebrew, and the author of *Flowers of Flame* (1949), *The Wind Rose* (1960), *The Glass Cage: The Eichmann Trial in Jerusalem* (1962), and *The Vision of Gehazi* (1974). **YITZHAK ORPAZ**'s *The Death of Lysandra* was published in English translation by Jonathan Cape in 1964. He is the author of a number of works, including *Skin for Skin*, which won the Asher Barash Prize for

339

Literature. **URI ORLEV** was born in Warsaw in 1931 and was imprisoned at Bergen-Belsen from 1943 to 1945. His first book, *Lead Soldiers* (1956), is an autobiographical novel about the Nazi occupation of Poland. He has also written a novel about Israel, *Till Tomorrow* (1958), and a book of stories, *The Last Vacation* (1968). **AMOS OZ** served in the tank corps during the Yom Kippur and Six-Day wars. He is the author of *My Michael* (Knopf, 1972) and *Touch the Water, Touch the Wind* (Harcourt, 1974). His most recent work is a collection of novellas, *The Hill of Evil Counsel*, which Harcourt Brace Jovanovich will publish this year. **PINCHAS SADEH** fought in the 1948 War of Independence and has worked as a librarian, a night watchman, and a shepherd. He has published two volumes of poetry, two novels, and several novellas. **DAVID AVIDAN**, Israel's leading avant-garde poet, is also a filmmaker and painter. English editions of Avidan's work include *Megavertone* (1966), poems; *No*, bilingual poems and essays; *My Electronic Psychiatrist*; and *Cryptograms from a Telestar*. **T. CARMI** (Carmi Charny) was born in the Bronx and studied at Yeshiva University, Columbia, and the Sorbonne. In 1964 his *The Brass Serpent* was published by Ohio University Press, and in 1971 *Somebody Like You*. Carmi has translated into Hebrew the plays of Shakespeare, Sophocles, Christopher Fry, Bertolt Brecht, and Edward Albee. For three years he was the editor of the Jerusalem literary magazine *Ariel*. The poems by **RAQUEL CHALFI** included here are selected from the "Submarine Cycle" of her first, recently published book of poems, *Submarine and Other Poems*. She has written plays and film documentaries, and now teaches film and television at the University of Tel Aviv. **MOSHE DOR** has written ten books of poetry, three books of poems for children, one collection of literary essays, and one collection of interviews with writers. He is presently Israel's Counselor for Cultural Affairs in London. **ANADAD ELDAN** is a son of one of the first kibbutzim in Israel and a teaching member of Kibbutz Beeri, near the desert border. Eldan has published five books of verse, among them *The Flowing Darkness and the Fruit* (1959), *Not by Stone Alone* (1967), and *Interior Light* (1973). **AMIR GILBOA** has been awarded the Shlonsky, Ussishkin, Brenner, and Bialik prizes and the Prime Minister's Award. Gilboa's books of poetry include *Seven Domains* (1949), *Blue and Red* (1963), *To Write the Lips of Those Asleep* (1968), and *Gazelle, I'll Send You* (1972). The most recent of **ZERUBAVEL GILEAD**'s books of poetry are *The Radiant Dust: Selected Poems 1939–1960*, *Reflected Light* (1970), and *In the Shiloh Valley* (1974). He has written five volumes of short stories, has collected documents and eyewitness reports relating to Zionist action against the Nazis (*Hidden Shield*, 1948), and has edited *The Book of the Palmach* (1953). Gilead has been awarded the Holon Prize, the Histadrut Prize, and the Prime Minister's Award (1976). **URI ZVI GREENBERG** was born in Bialykamien, Galicia, in 1894 and fought in World War I with the Austro-Hungarians. In 1949 he became a member of the first Knesset. Greenberg has aligned himself with expressionism, anti-aestheticism, and messianism.

His latest and most popular book of poems is *Streets of the River* (1951), a lamentation for the Jews exterminated in Europe. Among **YA'IR HURVITZ**'s books of verse are *Poems for Louise* (1964), *The Season of the Witch* (1970), *Narcissi for the Kingdom of Mud* (1972), and *As I Sit Alone* (1967). Hurvitz is on the editorial board of *Siman Kria Literary Quarterly*. **ABBA KOVNER** fought in the Lithuanian resistance in the Vilna ghetto, and after the war helped organize the Berihah, which brought many thousands of Jews to Israel. Penguin has published in one volume the poems of Kovner and Nelly Sachs (1971), and his *Canopy in the Desert* was published by Pittsburgh University Press in 1973. **DAN PAGIS** is professor of medieval Hebrew literature at the Hebrew University in Jerusalem. In 1968–1969, he was a visiting professor at the Jewish Theological Seminary in New York. Among his volumes of verse are *The Shadow-Dial* (1959) and *Transformation* (1970); another volume contains Stephen Mitchell's translations of the selected poems of both Pagis and T. Carmi (Penguin, 1976). Most of the poems of **GABRIEL PREIL** have not yet been translated into English. Titles of his collections of Hebrew verse (rendered by the author) include *Landscape of Sun and Frost*, *Candle Against Stars*, *Fire and Silence*, and *The Map of Evening*. Preil was awarded an honorary degree at Hebrew Union College in New York in 1972. **ESTHER RAAB** was born near Tel Aviv in 1899 and lived for many years in Cairo. Her three books of poetry are *Thistles* (1930), *The Poetry of Esther Raab* (1963), and *Ultimate Prayer* (1972). **DAHLIA RAVIKOVITCH** has published four books of poetry: *The Love of an Orange* (1959), *Winter Is Hard* (1963), *Third Book* (1969), and *All Your Little Waves and Big Waves*. She lives in Tel Aviv. **DAVID ROKEAH** has worked as a road paver and orange picker, has studied law and literature, and currently works as an electrical engineer. He has written nine books of verse, among them *Red Earth* (1974) and *A Town—The Time Is Summer* (1975). **TUVIA RUEBNER** has received the Anne Frank and ACUM awards (in 1960 and 1966) and most recently the Prime Minister's Award (1975). His poems have been published as *The Fire in the Stone, As Long As,* and *Unreturnable*. **AVNER TREININ** is a professor of physical chemistry who has lectured at Brandeis and at the Hebrew University, Jerusalem. During 1973–1974, he was a visiting scientist at the U.S. Army Natick Laboratory in Massachusetts. In 1969 Treinin received the Millo Award for his book of poems *Mount and Olives*. Born in Israel in 1945, **YONA WALLACH** has published three volumes of poetry: *Things* (1967), *Two Gardens* (1969), and *Poems* (1975). **MEIR WIESELTIER** was born in Moscow in 1941 and currently lives in Tel Aviv. He has published four books; the most recent is *Take* (1973). **NATAN ZACH** was born in Berlin in 1930. Among his volumes of poetry in Hebrew are *First Poems* (1955) and *All the Milk and Honey* (1966). His attack on the older generation of poets, *Time and Rhythm in Bergson's Thought and Modern Poetry,* was published in 1966. He lives in England. **ZELDA** (Mishkovsky) has written *Time, The Invisible Carmel,* and *Be Not*

341

Far. A fourth volume of verse is in preparation. She has received the Rivka Alper and Brenner prizes. **ODED FEINGERSH**, who did the illustrations, is a painter and graphic artist who has exhibited his drawings and paintings in Paris, Brussels, Antwerp, Madrid, Jaffa, Tel Aviv, and Amsterdam. Feingersh has defined the three periods of his work as the Zionist (until 1968), the pop (until 1973), and the present period of a new personal mythology.